A COACHING LIFE

THE SWAIM-PAUP-FORAN SPIRIT OF SPORT SERIES

Sponsored by James C. '74 & Debra Parchman Swaim,
Nancy & T. Edgar Paup '74, and Joseph Wm. & Nancy Foran

A COACHING LIFE

BY GARY BLAIR

FOREWORD BY
MIKE NEIGHBORS AND NELS HAWKINSON

Texas A&M University Press | College Station

This paper meets the requirements of ANSI/NISO
Z39.48–1992 (Permanence of Paper).
Binding materials have been chosen for durability.
Manufactured in the United States of America

Library of Congress Cataloging-in-Publication Data

Names: Blair, Gary, 1945– | Burson, Rusty, author.
Title: A coaching life / Gary Blair, Rusty Burson.
Other titles: Swaim-Paup-Foran spirit of sport series.
Description: First edition. | College Station: Texas A&M University Press, [2017] |
Series: The Swaim-Paup-Foran spirit of sport series | Includes index.
Identifiers: LCCN 2016038046 (print) | LCCN 2016039830 (ebook) |
ISBN 9781623495367 (cloth: alk. paper) | ISBN 9781623495374 (ebook)
Subjects: LCSH: Blair, Gary, 1945– | Basketball coaches—United States—Biography.
| Basketball for women—United States. | College sports for women—United States. |
Texas A&M University—Basketball—History.
Classification: LCC GV884.B57 A3 2017 (print) | LCC GV884.B57 (ebook) |
DDC 796,323092 [B]—dc23
LC record available at https://lccn.loc.gov/2016038046

CONTENTS

FOREWORD

*An Imaginary Telephone
Conversation between Mike
Neighbors and Nels Hawkinson*

NELS: Hey Nabes, you talked to Blair today?

NABES: No, I missed his call, but he left a four-minute message just to say "Howdy."

NELS: He wants us to write the foreword for his upcoming book.

NABES: Blair's writing a book? I didn't know an Aggie educated at Texas Tech could write!

NELS: Yes sir. If he writes like he talks, it'll be the first sports autobiography with more than 8,000 pages.

NABES: No doubt! It's quite an honor to be able to educate the readers about some of Gary's interests and passions. Where do we start?

NELS: Why don't we toss out a few suggested titles for the book?

NABES: That's great! I'll go first. How about *I'm Never Speechless*?

NELS: Good one. I was thinking either *The Candy Man* or *I Eat Pressure for Breakfast*.

NABES: Both perfect, based on what we know about Gary. Of course, one of the reasons he got into coaching was because he washed out of the baseball team at Texas Tech. How about *I Couldn't Hit the Curve Ball*?

NABES: Hmm. On the other hand, maybe we ought to leave the title to Gary and the publisher. Let's focus on Gary, instead, OK?

NELS: How about his favorite nonbasketball sport topic: baseball? Did you know his wife, Nan, asked Gary if he loved her more than baseball? Gary said "no," but quickly followed up that he loved her more than tennis.

NABES: He is a die-hard Texas Rangers fan. If his Rangers are playing, nothing else matters. He once left his best buddy, Joe McKeown (Northwestern coach), suffering from golf-induced heat stroke in a restaurant bar to race off to the old Arlington Stadium because Nolan Ryan was pitching.

NELS: Golf is another one of his huge passions. Since I don't play, what can you tell me?

NABES: He is crafty. He gets in your head. I consider myself to be a good golfer, but I've only beat him once. I think he's beat me 15 straight times.

NELS: I've stayed in his College Station home on Traditions Golf Course a couple times. It's on the fifth fairway. Everyone knows that after they tee off, his fridge is on the outdoor patio and is always well stocked. Golfers stop by for some free cold ones. I've known him almost 30 years, and that's just the kind of generous guy he is.

NABES: You are right on that, but he also is a cheap son of a gun.

NELS: Oh boy, which one of the hundreds of stories do we share about that?

NABES: Let's start with my favorite. In 2011, after A&M beat Stanford in the Final Four to advance to the national championship game, Gary celebrated both this huge victory and his wife's birthday by taking Nan to Steak 'n Shake. According to Gary, they went there because St. Elmo's Steak House closed at midnight. But there's more! On his way out, he asked for a free refill. The guy at the counter said, "Sir, that'll be 99 cents." He refused to pay, and so I slapped a one-spot on the counter to cover it.

NELS: Did you know that every day in College Station, he drives out of his way to the Hilton so he can run in and grab a free *USA Today* because he refuses to pay for a newspaper that's more than a quarter.

NABES: I think people get the idea. But let's describe "the real" Gary Blair!

NELS: Well, from the first time you meet him, he comes across as Jed Clampett from *The Beverly Hillbillies* and Gomer Pyle from *The Andy Griffith Show*, combined into one. He is a gosh-darn, aw-shucks kind of guy. He will talk to anybody, anywhere, anytime. His next job should be at Walmart as a store greeter. He'd be the greeter of the decade.

NABES: As his former assistant, I have waited for him probably hundreds of hours as he walks through hotel lobbies, restaurants, golf clubhouses, and arenas, all across America, giving candy to the young people and swapping stories with the older folks.

NELS: That's what I love about Gary. He truly cares about people. Never once have I seen him turn down someone who wanted to meet him. In fact, he seeks people out. He wants them to know that if times are hard, they are going to get better. If things are going good, they should feel blessed.

NABES: He is the same way with NCAA basketball. He has been a mentor to so many coaches. He will walk the concourses of away arenas to greet the opposing team's fans before the game begins. He works tirelessly to promote Texas A&M women's basketball, as you'll read in the book.

NELS: Besides giving so much of his personal time, he also has a heart for the Special Olympics since he has been at Texas A&M.

NABES: He sure does. The Gary Blair Golf Classic has raised over $1.2 million for the Special Olympics. The Special Olympics charity certainly benefits from this special guy.

NELS: We can't end our *"Blair*ing Comments" without mentioning the real special people in his life: his family. It's been tough living apart from Nan for 13 years, but somehow they make it work.

NABES: He loves Nan and his two kids, Paige and Matt. He especially loves playing the grandpa role to his grandkids. Family is really all you need, and he is blessed with a great one.

NELS: Definitely. And we are all blessed by having a friend and mentor like Gary Blair.

Mike Neighbors
Seattle, Washington
June 2016

Nels Hawkinson
Shoreline, Washington
June 2016

A COACHING LIFE

1 Stories, Memories, and Victories worth Preserving

I'll never forget the moment in August 2011 when I first heard that the legendary Pat Summitt, the winningest coach in NCAA basketball history at that time—men's or women's, regardless of division—had been diagnosed with Alzheimer's disease. The news literally sickened me, smacking me in the face like a haymaker knockout punch from Muhammad Ali in his prime. Not only was Summitt one of the most respected all-around coaches to ever live (in 2009, the *Sporting News* listed her as No. 11 on its list of the 50 greatest coaches of all time, regardless of the sport), but she is also a colleague and personal friend. I have an incalculable amount of admiration for her and all she accomplished as the head coach at the University of Tennessee from 1974 to 2012.

In 38 seasons as the Lady Vols' head coach, Summitt guided Tennessee to eight national championships. As I write this today, only two coaches (the late John Wooden of UCLA's men's program and Geno Auriemma with the University of Connecticut's women's team) have won more national titles in the history of NCAA Division I basketball.

Winning eight national titles in a career is simply amazing to me. To put that into context, I've been a college head coach since 1985, and in the ensuing three decades, I was part of one magical, memory-making, remember-it-for-forever run to a national championship. I was 65 years old when Texas

A&M won the 2011 title (it should be noted that I was not the oldest coach to win the NCAA Division I basketball championship in 2011, as UConn's men's coach Jim Calhoun was 68). That 2011 women's title was one of the most amazingly rewarding and fulfilling moments of my life. At my current rate of one national championship for every 30 years as a head coach, however, I'd need to continue coaching into the 23rd century, when I'd be 305 years old—roughly twice as old as Abraham from the Bible—to catch up to Summitt.

That's obviously not going to happen. The 23rd psalm will have been read at my funeral many, many decades before the arrival of the 23rd century. But I believe that offers some perspective on the magnitude of Summitt's magnificent accomplishments as a collegiate head coach.

After making one triumphant journey through the absolute mayhem of March Madness, I can only imagine how many glowing and precious memories Summitt possesses from her eight glorious runs to national championships. And quite frankly, that's why I was so utterly devastated by the news of her Alzheimer's diagnosis.

At one point or another, all coaches will eventually be required to leave the bench and hang up the whistle for good, creating a huge void in their lives. Father Time is undefeated in the long run. He's been held at bay various times, but he always wins, and that is difficult for a coach to accept when his or her time arrives.

You don't spend 30, 40, or 50 years in this profession without becoming absolutely addicted to the adrenaline rush of pregame introductions or last-second play calling and diagramming. Likewise, there's nothing quite like the energy infusion associated with the roar of a big and boisterous crowd when a plan comes together. While winning games is immensely rewarding, playing a role in the maturation or transformation of a young person's life is far more gratifying. And the joy of watching a group of typically self-centered individuals buy into the concept of becoming a self-sacrificing team in order to achieve their dreams is off the charts in terms of job satisfaction and fulfillment.

The losses can be tormenting and exasperating, but even the most difficult defeats can ultimately be uplifting when you watch young people learn, mature, and evolve through tough times. The intensity of the competition, the camaraderie of a team and others within the coaching profession, the exhilaration of winning, the passion of the players and fans, the pageantry of the sport, and so forth are all more energizing than any amount of caffeine and more intoxicating—in a memorable way—than any alcoholic beverage.

Those things obviously disappear in retirement, but at least we can count on reliving those memories and retelling those stories on bar stools, in coffee shops, and at banquets halls throughout our "golden years"—unless something as cruel, unmerciful, and degenerative as Alzheimer's gradually robs us of those memories. Winning trophies, cutting down nets after championships, and earning individual honors are all nice. I'd be lying if I claimed otherwise. But what I have most cherished collecting since I first entered the coaching profession in 1973 at South Oak Cliff High School are the memories associated with coaching and working with young people.

I'm certainly not alone in that regard. My guess is that most lifelong coaches—from the middle school ranks to the NFL or WNBA—feel the same way. So many of the games ultimately run together in my mind, but the faces of the players, the circumstances of their backgrounds, the details of their lives after basketball, the lessons learned, the halftime speeches, the clutch shots, the good hires, the questionable calls, the failed experiments, the agonizing losses, the uplifting wins, the first-class hotels, the broken-down buses, the missed opportunities, the magnificent comebacks—all fill my memory bank with so much more value than will ever accrue in my actual bank account.

That's not to say that I have not been well paid for my services as a basketball coach. Quite frankly, I've been blessed financially beyond my wildest dreams, especially considering what I earned when I first entered the teaching/coaching profession ($7,300 a year at South Oak Cliff in 1972–73; $7,000 for teaching PE and $300 for coaching). I thank God for the lifestyle and luxuries that my career has afforded my family and me. But in all sincerity—and unlike some professional athletes, I really, really mean this—I've never been driven in my career by money or material things. Never. What drives me is the need to make a difference in the lives of young people. What inspires me is that basketball can be used to build foundations for future success. What motivates me is the concept that victories and defeats, trials and triumphs, and adversities and accomplishments can teach life lessons that will be applicable to my players long after their basketball careers have ended. And what I cherish the most are the memories of those players and coaches, as well as the stories about all those seasons.

Hence the reason for this book. Following Summitt's Alzheimer's diagnosis, I was at least comforted by the fact that her most vivid memories and compelling stories had been preserved and protected in the pages of her three books: *Reach for the Summitt*, *Raise the Roof*, and *Sum It Up*. I've read them all and thoroughly enjoyed each one, primarily because all the remarkable anecdotes and the keen insights that she documented gave me an understanding of what made her so successful and so driven. Coaching against the fiery-eyed and combative coach throughout my tenure as an assistant coach at Louisiana Tech (1980–85) and as the head coach at the University of Arkansas (1993–2003), I grew quite familiar with her legendary scowl and how she snarled at players, referees, and opposing coaches like me. With her teeth and fists clenched and the veins protruding from her neck, she often seemed cold—even calloused—in the way she dealt with practically everyone.

Then I read her books and received a fascinating glimpse of exactly where she developed her no-nonsense, tough-love tactics and rigid coaching style. Summitt's father never hugged her or directly expressed any love toward her until she was 43. He instead instilled a fear-driven work ethic in Pat and her four siblings. I certainly understood her disciplinary approach after she revealed that her father frequently beat his children on the family's Tennessee farm with a belt, tobacco stick, switch, milk strap, or whatever else he could grab whenever they disobeyed him. He was relentless in his rigidness. Yet Pat possessed an immense amount of respect for him because he valued his kids enough to build a basketball court in the hayloft. And when Pat couldn't play for the local high school because it didn't have a girls' team, he moved the family. He wasn't warm, but he did care.

To read those stories, it's no wonder why the sport meant so much to her even though she often seemed to be coaching on the verge of an absolute rage to achieve perfection. To read the tales about what she said to some players made me cringe. Following a loss to Auriemma and UConn in the 1995 NCAA championship game, for example, Summitt blamed point guard Michelle Marciniak in front of the whole team. "You didn't show up," Summitt recalled of her brutal treatment of Marciniak. "If you had shown up, we'd have won." The following season, Summitt unapologetically pushed Marciniak to the brink—just the way her own father would have done to her. And at the end of the 1996 season, Tennessee beat UConn in the Final Four and went on to win the national championship. Meanwhile, Marciniak was named the MVP of the Final Four. After winning the championship, Summitt gave Marciniak the hug she had been withholding for years. Later that night, Summitt's father embraced 43-year-old Pat for the first time in her life.

What a story. What a remarkable perspective of what made Summitt such a sensationally successful, stern, and volatile coach. And while she could be brutal and brash, she is also beloved by so many of the players who benefitted from her coaching. Summitt mellowed somewhat as she aged, and her books were filled with one fascinating story after another that detailed how she evolved as a coach. I gained so much from reading those stories and perspectives; and, especially after she was diagnosed with dementia, I was grateful she had shared so many intimate details and personal memories about her life and how she was affected by all her experiences.

After reading her third book, I finally vowed to do something I had been pondering for many years: write my own. Not because I consider my own coaching accomplishments comparable to Summitt or Auriemma, but rather because I've always believed there's more than one way to skin a cat, more than one way to cook an egg, and more than one way to lead and inspire young people to achieve their dreams. Summitt's motivating style was menacing, which came naturally because of her upbringing. But that's simply not my style, and it's not who I am.

Rest assured, I can be tough—even domineering, dictatorial, and militaristic—when times or situations call for it. I joined the Marine Corps in 1969—at the beginning of Richard Nixon's presidency and right in the midst of the conflict in Vietnam. I was 23 years old when I joined the Marines, and I was easily the oldest member of my platoon. For the most part, I was surrounded by a bunch of 18-year-olds in my platoon, and I was even a year and a half older than two of my drill instructors. Being older didn't make surviving the Marine Corps' boot camp any easier for me (perhaps nothing is more grueling and challenging on an emotional and physical level than the Marine Corps' boot camp, especially back in the late 1960s). But being older did give me a perspective on life and people that many of my fellow platoon members simply did not possess.

I had already been to college, trying in vain to play baseball—I could cover the outfield with the best of the best, but I couldn't hit worth a crap—and working my butt off at Texas Tech. I worked so hard at Texas Tech (mostly outside of the classroom setting) that I flunked out of architecture after my first year and burned out of the college life before I even reached my senior year. When I left school prior to my senior year, I definitely needed a break and wound up in Los Angeles, where my real-life education truly began. At Tech, after I scrapped the architecture plan, I began majoring in physical education with plans to eventually become a coach, and journalism was my teaching field. But in need of a break and a change of scenery, I thought I would go into advertising in Hollywood. I thought wrong.

I had some advertising doors slammed in my face, but I never managed to get my foot in the door. Looking back on it, I may have had more luck trying to become the next Cary Grant or Jimmy Stewart. Instead, I wound up attending a restaurant management training school in West Los Angeles through A&W Restaurants, which was arguably the first successful fast food franchise company, starting franchises in California in 1923. The company, named after the initials of partners Roy W. Allen and Frank Wright, became famous in the United States for its "frosty mugs": mugs were kept in the freezer prior to being filled with root beer and served to the customer. I actually started my training with United Fruit, which had purchased A&W and its Los Angeles training center. I learned every aspect of the restaurant business at the training center—from flipping burgers to bookkeeping—and I quickly discovered that I was pretty damn good at it.

I also met a woman out in Los Angeles, and we were so infatuated with each other that we became engaged. The engagement only lasted three months, however, because I was so good at the A&W training center that I was quickly promoted to run a brand-new 110-seat store on Harbor Boulevard in Costa Mesa, California, that was similar to Kip's Big Boy Restaurants (or Shoney's). In running the restaurant, I was putting in 90-hour workweeks, even though I had a night manager. There are only a total of 168 hours in a week, and my fiancée at the time decided that she was not willing to settle for using the remaining 78 hours each week to build a relationship. I can't say I blame her. But while I lost my engagement, the round-the-clock hours in that restaurant provided me with some lifelong lessons and perspectives that ultimately shaped my personality and coaching style.

First, I realized that on a Saturday or Sunday morning, it was practically inevitable—at least on one of those days every weekend—that the cook who was supposed to arrive at 5:30 a.m. wouldn't show up on time because he'd been out drinking too late the night before. I learned how to poach, fry, and scramble eggs while running the deep fryer and operating the order wheel in the kitchen. Let me emphasize that if you can run the order wheel in the kitchen of a fast food restaurant, you can do just about anything. That is the definition of pressure. Big-time pressure. And I discovered that I had a knack for handling it without cracking. My trademark phrase as a coach is that "I eat pressure for breakfast." Maybe that started because of those pressure-packed breakfasts as a cook.

Even more valuable than that, though, I truly began evaluating and studying people and appreciating the rare individuals who mastered and utilized great people skills. Case in point: my best waitress. A large portion of my regular customers came from the nearby new-car lots, and they could be pushy and brash. They effectively drove many of my waitresses to their wit's end, testing their patience to the limit with plenty of demands and a few tasteless comments and sexual suggestions. My best waitress, however, handled it all in stride and earned the loyalty and respect of some of the tackiest trash-talkers. She wasn't the best looking of my waitresses, and she came from a rather tainted background.

She was a 32-year-old former stripper who was sick and tired of the sleazy scene. Nothing the salesmen said fazed her, and she was always able to smile and interact with them no matter how rude some of the other waitresses thought they were. She utilized humor, kept a smile on her face, and made the most money of all the waitresses. She was so good that I finally convinced her to start training some of the other waitresses. More than anything else, though, she just exhibited great people skills and genuinely made her customers feel like she appreciated them. They reciprocated by paying her bigger tips, requesting to sit in her section, and recommending her—and the restaurant—to their friends. It wasn't the coffee or my poached eggs that were winning customers—it was her people skills.

That made a huge impression on me. People skills mean everything, regardless of whether you are coaching elite athletes or taking orders from cranky car salesmen. Watching that waitress and refining my own people skills helped me immediately when I was transferred to Chicago about nine months after taking over the restaurant in Los Angeles.

The previous manager of the upscale drive-in located in one of South Chicago's tougher neighborhoods was taking kickbacks from vendors, and the restaurant was barely making any money because it had become a destination hangout for some of the Windy City's motorcycle gangs. The gang members weren't necessarily dangerous or malicious—they were more like Fonzie and the gang than Hells Angels—but they would basically take over the parking lot and the restaurant, sitting wherever they wanted for as long as they wanted . . . even if they never purchased food or beverage items. In one of the most challenging and intimidating jobs I have ever had, I went to Chicago with instructions to change vendors, replace the existing staff, and clear the bikers out of the restaurant. Or, at the very least, I was tasked with transforming the motorcycle gangsters from freeloading loiterers into paying customers. I certainly wasn't going to accomplish those objectives with intimidation techniques or tough-love tactics. I did display some signs that notified patrons that they had to buy a cup of coffee or a soda— 50 cents at minimum—if they were going to sit at our tables, but primarily, I was able to turn the restaurant around by exhibiting some genuine people skills and training my staff to do the same. Our primary plan of attack was to win the hearts and favor of the bikers with kindness and genuine, straight-forward explanations instead of attempting to force them to do anything. We also wanted to bring the families and working people back as customers.

The strategy was working quite well until about a month later, when I received a phone call notifying me that I was to report to the Armed Forces Induction Center in Los Angeles in five days. To make a long story short—and I will elaborate on some specifics later—I joined the Marine Corps without even informing my parents. I certainly wasn't the typical square-jawed, muscle-flexing, chest-thumping, fight-seeking badass that defined the Marine Corps, but I figured if I was going to be drafted, I might as well see if I had the mettle to be a Marine. I was placed on a bus bound for San Diego, and I wound up in a platoon of 75 young men, mostly teenagers. Roughly one-third of those men were African American, and it was really the first time I had ever been in a multiracial melting pot.

Growing up in Dallas and attending high school at Bryan Adams in the early 1960s, I didn't even know a single black person. I most certainly didn't go to school with any African Americans, even though many years had passed since *Brown v. Board of Education*. Desegregation began gradu-ally afterward—and it began slowly, especially the farther south the school system was located. The Dallas Independent School District (DISD), for example, did not begin integrating schools until 1971. But I am jumping ahead of myself.

I, for one, did not see "color." I saw people. Period. At that time in America—even in places like Chicago and San Diego—it was not com-mon for white men and women to view African Americans as their peers or equals. To say that racist perspectives, undertones, and opinions were still accepted and proliferated in mainstream America in the late 1960s and early 1970s would be an extreme understatement. Many, many white folks still viewed themselves as superior to blacks, even if a particular African Ameri-can held an identical or superior job, title, or position. But perhaps nothing unifies a group of men of varying races, socioeconomic backgrounds, and cultures like a Marine Corps boot camp. Or a foxhole. When you are going through the hellacious conditions of boot camp in preparation for a pos-sible tour of duty in Vietnam, you'd better develop some trust, admiration, and respect for the guy next to you regardless of whether he is black, white, brown, or whatever else. Not all my fellow white platoon members thought and acted that way, but I believe I earned the trust of all my platoon members by the way I took care of myself and treated others.

Even though I did not know any blacks growing up in Dallas, I was not raised by parents who discriminated against any segment of society. I also had the benefit of observing and studying people from various socio-economic, educational, and geographical backgrounds—especially in Los Angeles and Chicago—and had drawn some strong conclusions about treating people with genuine respect and sincerity, regardless of where they came from or how they looked. I really believe that my attitude entering the Marine Corps and my encounters with all the men in my platoon won me the respect of my fellow black Marines because they were not accustomed to seeing a white man—especially a slightly older white man—treat them as equals in every way.

Fortunately, none of us in that platoon ended up in Vietnam. The Third Marine Division, which included our platoon, was pulled back from Vietnam two weeks before we were assigned. Instead, my platoon was sent on a noncombative assignment at Camp Hansen in Okinawa, Japan.

In Okinawa, some of the ranking officers discovered that even though I was merely an enlisted private first class, I had spent years in college studying kinesiology and had at least somewhat of a journalism background from my education. As a result, I ended up working in an office setting from day to day as the diary clerk, arranging leaves for all the officers and enlisted people. I pushed plenty of papers and pencils and missed most of the inspections and physically demanding assignments. Quite frankly, I had a pretty good time in Okinawa, and I managed to save enough money to buy a '71 Camaro and some gifts for my family, travel to Expo '71 on my R and R, and visit Osaka and Tokyo. Unlike many of my fellow Marines, I was not wasting all my money in the villages at night.

My total time in the Marine Corps was just 18 months and seven days—long enough to qualify for the GI bill—and then I took advantage of an early-out program in December 1970. By that time, I was ready to sprint back to Texas Tech to finish my degree and pursue a career that involved something more than poaching eggs or pushing pencils. My former fiancée, who had checked out on me when I was working 90 hours a week in Los Angeles, had a change of heart when I returned to the United States and suddenly wanted to marry me again. But I was no longer interested—at least at that moment—in settling down with one person. I wanted to finish my degree and I wanted to coach. I loved sports. I loved people. I believed I had developed some outstanding people skills, and I had this great vision of being an outstanding high school coach before moving on to the collegiate ranks.

The problem with that plan, however, was that I still needed a job while I waited for one of my dream jobs to become available. I had earned my undergraduate degree from Texas Tech and was working toward my master's when I was offered a teaching job within DISD. The position was at South Oak Cliff (SOC—pronounced "sock"), which opened in 1952 as the first DISD high school to be constructed since Lincoln High had opened in 1939. SOC initially served the developing areas of south and east Oak Cliff. In the late 1950s, before Kimball and Carter high schools were opened, SOC was one of the largest high schools in the city, and for its first 13 years, SOC was designated as a "white" high school by DISD. When I was a senior at Bryan Adams High School in 1963, our all-white squad defeated SOC's all-white team for the Dallas city championship in baseball.

After integration began in 1968, however, South Oak Cliff, along with many other DISD schools, became predominantly black almost overnight. SOC, which now generally serves an area of Dallas east of Interstate 35E and south of Illinois Avenue, offered me an opportunity to teach the physical education classes until a full-time coaching opportunity opened. I leapt at the opportunity and went to work at SOC in the fall of 1972. At that time, about 65 percent of faculty and administration were white, while the remaining 35 percent were African American or Hispanic, but a concerted effort was being made to increase the number of minority teachers and administrators. I absolutely loved the faculty and staff that I encountered at SOC. We had a great time working together, and we all truly felt like we were part of something really big in terms of providing equal educational opportunities and changing racial perceptions.

Again, I did not see color when I looked into the classrooms, walked through the hallways, or worked with my physical education classes. I saw promising young people with brighter futures ahead of them. I believed that the 1970s could be a great time of racial progress and unification in America, and I believed I could make a difference at SOC. I looked forward to going to work each day and working directly with "my kids" in the PE classes. And for the most part, I was genuinely treated with great respect and appreciation by the students. They could tell I cared, and they knew I was doing much more than merely collecting a paycheck. Practically any job ultimately comes down to relationships and people skills—the lesson I learned from my best waitress in Los Angeles—and I believed I was being received by the vast majority of the students quite favorably.

There was one young man, however, whom I simply could not reach. And he would not allow me to avoid him. In the hallways between classes, he always seemed to be lurking around a corner, staring at me and daring me to confront him in some way. To this day, I cannot remember anything I might have done to initially incite his wrath. I think the bottom line was that his heart was filled with hatred, and while I didn't see color, he certainly noticed an absence of color in me. Initially, he stared at me. Then the stares became scowls. Then, wherever I went inside the school, he passed me or bumped into me and constantly referred to me in the same derogatory two-word phrase: white mother—.

Over time, this became a more and more uncomfortable situation, as I began to sense that he was becoming increasingly hostile toward me. I anticipated a looming confrontation and wondered how I could avoid the worst-case scenarios that kept playing in my mind. What if he attacked me? How could I respond? He was 16 or 17, and even if I was merely defending myself, I knew that I could absolutely not become involved in a scuffle or fight of any sort. And to make matters worse, I really didn't feel comfortable talking about the situation with my principal (a black man named Louie McQuirter) or any of my fellow teachers. I believed that if I brought it up, I would be perceived as a racist.

Mostly, I fretted or tried to ignore the situation altogether . . . until one day when this particular young man showed up with a gang of other questionable folks—an entourage of troublesome teens—on the main football practice field. The front entrance of South Oak Cliff faces South Marsalis Avenue, and the school property has a gradual descent from east to west, with the school at the top and the football practice field at the very bottom, behind the parking lot, portable buildings, tennis courts, and a baseball/softball field. Because of the descent and the existing facilities on the grounds behind the school, it is impossible to see what is happening on the practice football field from the school. The young man, whose heart was so obviously filled with hatred toward me, had figured this out and had made the decision to confront me once and for all during my third-period PE class as I worked with 20 to 30 young people who would certainly not fall under the description of being particularly "athletic." For the most part, these were the kids—sophomore and junior boys—who were not talented enough or aggressive enough to play the primary sports. Some sort of physical education was a state requirement, and this third-period PE class was fulfilling the mandatory physical obligation.

My would-be assailant arrived at the bottom of the school property with five or six of his friends who were intent on making sure that I didn't run away. There were no cell phones or camera phones in those days to warn anyone inside the school, and as this young man began to saunter my way, he yelled out at me, "Hey, I am about to whip your ass, you white mother—!"

At that moment, I thought my coaching career was about to come to an end before it ever even began. My heart raced. My stomach churned. The palms of my hands were suddenly covered in a thin film of cold sweat. For the life of me, I could not think of a good solution. I could do nothing to defend myself, and I could only hope that he stopped short of killing me with his bare hands. Or I could fight and defend myself and likely face criminal assault charges and a ton of negative media scrutiny. I swallowed hard, clenching my fists, and hoped for some sort of miracle.

At that very moment, I experienced perhaps the greatest team victory of my life. People who know me—even people who really know me well—would probably guess that my greatest win came on April 5, 2011, when Texas A&M, which was once one of the worst women's programs in the country, defeated Notre Dame at Conseco Fieldhouse in Indianapolis to win the national title. Others might guess that the biggest win was actually knocking off Baylor in the regional final in Dallas on March 29, 2011. Or that maybe my biggest win was leading South Oak Cliff to their first girls' state championship or taking the University of Arkansas to the Final Four in 1998.

All of those are great memories, but none of them would have been possible without the great team victory on that day on the practice field at South Oak Cliff. Just as I was bracing for the worst, my PE class members surrounded me in a circle of protection. I don't remember the exact words that were said, but my PE class came to my defense and told this foul-mouthed bully that he would have to come through all of them to get to me. It was my proudest moment as a teacher or coach. Unlike so many of the basketball games I coached in the ensuing decades, not many people saw it and nobody wrote about it. But this group of black kids that most of the rest of the school would have considered "mild-mannered" or "meek" stood up for me against one of the most intimidating and menacing kids in the entire school.

They did it because they knew I cared about them. They stood around me because they knew my motivation was them, not me. They did the right thing for me because they knew I would do the right thing for them. And at that point, I knew I had found my calling.

If I could somehow connect with a bunch of kids so deeply that they would literally be willing to fight for me, I figured I just might have the people skills to make a difference someday as a coach. That's why I am the kind of coach I am today. I am a people person. I connect with people. Hopefully that's my legacy as a coach, and as you will uncover in the ensuing chapters, that's why I have been able to accomplish things that many people never could have envisioned. In that regard, this book is not as much about documenting victories or accomplishments as it is about detailing the importance of building great relationships, learning from others, and making a positive difference in the lives of others by making positive memories.

As it was once so eloquently stated by the late poet Mattie J. T. Stepanek, who died in 2004 at the age of only 14, "Keep all special thoughts and memories for lifetimes to come. Share these keepsakes with others to inspire hope and build from the past, which can bridge to the future."

Ultimately, that's why I felt compelled to write this book. I've learned so many great lessons from so many great people through the years, from legendary coaching figures like Pat Summitt to former employees like the 32-year-old waitress who taught me so much about people skills in Los Angeles. I feel obliged to share some of those lessons, and my hope is that in sharing some of my favorite memories, I can also serve as an inspiration to others. After all, as an anonymous quote I once read stated, "there's no need to be perfect to inspire others. Let people be inspired by how you deal with your imperfections."

As you will undoubtedly see in the ensuing chapters, I possess plenty of imperfections—and plenty of stories about those imperfections.

2 Growing Up and Outgrowing the "Meathead" Phase

On January 12, 1971, the sitcom *All in the Family* made its American television premier, featuring the colorful and incomparable Carroll O'Connor as the blue-collared, bigoted, beer-drinking, berating, short-tempered, set-in-his-ways Archie Bunker. Throughout much of the 1970s, *All in the Family* was the top-rated US sitcom, as the gruff and grumbling Archie Bunker—despite his many flaws and biases—became one of the most well-known and popular characters in the country. While Bunker was crude and calloused, he was also somehow lovable in a "that's-just-Archie, don't-be-offended" kind of way. At the very least, Archie Bunker was relatable because in those far less politically correct times, practically everyone knew someone who was as opinionated and crass as Archie.

Archie resided in Queens, a borough in New York City. But he could have just as easily lived in Detroit, Denver, Des Moines, Dallas, or any other city in the United States. In fact, Archie Bunker could have easily lived in my childhood home in Dallas.

When I first watched *All in the Family*, he reminded me in numerous ways of my own father, from his prejudices and his relentless work ethic to his passion for beer and reluctance to show any affection toward anyone, including my mother. Furthermore, the sweet, nonconfrontational, and often naïve Edith Bunker reminded me in many ways of my own mother. Like

Edith, my mother didn't drive anywhere, but she was much sharper and stronger than my father gave her credit for. Also like Edith, she chose her battles extremely carefully. My childhood home wasn't an exact replica of the show, as my parents had four children, not just one. But it would definitely be accurate to say that my older brother, younger two sisters, and I were raised in a setting with a "Bunker mentality."

My father, Lee, was the second youngest of 12 kids and was raised by my grandparents in Troup, Texas, which is still not much more than a dot on the map some 20 miles southeast of Tyler. My father dropped out of school in the seventh grade to go to work. He took every job very seriously, especially when he landed a position with the Ford Motor Company, which was really big deal in Big D. At one point in time, every vehicle that rolled off the assembly line in Dallas was equipped with a sticker that stated, "Built in Texas by Texans." That was a source of great pride for Texans who owned Fords and especially for the Ford employees who were producing automobiles in Dallas.

The facility in Dallas was one of 15 plants operated throughout the country and could produce 650 cars and trucks each day with two eight-hour shifts. Despite my father's lack of a formal education, he rose through the ranks at Ford because of his work ethic and his ability to manage people. He didn't possess great social skills, and he wasn't necessarily eloquent, but he had been blessed with an innate ability to lead and to manage people. He did well enough at Ford that the company began sending him to the headquarters in Detroit fairly often. While other people in a similar position may have viewed the travel as a major reward, my father was uncomfortable with it, as well as with the increasing responsibilities he was gaining with Ford in Dallas.

His solution was to leave Ford and join a couple of brothers in the Dallas area who were doing construction work. My father became "the plaster guy," which made him far more comfortable. And rest assured, my father did not like stepping outside his comfort zone for anything or anybody. He was man of habit who liked to be home at a certain time every day, eat dinner at a particular time every evening (usually 6 p.m.), sit in his favorite chair, drink his favorite beer, and hang out with his favorite friend, "Shorty," who earned his nickname naturally thanks to his 4-foot-11-inch frame. As I recall, we didn't lack for any necessities while I was growing up, but we also didn't have much disposable income. My father's idea of a vacation was driving the family from Dallas to Weatherford (roughly 30 miles west of Fort Worth) to spend the night with Shorty and his family. And my father's idea of a big night out on the town was going to the "Devil's Bowl Speedway," a dirt-track stock car facility in Mesquite that is still in operation. Sometimes I can still hear the buzzing of stock cars in my head when I think back to those times.

Generally speaking, my father was a good man who minded his own business, worked hard, and provided for his family. He just wasn't particularly caring, connecting, compassionate, or anything of the sort. He was a bit of a loner who minded his business, and he expected everyone else in the house to do the same. Although my brother, sisters, and I attended church regularly, he didn't go unless it was Easter and my mother forced him. He also didn't show any affection toward my mother unless he had consumed at least several beers, and he was not particularly involved in his children's extracurricular interests and activities. He wanted to do things his way, and he was quite opinionated about many things. Like I said, the man was Archie Bunker before anyone had even heard of Archie.

My father's hands-off, mind-your-own-business parenting style definitely had an effect on each of his children, particularly when we were young. Steve, who is four years older than me, was somewhat of a rebel. In fact, as a teen, he was a lot like James Dean in *Rebel Without a Cause*—and he even looked like James Dean. Steve was never a bad kid, and he was definitely more ornery than mean-spirited or criminal, but he and my cousin "Hammy" were in and out of trouble from time to time and often up to no good. Because he is four years older than me, we were never in high school together, and maybe that was a good thing, since he earned such a mischievous reputation.

While my high school days revolved around sports, sports, and more sports, Steve was more "diversified." Some injuries had ended his athletic career relatively early, but Steve stayed in shape by "dodging" the police and "chasing" girls. He also loved working on cars, remodeling cars, driving cars, and drinking beer with his buddies. Despite his rebellious spirit, Steve turned out to be a terrific person. Steve followed some friends to Texas A&M University in the fall of 1959, and although he didn't graduate from A&M, the year he spent in Aggieland helped shape him. Texas A&M really straightened Steve out in a number of ways, and to this day, one of his great regrets is that he didn't graduate. He left school to get married, but if he could do it all over again, he would have married my sister-in-law and lived in married housing in Aggieland. Nevertheless, his year at A&M played a big role in his life and helped him build a great business, Blair Graphics, in Plano, which he ran for more than 27 years before selling it in 1998.

His year in College Station also made an impact on me when I attended the 1959 A&M–Texas game on Thanksgiving Day at Kyle Field. The Aggies were awful that year, entering the game at 3–6 overall and 0–5 in the Southwest Conference. Just two years earlier, A&M had climbed to No. 1 in the national polls under the direction of Bear Bryant. But the '59 team, led by Jim Myers, was rather woeful. Nevertheless, the Aggies played an inspired and spirited game against the No. 4–ranked Longhorns before ultimately falling, 20–17. I was impressed with the game and even more impressed by the overall atmosphere.

My younger sister, Dianne, was basically the complete opposite of Steve—she did everything right and was never in an ounce of trouble. While Steve was focused on raising hell as a teenager, Dianne was angelic in her focus and deeds throughout her life. Dianne loved spending time at church, working with the church, and representing the church. For example, she was a really good athlete, especially in softball, where she played for the church team. Even as an adult, her life essentially revolved around the church and spreading the gospel of Christ to all parts of the world. With her husband, Larry, she was a Southern Baptist missionary for decades in hostile places such as Rwanda—where an estimated 500,000 to 1,000,000 Rwandans were killed in the mid-1990s—Mozambique, and South Africa.

Perhaps the amount of time and effort Dianne invested in the church as a child and teen had something to do with the lack of attention she received from our father, but she definitely channeled her energies into a worthy and wonderful endeavor. Her Christian faith provided her with a great deal of fulfillment, and her work as a missionary made a tremendously positive impact in the lives of many others.

My baby sister, Debbie, was a little more like Steve in terms of her early rebellious spirit. Debbie is 15 years younger than my brother and 11 years younger than me. She was practically a toddler when Steve was leaving for A&M. As a result, she was basically an only child in many ways because Steve, Dianne, and I were so much older that we more like uncles and an aunt. Like Steve, Debbie was never a bad kid, and she turned out just fine, but she just wasn't a particularly big fan of following guidelines or rules. She liked dating older guys, staying out late, dancing into the wee hours of the morning, and multiplying the number of gray hairs on my mother's head.

Looking back now, I have little doubt that my fanatical and fervent fascination with sports had something to do with my father's detached parenting style. Don't get me wrong—I possessed a strong competitive nature and would have loved playing, watching, following, and dissecting sports under any circumstances. But one of the things I always wanted in my preteen years—and one of the things that I most envied about some of my friends' home lives—was the opportunity to play catch with my father.

Like so many other baseball-adoring Americans, I loved the 1989 movie *Field of Dreams*, starring Kevin Costner, Amy Madigan, and James Earl Jones, for a variety of reasons. According to some critics, however, it was too farfetched to be considered one of the great baseball movies of all time. But I loved and related to it because it wasn't really about ghosts, magic corn fields, Shoeless Joe Jackson, or Moonlight Graham. Ultimately, the entire movie is about the lengths one man will go to in order to play catch with his father. Period. I know the feeling, and I would have absolutely gone to extraordinary lengths to play catch with my father as well. That just wasn't his thing, though. We never played catch in the front yard, the backyard, or anywhere else. Not once. I wouldn't say that scarred me for life or anything, but it was a tough pill to swallow at the time. Instead of begging my father to play and risking that rejection or allowing anyone else to know that it bothered me that he didn't want to play, I spent as many hours as humanly possible playing baseball, basketball, and football with my neighbors and also a few of their fathers.

When I was born on August 10, 1945, my parents brought me home to a little house in Mesquite. But I only lived in that house for about two weeks before my parents bought the home I was raised in at 8715 Forest Hills Boulevard near White Lake Rock in northeast Dallas.

We lived in a nice framed section of Forest Hills. It certainly didn't compare with the brick houses and large homes near other parts of the lake, but it was a safe working-class neighborhood. Like most of the other homes in the area, our house was a one-story, three-bedroom cookie-cutter home with a tiny front porch, a small one-car garage, and a front yard that was really only large enough for one big cottonwood tree. From my perspective, though, the best feature of our house was the number of neighbors with kids who were roughly the same age as me.

When it wasn't raining, a group of us would meet out front after dinner in the springtime and summer practically every night to play street ball, stick ball, or some type of ball until the sun went down. We'd use manhole covers and driveways as bases, then we'd take a baseball and wrap it tight with black electrical tape to extend the life of the ball and prevent it from getting too scuffed up from playing on the street. We didn't have a field or park that was close enough for us to walk or ride our bikes to and still have enough daylight to play a lengthy game after dinner, so we played on a narrow,

treelined street. Our number-one rule was that if any ball went into one of
the yards on either side of the street, it was a foul ball. Obviously, you had to
hit the ball up the middle to have any success. Pull hitters from either side of
the plate didn't last long on our street, partly because of our rules and mainly
because it was so easy to break a window if you didn't hit a ball right back
up the middle. Nothing ended a good game more abruptly than a broken
window and an angry homeowner asking for our names, where we lived, and
who the hell was going to pay for this!

I was as skinny as a string bean, so I wasn't going to be a power hitter
regardless of how hard I tried to pull a pitch. My only chance in street ball,
or real baseball, for that matter, was to bunt, hit line drives, and put ground
balls into play so I could use my speed to get on the bases. In the long run,
our neighborhood games probably helped develop my skills enough for me
to make it in high school and college. But back then, I wasn't thinking about
how baseball might lead me to one college or another; I just wanted to play.
And I also just wanted Judy Bouska to be on my team, regardless of who
else was playing.

Judy went to a Catholic school and was three years older than me. While
I didn't have a crush on her, I did love the way she could crush a baseball.
Judy was a helluva good athlete—better than all the boys in the neighborhood, including me—and we made a terrific team together, regardless of
whether we were playing street ball, football, or basketball. She would always
pick me when we were choosing teams, and I would do the same. Technically, she was the first female athlete I ever recruited. Even when we had no
one else to play against, we'd get together in her driveway with some tennis
balls and a broomstick and play ball against her garage while I pretended
to be Whitey Ford or Willie Mays and she pretended to be Duke Snider.
This was long before the Texas Rangers relocated from Washington, DC,
to the Dallas–Fort Worth area, so our childhood baseball heroes were from
all over the country. Judy was the slickest fielder in the neighborhood, as well
as the best all-around ballplayer. She ended up playing plenty of softball in
the summers, and she undoubtedly could have been a star collegiate athlete
if women's athletics was as prominent then as it is now.

In any event, Judy was one of my constant companions and greatest
competitive pals throughout much of my childhood. Perhaps I was des-
tined to be connected with female athletes. Regardless, Judy filled some
voids for me that may have otherwise been filled by my father, who simply
didn't have a desire to play catch or to support my development as a young
athlete. Fortunately, my father never discouraged my fanatical desire to be

an athlete—particularly a baseball player—but he also didn't do much to nurture that desire. In fact, when I think back to my childhood and once I actually started playing on organized teams, I'm sometimes amazed that my parents allowed me to ride my bike to practices and games at parks that were as far as 25 to 30 minutes away from our home, requiring me to cross busy intersections along Garland Road or Buckner Boulevard. As I mentioned previously, my mother didn't drive anywhere or under any circumstances, so it would have been up to my father to drive me to games or practices. Maybe he really trusted the navigation skills of an eight-year-old. Or maybe he just preferred to stay home and drink his beers.

I do recall one game when I was eight or nine that my dad attended at Tietze Park off Skillman Avenue, several blocks north of Richmond Avenue in East Dallas. On the rare occasions he attended a game—usually when the park was a really long way from home and I couldn't catch a ride with another teammate—my dad would typically sit in his car in the outfield and drink his beer in the front seat while we played. He was doing that when I made a game-saving catch in centerfield at Tietze Park, as the left fielder undercut me while I was chasing down a fly ball in the gap. It wasn't necessarily a great catch, but I had held on to the ball even after hitting the ground hard; the baserunners from the other team circled the bases, hoping that I had dropped it and they had just won the game. But the umpire ran out to me, looked in my glove as I was rolling in pain on the ground, and yelled "Ball game!" when he noticed that the ball was securely in my glove. My teammates, the coaches, and other parents ran out to centerfield to congratulate me and to see if I was going to need to be carried off the field. (I thought for a moment that I might die, but hitting the ground that hard just temporarily knocked the wind out of me.) My father, however, never left the car. That was just his detached personality.

As I got older, he did voluntarily attend a few more of my baseball games, but primarily, my father viewed quality time with his second son as those times we "bonded" early on Saturday mornings when he put me to work cleaning up a couple of slum duplexes he owned and leased in the Fair Park area. Dad had done well enough at Ford and then in his construction business that he entered the landlord business as well. But his renters tended to be extremely poor, and they never left the duplexes in good shape, which created quite a workload when they moved out or had to be evicted. I hated that work with a passion, and I tried using every excuse I could possibly imagine in hopes of getting out of it. But the excuses rarely worked, and deep down,

I think my father thoroughly appreciated me for helping him out because I was more reliable at that point in my life.

The only relative who really nurtured my love for baseball was my grandfather Claude, who was also the only one in the family who really knew anything about sports. I was named after him, but I go by "Gary"; I never really cared for the name "Claude." While there were no major league teams in Texas until the Houston Colt .45s (now the Astros) began playing in 1962, minor league baseball first began in the Dallas area in the late 1880s. The Dallas minor league franchise had many names through the decades, but during my formative years in the 1950s, the team was known as the Dallas Eagles. My grandfather took me to numerous Eagles games at old Burnett Field, a 10,500-seat ballpark in South Dallas near the intersections of Colorado Boulevard and East Jefferson Boulevard, just a couple long home runs from the Trinity River to the north and Interstate 35 to the east. Interestingly, Burnett Field was also the first practice home of the Dallas Cowboys when the NFL team began playing in 1960, but it was primarily known as the home of Dallas minor league teams from 1924 to 1964.

The stadium is long gone now, but the mere mention of it brings back a rush of great memories for me that involve spending quality time with my grandfather. Beyond that, the Eagles were really good, winning three Texas League pennants and the 1953 Dixie Series, a best-of-seven-games competition between the champions of the Texas League and the Southern Association. My grandfather, who had been an insurance agent with Rio Grande Life Insurance, smoked cigars and loved to talk baseball. And I loved listening to him talk as we watched the Eagles. I had actually won a contest and was the alternate bat boy for the Eagles when I was in sixth or seventh grade. But the regular bat boy never missed a single game. I hate to admit that I used to secretly pray that he would come down with the flu or chicken pox, but the thought definitely crossed my mind from time to time.

Nevertheless, I spent some really good times with my grandfather at Burnett Field, watching some good teams and some really good players. I don't remember a ton of the players now, but I do recall being really impressed with a right-handed pitcher for the Eagles named Red Murff, who made it to the major leagues with the Milwaukee Brewers in the mid-1950s. Murff's claim to fame, however, was not as a player but rather many years later as a scout for the New York Mets. Murff, who was born in Burlington, Texas, discovered and signed future Texas baseball legend Nolan Ryan. When Ryan was inducted into the Baseball Hall of Fame in 1999, he even mentioned his friendship with Murff during his acceptance speech.

Watching the Eagles and spending time with my grandfather at Burnett Field further solidified my love for the game and my desire to play it for a long as possible. When I wasn't playing baseball or going to a baseball game, I could often be found listening to Eagles games on the radio and keeping my own score book in a spiral notebook. My grandfather taught me how to keep score at the Eagles games, and even at home, I'd take my ruler out and draw out the lines in my notebook and then hang on the announcer's every word so that I could fill the scorebook out accurately. And when the Eagles weren't on the radio, I was listening to the MLB's Cardinals or the Browns on KMOX-AM out of St. Louis, the 50,000-watt clear-channel station, which permits its nighttime signal to be heard throughout much of the continental United States. I could also listen to some of the Chicago Cubs games on the radio back then, but the Cardinals became my team and I loved listening to announcer Buddy Blattner, who teamed with Dizzy Dean on the national broadcasts on the Liberty and Mutual national networks.

I loved, lived, and breathed baseball, which was a good thing because I certainly didn't have the body for football or basketball. I wasn't short, but I wasn't exceptionally tall either. I was only exceptionally skinny. In fact, I was so skinny at one point in my life that I could practically grate cheese on my rib cage. My football career ended in seventh grade, primarily because of my extremely slender frame. It wasn't until eighth grade that I finally crossed the 100-pound barrier. I continued to play basketball through middle school and into my early high school days at Bryan Adams, but by that time, it was obvious to everyone, including me, that my only future in sports was as a baseball player. I had a really good arm as an outfielder, I had a good eye at the plate, I possessed the speed to steal bases, and I had a great feel for the game. The one thing I lacked, however—and it was a big thing—was power. Throughout my entire high school career, I never had an extra-base hit. Not one homer, triple, or even a double. Occasionally, an outfielder would bobble the ball, and if he did, I was typically standing on second base. But I just couldn't hit for power. For that matter, I couldn't hit for average either. But I could drag bunt with the best of the best, and I took great pride in working a pitcher for a walk.

I weighed 128 pounds as a senior center fielder, and that probably would have been my batting average, as well, if not for my ability to lay down a drag bunt and beat it out for a base hit. My baseball coach at Bryan Adams, Bobby Griffin, was also a part-time scout for the Cincinnati Reds. After leaving Bryan Adams, he became one of the Dallas Cowboys' chief scouts in 1967 under the legendary Gil Brandt, and in 1998, he was inducted into the Garland Sports Hall of Fame, where he attended high school. Coach Griffin was an all-around sportsman; he knew baseball inside and out, and he certainly knew how to utilize his players to the best of their abilities. Coach Griffin put me as the leadoff hitter and allowed me to use my speed, making up for my deficiencies as a hitter. My primary deficiency was my complete inability to hit a slider. But I bunted my way to all-city honors, and our team won the city championship during my senior season. Interestingly, the school we beat to win the Dallas city championship was South Oak Cliff, where I would eventually begin my coaching career.

I had two real passions in high school: baseball and mechanical drawing. I had a great mechanical drawing teacher, Mr. Malone, and he really instilled in me a desire to be an architect, which was my backup plan. My big dream was to be the next Willie Mays, but if that didn't work out, I figured it would be pretty nice to become the next Frank Lloyd Wright. By the end of high school, I realized the Willie Mays scenario or reaching pro baseball at any level was a farfetched dream. But I still wanted to play as long as possible, so I bunted my way to Texas Tech following my graduation in 1963.

I was only 17 when I graduated from Bryan Adams, and in hindsight, I should have gone to junior college to mature as a baseball player and as a man. My mother wanted me to go to the University of Texas, and my father hoped that I would follow my brother's footsteps at Texas A&M. Naturally, I chose Texas Tech, but I suppose I did follow my brother's footsteps in at least one regard: I didn't last there for very long.

Following the 1929 baseball season, Tech dropped the sport from its intercollegiate athletic programs. It wasn't until 1954 that baseball was revived as a varsity sport at Tech thanks to the recommendation of then head football coach DeWitt Weaver, who carried plenty of clout following an 11–1 football season that included a whipping of Tennessee in the 1953 Gator Bowl. Beattie Feathers was selected to coach the baseball program, which had been dormant for some 25 seasons. Playing in the Border Conference, which included baseball powerhouse Arizona, the Raiders didn't have much success under Feathers, who went 41–56–1 in seven seasons. Berl Huffman took over the program in 1961 and had a moderate level of success.

Perhaps I chose Tech—at least partially—because I figured I had a better chance playing for a rather new and fairly mediocre program than I did playing at established programs like Texas A&M, University of Texas, or Oklahoma State. But I had struggled against Dallas area high school pitchers at Bryan Adams, and I really struggled against collegiate pitchers. I gave it the old "college try" at Tech, practicing throughout the fall of my freshman year, playing on the freshman team, and participating in a couple exhibition games. What I most vividly recall about that first year at Tech was practicing on the same field with the varsity team, which included legendary Red Raider icon Donny Anderson. Most people remember Anderson for his football heroics. Nicknamed the "Golden Palomino," Anderson was a two-time All-American running back who finished fourth in the 1965 Heisman Trophy race. He also had a sensational NFL career, primarily with the Green Bay Packers. In fact, he was part of the first two Super Bowl championship teams for the Packers. But what many people don't realize is that guy could flat-out hit a baseball—and he could hit it a helluva long way. Whenever I would shag balls when Anderson was hitting in the spring of my freshman year, I would position myself on the other side of the outfield walls, a 4-foot-high picket fence. Anderson probably thought I was the coach's kid or something.

Unfortunately, I didn't stick around long enough for him to realize any differently. In addition to walking on as a baseball player, I also was playing intramural sports. Lots and lots of intramural sports. It was like playing with all my neighborhood friends in Dallas—only better because we had real fields and courts. I never had to worry about hitting a parked car or breaking a neighbor's window, but I probably should have worried a little more about my grades. I only passed eight of the nine required hours in the fall of my first year at Tech. I really had a passion for and was genuinely intrigued by architecture, but my math comprehension was not strong enough. My freehand drawing wasn't so hot either, but I was still looking forward to taking freehand as a sophomore because we were going to be drawing live nude models in the classroom.

I never made it that far, though. I was on the team bus heading to a ball game when the freshmen coach informed me that I was no longer eligible to play in the spring due to my grades. I still stuck around and practiced during the spring, throwing plenty of batting practice and struggling like hell to keep my head above water in my architecture classes, but it was a losing battle, and I finally drowned at the drafting table. I flunked out of school in the spring of '64 and returned to Dallas with my tail between my legs. Humbled and in desperate need of money, I landed a job in the mailroom at Hartford Insurance. If that wasn't humbling enough, I didn't have a car, so I had to take the city bus to and from work every day. After several trying months in the mailroom, I raced back to Lubbock in January 1965 with a renewed focus and appreciation for the college experience. I switched my major to kinesiology and did better in the classroom (better than flunking, at least) over the next couple of years, although I worked my butt off to earn enough money to stay in school.

My father helped me financially my first year at Tech when I flunked out, and he did what he could to help when I returned. But I had to cover the vast majority of my college expenses, and I was scrambling to keep up my grades and make ends meet. I did a little bit of everything to make a buck, including working as a checker at Furr's Supermarket on Thirty-Fourth Street in Lubbock. The Furr name was legendary in Lubbock. Roy Furr had moved to town in the late 1920s and started his entrepreneurial empire by purchasing six grocery stores in Lubbock. By the time he died in 1975, he had 68 supermarkets and 57 Furr's Cafeterias in seven states. I'm proud to say that I worked for the man, although I made much more money umpiring and officiating—$2.50 for officiating intramural games, $5 for city league games, and anywhere from $7.50 to $10 for junior high games. I even worked my way into the high school ranks, earning $12.50 per game. I was hooked on officiating basketball games, but that didn't stop me from devoting massive amounts of time to playing intramural sports. I was like a junkie with an uncontrollable addiction to competition.

In one year, I participated in 22 of the 27 intramural sports Tech offered. My addiction to competition earned me the prestigious award for most outstanding intramural player at Tech in 1968. I still have the picture of me accepting that award. Rest assured, I had put in plenty of time, and it really was the biggest individual award I had ever received at that point in my life. But all the competing, the officiating, the clerking at Furr's, and the scrambling to keep my grade point average above the passing level led me to a complete burnout just before my senior year. I desperately needed a break from college and Lubbock, and something kept pulling me toward the West Coast.

I had spent the previous summer in California with my roommate, George Dowling, a chemical engineer who had landed a gig with Texaco. We lived in South Pasadena, and I worked two jobs (one with Kelly Services, an employment/temporary services agency, and one with Hughes Supermarket). I worked 16 hours a day four days of the week and eight hours on the fifth day. The work weeks were brutal, but the weekends in Manhattan Beach, a small coastal city in southwestern Los Angeles County, were fantastic. All the flight attendants lived close to Los Angeles International Airport (LAX), and Manhattan Beach was a dream destination for a single guy with a sudden fascination for California girls. We'd play volleyball, go to clubs, and take scenic drives along the Pacific Coast Highway. It was a fabulous summer on the West Coast, and I longed for the opportunity to return when the time was right.

After reaching the burnout point at Tech in May 1968, with a GPA that was hovering around the 2.0 mark, I figured the time was right to leave the South Plains for the West Coast once again. I really had no idea exactly what I wanted to do or how long my West Coast journey would last, but I packed my bags and left. On a whim, I figured I would go to Hollywood and perhaps make a career in advertising. I'm not really sure why advertising sounded so good. Maybe I was hoping to sell ads for television shows like *All in the Family.*

Instead of launching a career in advertising, however, my West Coast relocation helped me outgrow my "meathead" phase. After 18 months in the Marine Corps, I sprinted back to Texas Tech to finally finish my degree. As it turns out, the third time really was the charm for me when it came to finishing college.

Baseball had always been my true love, and I was going back to Dallas to teach and to wait for the right opportunity to coach the game I knew so well and loved so much. Little did I know that the "right" coaching opportunity would come along soon enough, but not in the sport—or even with the gender—that I had envisioned.

3 Seize Your Opportunities . . . Any Opportunities

Following his graduation from Kansas University in the mid-1950s, Dean Smith—one of the greatest names in the history of men's college basketball—served in the US Air Force in Germany and later as the head coach at the Air Force Academy in Colorado Springs. But Smith was not the head coach of the Falcons' basketball team; the legendary future leader of the University of North Carolina men's basketball program—the man who coached Michael Jordan, Sam Perkins, James Worthy, Vince Carter, Jerry Stackhouse, Billy Cunningham, and Phil Ford, to name a merely a handful—earned his first collegiate head coaching jobs with the USAF's baseball and golf teams.

While it may be difficult to envision Dean Smith in a baseball uniform pacing the dugout and teaching hitting mechanics, it's certainly not uncommon for coaches to start off their careers in a sport other than the one in which they ultimately gain recognition. For example, the great Marv Levy, who led the Buffalo Bills to four straight Super Bowls in the early 1990s, won his first championship as a head coach with the basketball team at St. Louis Country Day School. Almost a decade later, when he was hired as the head football coach at the University of California, Levy hired an assistant and future NFL Hall of Fame coach by the name of Bill Walsh, who had begun his coaching career as a high school football and swimming coach.

Undoubtedly, there are many other similar stories throughout the coaching ranks because, quite frankly, it's extremely rare that your dream job is also your first job. That's true in the coaching profession, as well as just about every other one.

Nowadays, I find it alarming that so many young people graduating from college expect to be handed prestigious jobs with lucrative salaries and luxurious benefits. On rare occasions, and perhaps in a few prominent career fields, that may be the case, but that certainly isn't the norm in most professions, especially coaching. In virtually every career field, a college degree—even a postgraduate degree—may only allow you to get your foot in the door. That door is probably not the grand entrance to your dream job or to "Easy Street." It may lead you down a winding path that you could have never imagined and one that you would have never initially chosen. That's perfectly OK. Bloom wherever you are planted. Besides, it's always been my observation that fate is much kinder to people who make the most of any opportunity at hand instead of waiting for a golden opportunity. Opportunities generally increase and improve as they're seized.

That's certainly been the case with my career as a coach. My dream scenario was to be a baseball coach. After my major league dreams as a player faded, I could eventually see myself as a great manager like Casey Stengel or Ralph Houk. I would have never been as volatile as Billy Martin, Leo Durocher, or Earl Weaver, but I could have seen myself as a Tommy Lasorda type. Practically every one of my dream coaching scenarios involved baseball, and I believed that I had a gift as a baseball coach. Not only did I know the game, but I also possessed a proven track record before having ever accepted my first official full-time job as a high school teacher.

While working toward my master's degree at Texas Tech in the early 1970s, I coached the summer baseball programs in Roosevelt, a small public school district about 10 miles east of Lubbock that serves the unincorporated communities of Acuff and Roosevelt, along with the incorporated towns of Buffalo Springs and Ransom Canyon. I coached eight teams of various age groups—from about 6 or 7 years old up to the junior and senior American Legion teams, with players aged 13 to 19—and I was paid a base salary of about $500. But I also had a "lucrative" bonus package: for every one of my first-place teams, I received a bonus of $100. That was a helluva lot of money to me in the early 1970s, when a gallon of gas was about 35 cents and postage was six cents.

For second place, the bonus was $75, and for third, it was $50. I needed all the extra money I could possibly make to pay for school and rent, and I literally coached my tail off, teaching those kids the fundamentals, drilling the basics, and watching them evolve as players. I may have designed and constructed more drills at that point in my life than Black & Decker and DeWalt combined. After all, I was basically coaching for my next trip to the grocery store, and how we performed as teams would ultimately determine whether I would continue eating cereal for breakfast or bring home the bacon . . . and beer.

Many of the kids I coached were from single-parent homes and some were from the Lubbock Children's Home, which meant they were orphans. No matter their background, however, I studied them all and learned how to push the right buttons to bring out the best in them. Most significantly, I made a great effort to connect with them as boys and young men and not just as baseball players. Bonus money was certainly my initial motivation, but I discovered that I was genuinely invigorated and uplifted when my kids learned new skills, improved on those skills, and gained confidence as a result. The more I connected with the kids and the more my teams won, the more I believed coaching baseball was my calling. At that point, coaching baseball was my sole dream scenario.

My first official job offer, however, didn't include a coaching position of any sort, and when I finally received an opportunity to coach, it wasn't at all what I had envisioned. My first coaching opportunity was as the golf coach at South Oak Cliff High School, which technically didn't have a golf team and didn't have any students—at least none that I could find—who had ever played golf, let alone played it well enough to be considered a potential golf letter-winner. My guess is that when Bill Walsh was starting off as a coach, at least some members of his swim team had been in water before. Let's just say that my first coaching gig wasn't what most people would perceive as a "golden opportunity." But it was at least an opportunity in coaching, and I leapt at it. Then I made the most of it. But first, let me back up to that initial job offer.

My ideal plan was to earn my master's degree at Texas Tech and stay in the Lubbock area for my first teaching and coaching job because I had become a friend and a huge fan of Pete Ragus, a former football coach and the Lubbock Independent School District (LISD) athletic director at that time. Ragus was a fantastic person and first made a name for himself when his 1960 Corpus Christi Miller football squad became Texas' first integrated team to win a University Interscholastic League (UIL) state championship. I had officiated so often for LISD during my multiple tenures at Texas Tech that Ragus really liked me, and I absolutely loved the idea of working for him. However, LISD couldn't offer me a job—if there was an opening—until August of 1972. DISD, on the other hand, offered me a position as a physical education teacher at South Oak Cliff in May of 1972. There wasn't a coaching position in Dallas, but I felt like I had to take the teaching job. When you're living paycheck-to-paycheck and you're banking on a first-place finish by a baseball team of 12-year-olds to pay your bills, the security of a full-time offer—paying a whopping $7,000 a year—is too good to not accept. It wasn't part of my perfect plan—merely writing that reminds me of the famous Woody Allen quote, "If you want to make God laugh, tell Him about your plans."

Taking the job in Dallas was a godsend and ultimately proved to be a great personal and career move for me, allowing me to meet my wife and opening some great doors to other opportunities. But at first glance, it didn't immediately seem that way. When I started at South Oak Cliff (SOC) High School in the fall of 1972, I inherited a physical education program that had become a major afterthought since full-scale integration had turned SOC into an all-black school. Apparently, some of the previous physical education teachers believed that rolling out the basketballs and making sure no one was seriously injured during the ensuing PE hour was good enough exercise for the students who weren't part of the official athletic programs at SOC.

That wasn't my idea of teaching, though—I was intent on making an impression and making a difference. I had learned so much about organization while working with the intramural programs at Texas Tech, and I had a great deal of confidence about working with people of all ethnic and socioeconomic backgrounds from my time in the Marine Corps and in running restaurants. I entered the fall of '72 with a comprehensive plan to turn what had been a ho-hum physical education department into a multifaceted intramural program incorporating numerous sports. The kids would still play basketball, but I was going to teach the fundamentals of the game. I also organized intramural football, baseball, softball, volleyball, soccer, gymnastics, and even wrestling. I didn't merely roll out the balls or point the kids to an appropriate field or court while I read a book or took a nap. I took great pride in introducing the various sports to the kids, instructing them on the finer points of each sport, and providing plenty of hands-on examples. That was fine in sports like volleyball and soccer, but I quickly learned that teaching wrestling was far more challenging and dangerous because practically all the boys desperately wanted to pin the white boy. And, of course, I was the white boy. I would teach them a move and then try to keep from being knocked around like a bowling pin.

Even when some of the kids were wearing me out, though, I could tell that they were having a good time, and I really believed that I was connecting with them, which was my goal and my motivation right from the start. As a teacher and a coach, I have always believed that students and athletes don't really care how much you know until they know how much you care. I am quite certain that the kids at SOC could tell right away that I really cared, and they certainly proved that they liked me when the one troublemaker I mentioned earlier challenged me to a fight. When my physical education kids came to my defense, I knew that I had made a positive impression on them.

I also felt good about the impression I was making on my fellow teachers and administrators, especially SOC's head football coach and campus athletic director, Norman Jett, who was a great coach and a tremendous role model for a first-year teacher and aspiring coach like me. Jett, a white man, first began coaching at SOC as an assistant in 1962 and was named head coach and athletic director at the school in 1970, the year the racial composition at South Oak Cliff changed from predominantly white to essentially all black. But the only color that ever mattered to Jett was gold—the South Oak Cliff Golden Bears. I admired Coach Jett right from the start, and I constantly reminded him that I wanted to be a coach, preferably the baseball coach. He could see my passion for coaching and how deeply I cared for the kids, and he constantly reminded me to stay patient and to wait for a coaching opportunity to arise.

That opportunity "arose" a couple months later at a staff meeting when Jett asked for a volunteer to coach the golf team, which had been dormant for the last couple years. Naturally, I raised my hand quickly and happily accepted the role without hesitation and without even knowing I would be paid an extra $300 annually. But the truth of the matter was that I would have done it for free, and considering all the out-of-pocket money I spent on that golf team, it actually cost me to coach. Nevertheless, I was thrilled to have the chance to actually coach a team, which is why I never thought twice about raising my hand that day.

Looking back at it now, perhaps I should have hesitated—or run the other way. It wasn't just a coaching job that I was accepting; I also had to recruit a team ("begging" practically everyone in my PE classes would be a more accurate description), provide equipment for the team (we didn't have a full set of clubs), find uniforms for the team (we didn't even have matching collared shirts), and even drive the team to practices and tournaments (my entire boys and girls teams had to fit into the 1971 Camaro I had purchased at a discount—$3,100—while I was still in the Marine Corps because SOC didn't have a bus or van for the team). But even with all the challenges and obstacles I inherited, I loved having the opportunity to build the golf program at SOC from the ground up again.

Sure, it would have been easier if I was coaching golf at a place like Jesuit Preparatory School of Dallas, where Jordan Spieth played many years later, or even Lake Highlands, where Justin Leonard honed his golf skills. But developing future PGA Tour players was never my goal. I wanted to teach some young people a sport that they could play the rest of their lives. My desire was to teach them some life lessons through a sport that involves so many mental challenges and so much self-control. I wanted to use sports to somehow prepare the kids I influenced for a better future. And I wanted to be a positive role model and to prove myself as a leader of young men and women, regardless of the sport I was coaching. Besides, I figured that if I could recruit a golf team, equip and uniform the team, and actually teach the game to kids who had never played before, then I could certainly make an impression on Norman Jett and the administrators at SOC so that I would be the first name that came to mind whenever the baseball job did open up.

Once I began assembling a squad for the spring of 1973, I knew right away that the SOC golf team would undoubtedly make an unforgettable impression everywhere we went, although it was probably not going to be a positive one on most occasions. One of the numerous challenges I faced in recruiting a team was that golf was considered a rich white man's game. There weren't any rich kids in Oak Cliff, and there weren't any white kids at SOC. So while the SOC hallways were filled with an abundance of great athletes, most of them were extremely reluctant to even give golf a try because of how they might be perceived by their fellow students. Remember that this was still a couple of years before Lee Elder became the first African American to play in the Masters and six years before Calvin Peete won the first of his 12 career PGA Tour victories in 1979. There were just not many successful African American golfers whom I could cite in recruiting my own team.

So I begged. And pleaded. And implored. Somehow, I convinced five boys and two girls to give golf a shot. In the meantime, I was also hustling around Dallas to pawn shops and pleading for donations, loans, or drastic discounts from practically every golf pro shop in Dallas for clubs and bags for my ragtag team. I bought some of the clubs myself and accumulated enough others to fully equip the team. I also managed to find enough hand-me-down yellow or gold collared sport shirts to provide uniforms for the team, although none of the shirts actually matched, and all the kids wore tennis shoes, not golf spikes.

With a team, equipment, and uniforms, all that was left was for me to teach the game to a group of kids who didn't even know the difference between a seven iron and a cast-iron skillet. The good news is that they didn't have any bad habits to correct; the bad news is that we generated more swing-and-misses at a typical practice than Nolan Ryan did in his entire career. And when we did connect with the golf ball, the flight path was as unpredictable as a Mexican free-tailed bat. The original *Bad News Bears* movie, starring Walter Matthau and Tatum O'Neal, was released in 1976. I am still convinced that the screenplay was somehow inspired by my first golf team, the real-life Bad News Golden Bears. Of course, back then I looked more like a skinny Jimmy Stewart than a Walter Matthau. Nowadays, the Matthau comparison fits well.

After a few weeks of practice, we were finally ready to make our debut at a miniature golf course—the kind with multicolored golf balls, windmill obstacles in front of the cup, and animated dinosaurs on the final hole. Unfortunately, it was time to actually play our first tournament at a real golf course. My best golfer was a young man named David Kenny, a wonderful young man who sat in the front seat of my Camaro, which was my pride and joy even though I couldn't afford to have air conditioning, as we traveled from Oak Cliff to Cedar Crest Park in South Dallas. David was allowed to sit in the front seat not because he was our best golfer (although he was) but because he was about 280 pounds and literally couldn't fit into the backseat of my blue-and-white sports car. One of the two girls sat in David's lap and the other five players—four boys and the other girl—crammed into the back. We somehow also managed to fit all our equipment, and I will never quite forget the looks on the faces of our competitors as we pulled into the parking lot at Cedar Crest, a storied golf course south of downtown that opened in 1919 and was the site of the 1927 PGA Championship. When we piled out of my Camaro, with mismatched shirts and golf bags, jaws literally dropped on the faces of our stunned competitors, who had come from places like Highland Park, Irving, and Thomas Jefferson High School.

If only we could have dropped putts with the same frequency. Unfortunately, my players looked as if they were allergic to greens. And fairways. And definitely the center of the cup. My best player, David Kenny, produced our team's low score at our first official tournament, which was—and this is no joke or exaggeration—a 127, which was 55 over par. And here's the thing about that: Kenny probably cheated. It wasn't intentional; he just didn't know all the rules. It's really not a stretch to say that the best wood in any of my players' bags was a pencil.

It was a challenging season, to say the least, but we continued to make progress, and I continued to thoroughly enjoy working with the kids on the golf team and with my intramural teams. I knew something about leadership before I ever took the job at SOC, but I learned so much more about working with young people and being a leader in that first full year at SOC. The biggest realization I made that year—aside from the fact that I really could fit eight people into a Camaro—was that I didn't necessarily need to be a baseball coach to experience a sense of career fulfillment. The bottom line was that I just loved to coach, regardless of whether I was leading one of the worst golf teams in DISD history or teaching wrestling moves so that my students could pin the white boy.

Entering my second year at SOC in the fall of '73, I was still hoping for a more significant coaching job, preferably as the next head baseball coach, but I was prepared to take on whatever challenge that was presented to me. In other words, I was in the right mind-set in October of 1973 when opportunity literally knocked—or banged—on my gym door while I was running a boys' intramural program. This was just one year after the passage of Title IX of the Education Amendments of 1972, which stated (in part), "No person in the United States shall, on the basis of sex, be excluded from participation in, be denied the benefits of, or be subjected to discrimination under any education program or activity receiving federal financial assistance."

When President Richard Nixon signed the bill and it became law on June 23, 1972, it never crossed my mind that Title IX would ever have any kind of impact on me personally or on sports in general—but it did. I opened the door and opened myself to a world of unforeseen opportunities. Three young women were on the other side of the door with a request. They wanted to know if I would be interested in coaching the new girls' basketball program. Naturally, and once again without hesitation, I said yes. It wasn't even a paying job, but it obviously proved to be one helluva opportunity.

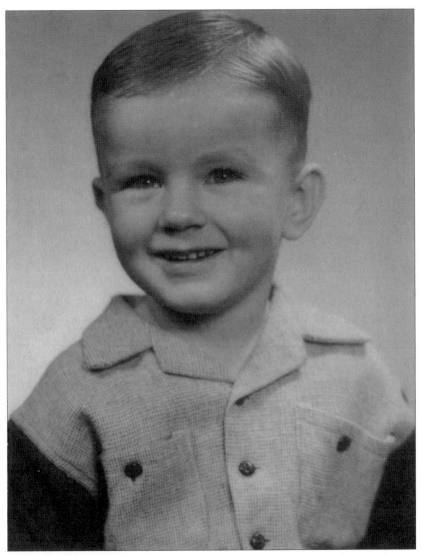

Gary as a young child.

Gary as a Cub Scout.

Gary as a sophomore in high school.

Gary as a US Marine 1969.

Gary and Nan at their wedding in Abilene, Texas, July 21, 1979.

South Oak Cliff women's team, 1976. They were state semi-finalists.

The 1977 state championship team of South Oak Cliff High School, coached by Gary Blair. This was the first all-African American women's team to win a state title. The South Oak Cliff men's team won it the next year.

State championship team, 1978. They played the last 6-on-6 game in Texas. Eleven of these players received college scholarships.

Gary Blair and three All-State players on his South Oak Cliff High School women's basketball team. Pam Green (#5), who attended the University of Missouri; Lorretta Lister (#13), who went to McClennan Community College in Waco; and Anita Foster (#22), who played at Southwestern Oklahoma State.

Gary Blair and the Louisiana Tech women's basketball team; Kim Mulkey is third from the right. This team won the national championship in 1981.

Gary and Nan, his wife, around the time that Gary was coaching at South Oak Cliff.

Family picture of Gary from a 1985 program of the Stephen F. Austin State University women's basketball team. Pictured with him are Nan, his wife, and Paige, their daughter.

**1985-86
Ladyjack Basketball**

A Change of Seasons

**Stephen F. Austin
State University**

*Gary Blair pictured on the cover of an early SFA women's basketball media guide.
Pictured with him are seniors Janice Joseph (L.) and Rosalind Johnson.*

The 1989–90 SFA women's basketball team, coached by Gary Blair. This team was ranked third in the nation at the end of the regular season. Eight of these players have been inducted into the Stephen F. Austin University Hall of Fame.

The 1990–91 SFA women's basketball team, coached by Gary Blair.

Gary Blair and his two assistant coaches from Stephen F. Austin, 1991. Sue Donohoe (L.) and Julie Thomas (R.)

Gary and his daughter Paige, dressed for a social event in Nacogdoches.

President Bill Clinton with members of the 1994 University of Arkansas women's basketball team, which was coached by Gary Blair.

Gary Blair at a podium in front of a White House backdrop in 1995, when his Arkansas team was invited to visit the Bill Clinton White House.

Members of the 1994–95 Arkansas women's basketball team on a team bus.

Members of the Arkansas women's basketball team wearing t-shirts showing their 1998 regional championship. This team went to the Final Four in Kansas City.

Tennille Adams hit the basket to give Arkansas the lead against Duke that enabled the Razorback Women to go to the Final Four in 1998.

Gary Blair, discussing a call with the referee.

Scoreboard of the 1998 regional championship game in which Arkansas defeated Duke.

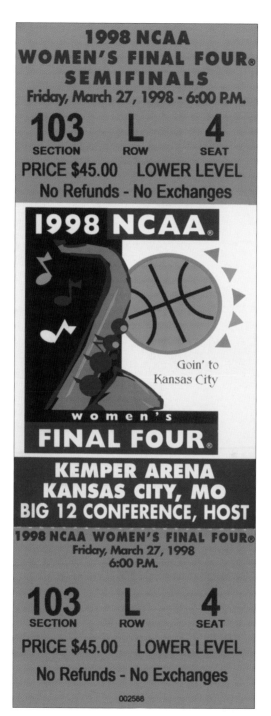

Ticket stub for a 1998 Final Four game in which Arkansas women lost to perhaps the best Tennessee women's team in history. Pat Summitt's Volunteer squad featured the "Three Meeks": Chamique Holdsclaw, Semeka Randall, and Tamika Catchings.

Gary Blair and Kemara Stencil, on an Arkansas team trip to Australia in 1999. The snake in this picture is very much alive.

Gary Blair in a Brazos Valley Bombers uniform, participating in a promotional event in Bryan, Texas. He was the designated hitter in the first inning. He struck out after working the count to 3–2.

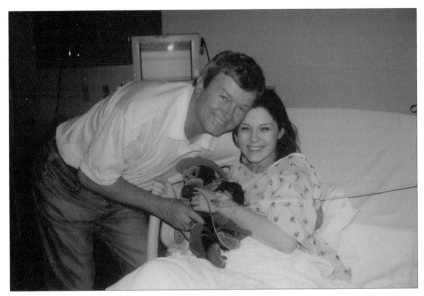

Gary Blair at his daughter's hospital bedside, at the birth of his grandson Logan, in 2004.

Gary and Nan Blair, hositng a group of traveling Aggies on a trip to the Great Lakes, 2015.

Gary and Nan Blair walking under an arch of swords provided by the Ross Volunteers at a "Gary Blair Roast" held for the benefit of a local nonprofit group. Blair says, "I was roasted more than toasted."

Nan Blair speaking at the roast, as Gary Blair looks on.

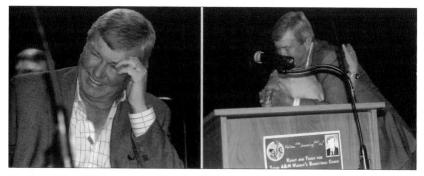

Gary and Nan Blair embrace after her speech at the roast.

Gary Blair, posing with the cut net, just after TAMU women's basketball team won the 2011 NCAA national championship game.

Photograph courtesy Texas A&M University Sports Information Services.

Gary Blair and members of the TAMU women's basketball team holding the trophy for winning the 2011 NCAA women's basketball championship.

Photograph courtesy Texas A&M University Sports Information Services.

Gary Blair and team member Danielle Adams at a press conference following the championship game. ESPN announcers (from L.): Trey Wingo, Kara Lawson, and Carolyn Peck.

Photograph courtesy Texas A&M University Sports Information Services.

Gary Blair and his son Matt at a Texas Rangers baseball game after the Texas A&M women's basketball team won the NCAA national championship.

Gary Blair and his grandson Logan meeting President Barack Obama at the White House, fall 2011. President Obama is writing Logan a pass for an excused absence from school.

Photo courtesy Courtesy Texas A&M University Athletics.

*Gary Blair at his induction into the Women's Basketball Hall of Fame in 2013.
He is pictured with Marsha Sharp (L.), Texas Tech University, and Tody Conradt
(R.), University of Texas. Conradt's women won the national championship in
1986, Sharp's team won in 1993, and Blair's Aggies were champions in 2011. All
three coaches were born in Texas, coached high school and college in Texas, and won
national championships in Texas. Sharp is giving the Tech "guns up" sign, Blair is
flashing the A&M "gig 'em," and Conradt displays "Hook 'em, Horns."*

Gary with associate head coach Kelly Bond-White after his 2013 Women's Basketball Hall of Fame Induction celebration. Blair says that he continues to hire the finest coaches, so he is able to sustain coaching the best.

4   Building a Dynasty in Big D

In late January 1973, the Dallas Cowboys used the first pick in the third round of the NFL Draft—the 53rd overall selection—to choose a defensive end by the name of Harvey Martin. From a media standpoint, the pick probably didn't even register as a blip on the national sports radar. It was, however, a rather big and intriguing news item for sports fans across northeast Texas.

First and foremost, anything the Dallas Cowboys did was (and still is) big news in northeast Texas. In January 1973, the Cowboys were just one year removed from their first NFL title, with Dallas having beaten the Miami Dolphins in Super Bowl VI on January 16, 1972. The Cowboys had just moved into their new home with a hole in the roof (Texas Stadium) during the 1971 season. The fact that they had drafted a young man from a small college some 65 miles northeast of downtown Dallas (East Texas State University, which is now Texas A&M–Commerce) added to the regional newsworthiness.

To top it all off, though, Martin was raised in Dallas and had begun his football career at South Oak Cliff (SOC) High School. As a young teen, Martin worked at a department store, dreaming of becoming a store manager and making a career in the industry. But in his autobiography, *Texas Thunder*, Martin recalled his truck-driver father telling his mother, "All the guys at the [golf] club are bragging about their boys being on the football field. I can never brag about my boy."

In 1967, as a junior, Martin suited up for Norman Jett's South Oak Cliff football team for the first time, wearing shoes one size too small and a helmet so tight that it left a dent in his forehead for years. Martin rarely played his first year, but in his second season, he moved from the offensive line to defensive end and helped lead SOC to an unbeaten regular season. Nevertheless, if not for Jett actively promoting him, Martin probably never would have received any scholarship offers, not even from a National Association of Intercollegiate Athletics school like East Texas State. But Martin obviously developed and matured, leading the Lions to a national championship as a senior in '72 and earning All-America honors. So when Martin made his debut with his hometown Dallas Cowboys in the fall of 1973, it was big news throughout the Dallas–Fort Worth area. There was tremendous excitement at his high school alma mater, as Martin played a huge role in helping the Cowboys build the "Doomsday Defense" and a dynasty in the 1970s.

And that is just one example of some of the fine young people who attended SOC. Another is a young man who was in my PE classes, David Brown. He would go on to rise through the ranks in law enforcement, becoming Dallas Chief of Police and providing steady leadership during the wrenching events following the fatal sniper attack on Dallas police that occurred on July 7, 2016.

On a much smaller and far less trumpeted scale (not even "harmonica-ed," for that matter), South Oak Cliff was at the center of another sports news item that would also generate a dynasty of sorts for years to come. When I heard the knock and opened that heavy wood gym door in October 1973, I listened to the three young ladies and quickly agreed to coach the newly founded girls' basketball team. It would probably make for a better story if I said that a lightning bolt immediately darted across the sky outside the SOC gym, revealing to me that I was experiencing a life-defining, fate-forming event that would forever shape the destiny of my career.

In all sincerity, though, it initially didn't even strike me as a big deal. For one thing, it paid exactly $300 less than my job as the golf coach, for which my total salary was . . . $300. For another thing, women's sports just weren't particularly significant at practically any level in the fall of '73. For example, the NCAA had nothing to do with women's athletics until the early 1980s, and the Association for Intercollegiate Athletics for Women (AIAW) had only been founded in 1971. In the early years of the AIAW, female student-athletes were allowed to transfer freely among schools from year to year, and to prevent unfair advantages, programs were initially forbidden from offering scholarships and recruiting off campus. A lawsuit ended the ban on scholarships in 1973, but it is estimated that the average public university spent less than 1 percent of its athletic budget on women's sports in the early 1970s.

At Texas A&M, women's sports weren't even under the athletic department's umbrella until the 1974–75 school year. While some women's sports teams were already participating in intercollegiate competitions as early as 1971, the Texas A&M Athletic Council did not approve financial support for women's athletics until June 15, 1975. And it wasn't until 1981 that the NCAA finally decided to offer championships in women's sports.

Besides, girls' high school basketball in the Lone Star State in the early 1970s wasn't even remotely the same sport that the boys played. Girls played a six-on-six game instead of five-on-five, which had been the case practically everywhere in the country from the time the first high school girls' games were ever played in Iowa in 1898 until 1971, when the Amateur Athletic Union (AAU) and Division for Girls' and Women's Sports (DGWS) adopted the five-person, full-court version of the game that the boys played. However, not all states immediately switched from six-on-six. Texas played six-on-six until 1979; Iowa had women's championships for both five- and six-person teams until 1984, and Oklahoma did not fully make the change to five-on-five until 1995.

Officially, girls' basketball joined the state of Texas' University Interscholastic League (UIL) slate of athletic events during the 1950–51 school year, decades prior to Title IX. But for the most part, it was a rural sport in Texas—like it had long been in Iowa—and if you look at the girls' state champions from 1951 to 1971, the biggest "city" schools are from Lubbock, Corpus Christi, and Waco. Most of the big winners then were from tiny towns and farming communities like Claude, Buna, Tulia, Brock, and Nazareth. One of the theories behind the rural dominance was that the farmer parents of those girls realized that sweating and hard work wouldn't "harm" their daughters, many of whom worked in the fields. But in the larger cities, there still seemed to be a prevailing belief that a physically demanding and occasionally aggressive game like basketball could be detrimental to females. In fact, that belief was partly why girls played six-on-six basketball in Texas and other states for so long.

Janice Beran, author of *From Six-on-Six to Full Court Press: A Century of Iowa Girls' Basketball*, cited plenty of old-school medical experts who truly believed that athletics affected menstrual cycles and women's capacity to have children. Whatever the case, the six-on-six game was thought to be "safe enough" for even the girls to play because it limited running and was not nearly as taxing as the five-on-five game. In six-on-six basketball, it was illegal for players to ever cross the center line. Three girls (the guards) played only defense while three others (the forwards) played only offense, and in order for the ball to cross from the backcourt to the frontcourt, it had to be passed. That game was very fundamentally sound, and it drew great crowds, particularly in the small towns of West Texas.

However, the pace of the game was much slower than today's game, and the rules of play typically allowed average athletes to compete with superior ones. But my hunch was that if you could put together a team of outstanding athletes from the inner city, then it wouldn't remain a rural-dominated sport for long. What I initially underestimated, however, was the incredible talent of the female athletes at South Oak Cliff. I knew the boys were remarkable. South Oak Cliff, after all, was the Dallas Cowboys of high schools as far as boys' teams were concerned in DISD. Based on my physical education classes, I could see that the young women were also extremely athletic. But I really had no basis for comparison until we started competing against other schools in something other than golf.

I took over the girls' basketball program at SOC primarily because those three girls had asked me to, and I had already won the approval of Mama Reeves. Even though she was not technically an administrator (she was the senior class sponsor and home economics teacher), Lillian "Mama" Reeves basically ran the school. She had more influence with the kids than any other person in the school, and she was respected by all the teachers and administrators. Her approval was enough to earn me a shot at the first-year job. Besides, there wasn't exactly much competition for the volunteer position. The two female PE teachers were Mary Been, who coached the cheerleaders, and Edna Osborne, who coached the drill team. Like every other athletic-oriented extracurricular activity at SOC (aside from golf), the Golden Bears cheerleaders and drill team were great. We're talking award-winning great. The girls could practically leap out of the gym, and the drill team was sensational.

Been and Osborn didn't have the interest or the time to take on the girls' basketball team, especially one that didn't have any uniforms or even a roster. Indeed, coaching was only part of my role, and I was determined not to do things haphazardly. Dallas was one of the first big cities in Texas to give girls' basketball a shot, but there was no budget, and the citywide preseason planning/organizational meeting was obviously never planned. Right away, I started selling Tootsie Rolls, Snickers, and other candy along with hotlinks on Friday afternoons to my PE classes to raise money for uniforms. We also organized a community- and school-wide Halloween carnival, and we held talent shows as fundraisers. In future years, I would have the girls on the team borrow clothes from chains like Sanger Harris and Titche's, and we would stage an elaborate annual fashion show that included students, teachers, and administrators. Its popularity grew, and we eventually raised enough money to outfit our girls with the same uniforms worn by Duncanville, which at the time was a white suburb that probably only had one African American resident—Mean Joe Greene, the University of North Texas graduate who, in the mid-1970s, was on his way to becoming a legendary defensive lineman with the Pittsburgh Steelers. We also were able to set aside a travel budget that allowed us to play teams around the state instead of just the Dallas area.

During the first two seasons (1973–74 and 1974–75), we were not eligible for UIL play or the state playoffs because of a mandatory waiting period. In the first season, we played at the "extramural" level, which allowed us to compete against teams from DISD and also play practice games against Metroplex-area teams like Duncanville. Our girls picked up the game well—really well—and we went 18–3 that first season, with two of the losses coming to Duncanville, an established program at the time. I had a blast coaching that first season, and I quickly realized that not only could I coach girls, but I was probably also one of the better girls' coaches in DISD—and the only male coach that first year.

That may sound like braggadocio, but honestly, there wasn't a tremendous amount of competition. Most of the other schools had filled their girls' basketball coaching vacancies with female physical education teachers who had very little interest in actually coaching a team, especially on a volunteer basis. But I loved it, and once I tasted a little success—as opposed to what I had tasted the previous spring with the golf teams—I was hooked. Not only did I coach the girls' basketball team that first year, but I also coached girls' volleyball, girls' track-and-field and cross-country, and girls' and boys' golf in the spring. I knew just enough about track-and-field to allow my supremely talented girls to run really fast and veer to the left. Mama Reeves, who had once played basketball at Prairie View, assisted me with those first basketball and track-and-field teams. She didn't really help me instruct the girls, but she certainly bridged a communications gap, helping a blue-eyed white man develop a level of trust and a real bond with a group of young black women, many of whom didn't have a father at home.

Again, I can't emphasize this enough to any young coach or someone who might be considering the coaching profession as a career: For me, the key to winning at South Oak Cliff—or any other school at any level—was winning the hearts of my players. Different coaches have different styles in accomplishing that objective, and Pat Summitt, Muffet McGraw, Kim Mulkey, Sue Gunter, Kay Yow, Jody Conradt, Geno Auriemma, and every other coach each motivate and inspire players in different ways. But most all of the successful ones develop a relationship with the players that supersedes what happens on the courts or fields. Especially with girls—but I think it almost always applies with boys, as well—the players simply do not care how much you know until they know how much you care. Many young coaches are focused only on what a player can do for their own careers or the team's season, which is a huge mistake.

Bottom line: You want to be a great coach? Take the focus off of yourself and place it on the players. Focus on how to make your players better athletes in the short term and better young men or women in the long term, and more times than not, everything will fall into place. I am not suggesting you pacify or pamper your players. My point is to find a way to connect with the players and then to follow through with connecting. Some players need discipline, some need a pat on the back, some need structure, and others need a hug.

I recognized right away that the two things my female student-athletes really needed were a safe ride home after practices and something to keep them away from the temptations and potential dangers that loomed in prac- tically every nook and cranny in Oak Cliff. To be clear, South Oak Cliff was not in the slums or the "hood" of Dallas. But if you were looking for trouble, it could easily be found and also find you.

While many of the administrators in DISD were black, about 65 per- cent of the teachers were white. At SOC, many of those white teachers left the neighborhood and crossed the Trinity River or Interstate 35 as soon as the school day ended. Where I connected with my student-athletes was my simple willingness to make sure they made it home safely after practices. I would load up my players in my '71 Camaro and take them home after practice, while Mama Reeves would load up other kids—playing whatever sport was in season—in her Oldsmobile, which she called "Betsy," and take them home. The girls didn't care that my Camaro didn't have any air condi- tioning. They were just happy to not be walking. But it was more than just making sure the girls made it home safely; we laughed, told stories, cracked jokes, and bonded on those car rides. While making those rounds to their homes—houses that were often empty because a single-parent mother was working late to make ends meet—I also realized the importance of keeping my players busy year-round. I decided then that if I was allowed to continue coaching at SOC, I was going to make participation in multiple sports mandatory by all my girls. If a girl wanted to play basketball, she was also going to run track, play volleyball, and run cross country. The mandatory participation requirement would be good for SOC girls' athletics, and it would also be great for all the girls. It was much better to keep them active, to keep them with their friends, and to keep them participating in something positive than to send them home alone.

Before I could actually implement that policy, however, I first had to be awarded the full-time girls' coaching position. Entering the 1974–75 school year (my third at SOC), the decision was made by DISD to pay the girls' head coaches at each school an additional $2,500 a year. At many of the other schools, the money was split among several people who served as the head coach of different sports. But I wanted to be the head coach of four sports—volleyball, cross country, basketball, and track-and-field—so I could make sure the girls were able to participate in multiple sports.

The additional $2,500 was certainly not a lucrative offer—even in the mid-1970s—but the money did raise interest among other teachers at SOC, including numerous black teachers, meaning I was not guaranteed the position simply because I had volunteered the year before. But my assurance came from Mama Reeves. At the first teachers meeting of the year, our principal, Louis McQuirter, asked who was interested in the girls' athletics head coaching position. Before anyone could raise his or her hand, including me, Mama Reeves spoke quickly and fervently on my behalf: "Blair took that job when nobody else wanted that job, including us black folks," she said. "He took that job and look what he did last year. You're going to give him that job." Mama Reeves was a lot like the old E. F. Hutton commercials: when she spoke, people listened.

Nothing else needed to be said. I was awarded the job right then and there. During our second season (1974–75), we could play any school that we could schedule, but we were still not eligible for the UIL playoffs. We played 30 games our second season, which was more than the 21 games our first season. We went 25–5 and played for the Dallas city championship, losing the title to my alma mater, Bryan Adams. They beat us fair and square, but it certainly helped that Bryan Adams head coach Obenna Hartford had a superstar in Carol Reeves, a 6-foot-3 post who played outside, facing the basket, and averaged over 30 points a game in her high school career. Reeves went on to star at Baylor, where she was later inducted into the school's Athletic Hall of Fame.

That's not to say that we didn't have our fair share of superstars. We most certainly did. We had some really good players in the early years of the program, and we featured some great ones as time progressed. One of our first really big stars—literally and figuratively—was 6-foot forward Barbara Brown, who was worried she would not be able to play for me because she was a teenage mother. There was a DISD rule that a teen mother could not play team sports, which I thought was ludicrous and counterproductive. I challenged the rule, and thankfully, it was changed. Barbara wasn't just a great player; she was our "team glue." She eventually earned a scholarship to Stephen F. Austin State University and made the school's Athletic Hall of Fame. She also was an alternate on the USA basketball team that took part in the 1980 Summer Olympics boycott. She later returned to DISD as the girls' basketball head coach at Bryan Adams and then South Oak Cliff, where she ultimately became the first female athletic director. She made a positive impact in the lives of so many young people, which may have never happened if the rule had not been changed.

Fortunately for everyone, Brown was allowed to play, and what a player she was for us. Brown was one of the primary leaders on the 1975–76 team— the first team eligible for the UIL playoffs. We raised money for travel and participated in a couple of tournaments that I believed would toughen us up and prepare us for our first postseason run. We won District 6-4A and advanced to G. Rollie White Coliseum in College Station for the regionals. I still remember that Wally Groff, who would eventually become the Texas A&M athletic director, was the ticket manager at the time, and Penny King, who would become the associate athletic director, was his assistant. We won the 1976 regional championship in College Station, which was the start of a great run in Aggieland. We made it to the regionals in College Station for five straight years, and we never lost a game inside G. Rollie White. With all those great memories, it's unlikely anyone was more upset than me when the building was demolished in 2013.

But let's go back to 1976 and SOC making it to Austin for the high school "final four" for the first time. No girls' team from DISD in any sport had ever made it to Austin before we accomplished the feat in '76, so our administrators didn't really know what to expect or how we were supposed to conduct ourselves once we arrived—a fact that would soon become frustratingly obvious.

We rode the bus to Austin the day of our first game, leaving at 8 a.m., because DISD didn't want to pay for an extra night's stay in a hotel. We arrived in Austin around noon, checked into our hotel, and then went to

Luby's Cafeteria, which was a real treat for many of the girls. We were scheduled to play the early game of the girls' Class 4A championship bracket against Victoria, and we arrived at Gregory Gym on the University of Texas campus about an hour and 15 minutes before the start of our game. Without going into all the gruesome details, Victoria, which had won the state championship in 1971, overwhelmed our girls and me, 60–44. Losing on our first trip to the state tournament was disappointing, but it wasn't stunning, especially since we lost to a former state champion team, coached by the legendary Jan Lahodny. But even after losing the semifinal game, I wanted my team to experience everything about the state tournament, since so many of my players were underclassmen.

After the loss to Victoria, our plan was to go to Hill's Steakhouse—an even bigger treat for the girls—and to return to Gregory Gym to watch Duncanville play Weslaco in the other Class 4A semifinal game. We would then spend the night and stick around to watch the championship game between Victoria and the Duncanville–Weslaco winner. On the way to dinner, however, we were told by an administrator that we were to return to Dallas. Immediately. I protested vehemently, pointing out that we had already checked into our hotel rooms. It didn't matter, though. We were told that in DISD, if you lose the first game, you come home. I was tempted to raise the Title IX flag, but it was not particularly strong at the time, and I decided to find another way.

There was no point in fighting it. The bus was going back to Dallas. End of discussion. But that didn't mean we had to *stay* in Dallas. Before the bus left Austin, I instructed my players to call their parents to let them know there would be a slight change in plans. I stayed in Austin as the bus departed, and once the team arrived at SOC at about 2 a.m., our athletic sponsors—Mama Reeves, Mary Been, and Christine Walker—loaded up the girls in their vehicles. They immediately hopped back on the road and made it back to the hotel. We slept a little bit and then headed over to Gregory Gym, where we watched all five of the girls' state championship games: Class B, 1A, 2A, 3A, and 4A. In the Class 4A championship, Duncanville beat Victoria, 70–69. My girls soaked it all up, watching every celebration and studying what it took to win a title. It was an invaluable experience for each and every one of them. We loaded up the vehicles at the end of the night, arrived in Dallas in the wee hours of Sunday morning, and started track-and-field practice the following Monday. But the championship experience made an indelible impression on my girls that paid huge dividends the following basketball season—just as I expected.

During the 1976–77 season—Barbara Brown's senior season—we were loaded with future collegiate players, including Brown (Stephen F. Austin), Jackie Valentine (Baylor), Pam Green (Missouri), Lorretta Lister (McClennon County Junior College), and our leading scorer, Anita Foster, who started at Stephen F. Austin and finished as an All-American at Southwestern Oklahoma. In future years, we also had Ramona Dozier (LSU), Bridget Phillips (Texas Woman's University), Angela Jones (SMU), Fran Harris (University of Texas), Vickie Green (Louisiana Tech and Oklahoma), Debra Rodman (Louisiana Tech), and Kim Rodman (Stephen F. Austin). The Rodman sisters had an older brother named Dennis, who wasn't nearly as good as either one of his sisters in basketball or any other sport. Dennis had been cut from the SOC football team early in his high school career, and he didn't make the basketball team, which is how he ended up in my PE classes. The only sport he could play with any proficiency was table tennis, and even though he was pretty good, I beat him regularly. But Dennis, who was about 5-foot-11 when he graduated from SOC in 1979, was a good, well-mannered young man who was proud of his talented younger sisters. I really liked Dennis, but I would have never thought he'd eventually become a member of the Naismith Memorial Basketball Hall of Fame and a five-time NBA champion with Detroit and Chicago. His story is even more unlikely than Harvey Martin's, as Rodman's first job out of SOC was as a janitor at the Dallas/Fort Worth International Airport. Once he hit his growth spurt and shot up to 6 foot 7, he enrolled at Cooke County College in Gainesville, Texas, where he dominated on the court before flunking out of school. Then he became a star at Southeastern Oklahoma State (an NAIA school), and the rest is well-documented history.

Dennis Rodman's remarkable story is yet another example of the number of incredible athletes walking around the hallways at South Oak Cliff. Pam Green is another. During the 1975–76 school year, we made an announcement that we were looking for a volleyball manager. Pam showed up to fill the position, but I noticed her hitting the ball one day and asked her to try out for the team. She was a natural athlete, and she made the volleyball team. After that, she also tried out for the basketball team at my urging, although she had never played previously. Once again, she proved to be a natural. She started slowly on the junior varsity team and didn't score in the first three games of the 1975–76 season. But once things clicked, she was remarkable. She scored 19 points in her fourth game, and her confidence continued to build throughout the rest of the season. I put her on varsity once the playoffs began because I wanted her to experience the run to Austin. I suspected she could play a key role for us in the future, and she did just that beginning in 1977–78.

With a roster that included future college stars like Jackie Valentine and Pam Green, along with talented high school stars like Loretta Lister, Anita Foster, and Bridgett Phillips, we once again won the District 6-4A championship, and we cruised through the regionals in College Station. During that regular season, one of the pre–district tournament games we played was against Lockney, which was coached by future Women's Basketball Hall of Famer and Texas Tech legend Marsha Sharp. I remember that game so vividly because it involved one of the worst calls I have ever seen by an official—and rest assured, I've seen some awful ones.

We were playing in the Wayland Baptist tournament in Plainview, north of Lubbock, and the gym was packed to see my all-black team play against so many all-white schools. As I've noted, Barbara Brown was a tremendous athlete who had a vertical jump that was worth the price of admission. But she was only 6 feet tall, and it wasn't like she could dunk or play above the rim. Nevertheless, she was called for goaltending in a truly awful call. Barbara and Marsha ran into each other at a coaching school in Arlington almost 40 years later, and Marsha still recognized Barbara as the player that "allegedly" swatted the ball away from its downward trajectory toward the rim. Technically, she got the ball on the way up, not on the way down, but it makes for a great story.

At the time, the call was so awful that I pulled the blue suede sports coat I was wearing over my head and just walked back to the bench. I made a scene, but I didn't say anything because I knew I would have been kicked right out of the gym. The funny thing is, that call took on a life of its own—long before the days of the Internet—and as we made our way through district and the playoffs, our opponents would often stop during pregame warmups and try to figure out which one of our girls had been called for goaltending. Strictly from an intimidation standpoint, that call may have been worth five points a game as we made our way back to Austin in 1977 for the final state tournament to ever be played in Gregory Gym (the Erwin Center opened in 1978). This time, however, we were not just happy to be in Austin or to eat at a steakhouse; we were on a mission to win it all—and to at least spend a full night in our hotel rooms.

We opened the 1977 state tournament by playing Angleton, and we whipped the Wildcats relatively easily, 79–61. That set up the championship game against San Antonio Schertz Clemens, which had beaten Arlington,

70–54, in the semifinals. Before the game, the Clemens girls presented each of our team members with a Bible. We didn't really know how to respond— were they just being generous or did their team members believe we were a bunch of heathens who desperately needed God's word? If I had been on top of things, I would have had our girls open the Bible to Romans 8:37, which states that we are more than conquerors through Christ. But instead, we thanked the Clemens players and went to work.

Clemens was a solid team, but once we started rolling, we were practically impossible to beat. We beat Clemens, 79–65, to win the first state championship in girls' athletics history among DISD schools, finishing the year with a 37–2 record. One week later, our South Oak Cliff boys beat Fort Worth Dunbar and also claimed the state championship; SOC truly ruled Texas high school basketball in 1977. Like I've said over and over again, the athletes walking through the hallways at South Oak Cliff transformed good coaches into elite coaches.

Jimmy Gales had done a great job building the boys' program at SOC in the early 1970s, compiling a 104–15 record from 1972 to 1975. In fact, Gales did such a good job at SOC that he was hired as an assistant coach at North Texas State University in '75 (he later returned to SOC as head coach and then became North Texas State's head coach in 1986). Because of the success we were having at South Oak Cliff in all sports and the number of college-caliber athletes we were producing, it was quite common for college coaches like Bill Blakeley (the head coach at North Texas from 1975 to 1983 who hired Gales) to be walking through our hallways. In fact, I first met Sonja Hogg, the legendary head coach at Louisiana Tech who ultimately hired me as an assistant coach in 1980, when she was recruiting Debra Rodman at SOC. But long before I made the move to the college ranks, I was presented with another difficult coaching decision.

Following our 1977 run to the girls' state championship, the great Norman Jett, who compiled a 201–59–3 record in 21 seasons as the head football coach at SOC, offered me what had once been my dream job: baseball coach at South Oak Cliff. Technically, I would be starting off as a coordinator for the junior varsity football team. However, Jett assured me the varsity head baseball job would be mine if I took the position he was offering. To say I was tempted to take the job would be a major understatement. As long as I could remember, making a career in baseball had been my focus and my greatest ambition. This was my chance to follow my dreams and to also join so many of my friends in the coaching world, most of whom were coaching boys' sports.

While I gave baseball some serious thought, I just couldn't pull the trigger. The bottom line was that I was having too much fun coaching the girls, and there was certainly no guarantee that I would ever sniff a state baseball championship at South Oak Cliff. But I knew that the odds were pretty good that we could make a serious run at Austin virtually every year with the elite athletes in our girls' basketball program. Besides, while coaching the South Oak Cliff girls, I had already achieved some of the dreams that seemed rather farfetched a couple of years earlier.

I've always loved reading multiple newspaper sports sections every day. I didn't just read the sports sections for information; I read them because I was often intrigued—and sometimes mesmerized—by the way my favorite sportswriters would paint vivid and colorful pictures with their words. Jim Dent, who eventually wrote the *New York Times* best-selling book *The Junction Boys*, was my first beat writer, and my second was Richard Justice, who became one of the great baseball journalists. But following our 1977 state championship, two of my biggest personal highlights were being interviewed for a newspaper story by the great Frank Luksa and doing a radio show with longtime Dallas Cowboys radio voice Brad Sham. Luksa's 40 years in journalism included stints at the *Fort Worth Star-Telegram*, the *Dallas Times Herald*, and the *Dallas Morning News*, and he was the consummate print journalism professional, just as Brad Sham was the best of the best in the broadcasting business—and still is. Being interviewed by those two pros in the same year was a "bucket list" accomplishment for me.

Selfishly, I knew I might have more opportunities to do those kinds of things and to build something really special if I stayed with the girls' programs. Looking back, that was one of the best decisions I ever made. Thanks to the array of remarkable players that continually arrived at South Oak Cliff year after year, we didn't just become a consistent winner—we built a dynasty.

In 1977–78, we made it to Austin for the state tournament for a third consecutive year, where we were able to christen the Erwin Center on the University of Texas campus by destroying League City Clear Creek in the semifinals, 86–47, and avenging our loss to Victoria two years earlier. In the 1978 Class 4A state championship game—the final six-on-six game in Texas—we beat Victoria, 70–62, to win our second straight state title and finish the year at 41–3 overall. Incidentally, it was in 1978 that Coach Jett pinned a nickname on me that stuck for quite a while: The White Shadow. The CBS television drama of the same name, starring Ken Howard as head coach Ken Reeves, had debuted that year. Upon his retirement from the NBA as a player, Reeves took a job as a basketball coach at Carver High School, a mostly black and Hispanic urban high school in South Central Los Angeles. The show was popular for several years, and it seemed like all my kids—from the female athletes to the students in my PE classes—loved referring to me as "The White Shadow." Considering some of the other nicknames I had received when I first showed up at SOC, that suited me just fine.

The nickname probably gained more popularity beyond the hallways of SOC a year later, when we went into the 1979 state tournament undefeated and beat Alvin, 68–48, in the semifinals. At that point, we had won 65 straight games dating back to the previous year. We may have felt invincible, but we were not. Victoria gained its redemption in the 1979 championship game, slowing the game down and holding on for a 43–41 victory that left an extremely sour taste in our mouths.

We used that loss as motivation the next year, going undefeated en route to a fifth consecutive trip to Austin for the 1980 state tournament. Once we were in Austin, we took care of business, beating Pearland in the semifinals and Lubbock Monterey in the championship game to win our third state championship in four years. At that point, we had won 105 of our previous 106 games. And in seven years at South Oak Cliff, we had compiled an overall record of 239–18. Quite honestly, we had a well-oiled machine that was operating at a high capacity, and I really believed that we could continue doing great things at South Oak Cliff for many years. But following that 1980 championship, Louisiana Tech head coach Sonja Hogg (pronounced "Hoag") and her top assistant, Leon Barmore, offered me a job on the Lady Techsters' staff in Ruston, Louisiana.

I initially turned down the position, but eventually accepted—one of the best decisions in my life. When I turned down the baseball offer, I had been a single man. But when the offer came from Louisiana Tech, I was no longer thinking only about myself. That's because in 1978, I had made an even better decision that had absolutely nothing to do with basketball.

5 Investing Time Wisely Pays Off

On November 18, 2008, Little, Brown and Company published *Outliers: The Story of Success*, a nonfiction book by Malcolm Gladwell. The book, which debuted at No. 1 on the *New York Times* bestseller list, has sold millions of copies and has probably been reviewed, dissected, and debated that many times. I won't bore you with my own synopsis, but one of the themes throughout the book that is most often discussed, deliberated, and disputed is the "10,000-hour rule." To summarize, Gladwell states that it takes 10,000 hours of practice to become an expert on any subject or to become great in practically any field.

Among other things, Gladwell cites the Beatles, who performed live in Hamburg, Germany, over 1,200 times from 1960 to 1964, amassing at least 10,000 hours of playing time before really hitting it big, especially in the United States, in 1964. He also notes that Microsoft cofounder Bill Gates spent at least 10,000 hours of programming time on a high school computer in the late 1960s. In writing the book, Gladwell interviewed Gates, who said that the unique access he had to a computer at a time when they were not commonplace helped him tremendously in his success.

In all sincerity, I don't know if there is anything truly magical about 10,000 hours of anything. But I have always believed that if you want to be great at something, there is simply no substitute for putting in the time. You want to be a great auto mechanic? Put in the time under the hood. Want to be a great golfer? Spend your time on the practice range. My philosophy has always been that time spent working on your profession or your passion is often time well invested. At least that's what I tried to convince my parents of when I probably spent at least 10,000 hours playing intramural sports during my multiple tenures at Texas Tech.

That's a joke. But in all seriousness, investing thousands upon thousands of hours playing all those intramural sports at Texas Tech—as well as all the other sports I played while growing up—was probably the perfect preparation for teaching PE classes at South Oak Cliff and coaching numerous sports when I first took over the girls' athletics program. After all, it's much easier to teach a sport when you can actually demonstrate the proper techniques and finer points of the games. And to know the finer points of a particular game, it was practically a necessity to have played it, especially in those archaic days before YouTube instructional videos.

Coaching basketball came naturally to me because I'd played so much of it growing up. Ditto with golf and track-and-field. But as the head coach of the girls' athletic programs at South Oak Cliff, I considered volleyball my weakest sport. So naturally, I decided to play volleyball—a whole lot of volleyball—and signed up to play in the Dallas-area city leagues. At first, I played at Fair Park and recreation centers around the Dallas area. We then began traveling to tournaments in Austin, San Antonio, and other destinations within the Lone Star State. My goal was never to become the next men's volleyball superstar like Karch Kiraly, especially since this was the late 1970s and most of the country hadn't heard of Karch Kiraly until he helped the United States win the Olympic gold medal in the summer of 1984. He would later coach the USA women's volleyball team for the 2016 Olympics.

Obviously, I loved competing, and I certainly had fun meeting new friends while playing volleyball. But my primary purpose for playing was to become a better player so that I could be a better coach and instructor to the girls on my volleyball teams. Going the extra mile—whether that meant driving back to Austin in the middle of the night so my team could see the championship games at the state basketball tournament or driving to San Antonio to play volleyball—has always been my key to coaching success. It has also made a huge difference in my personal life.

I played volleyball for a couple of years, and my fascination and love for the sport played a role in meeting my wife during the summer of 1978. At that point, I was in my early 30s, and while I was certainly not desperate to find a spouse, I was ready to settle down and share my life with the right person. After all, I had made the most of my single life: I had previously been engaged; I'd lived on the West Coast as a civilian and had been overseas in the US Marines; I had earned two degrees, finishing my master's in 1975; I had sown my "wild oats"; and I had even spent the summer of 1975 traveling around Europe. Looking back, that trip was one of the smartest and most economical decisions I made in my late 20s. I went by myself, and I spent the entire summer traveling to Florence, Amsterdam, Venice, London, Barcelona, Monte Carlo, Madrid, Zürich, Vienna, and Munich. I stayed in cheap hotels, didn't buy a single souvenir, discovered that I loved German beer but didn't like warm beer or ale in London, fell in love with Spain, and survived the entire summer by spending less than $2,000. That included my $400 airfare and my $200 Europass, which allowed me to travel the train/rail systems throughout Europe. I did a whole lot of sightseeing and even more growing up on that trip, and by the summer of '78, I was open to finding the right person for the right long-term relationship.

As fate would have it, that person showed up at my apartment complex on Moser Street in east Dallas, which was one of the coolest paces to live in the '70s. In the summer of 1978, a group of us were playing water volleyball. I was in my element, and I may have been an "eight" on a scale of 1 to 10. Under normal circumstances, I was probably a six, at best, even with my hip mustache. But I was so well known at that apartment complex—the same apartment complex where legendary Dallas sportswriter Blackie Sherrod lived—that I might have been up to an eight, especially with my "dominant" volleyball skills in the swimming pool.

That's a major joke, but in all sincerity, I was a pretty good volleyball player. I also had a good job; I owned a cool car; I had plenty of friends who would vouch for me, especially in that apartment complex; and I had enough confidence in myself—and in my surroundings—to make my move when I first spotted Nan, a brand-new resident at the complex, in her all-white nurse's uniform as the apartment manager, Willetta Stellmacher, was showing her around the place.

Inside Willetta's office was a keg of beer, which cost a quarter per cup. As I saw Willetta escorting Nan around the complex, I made sure to make a beer run so that I could say hello to the young redheaded nurse. To make a long story short, I did say a flirtatious hello to Nan and then went back to playing water volleyball with the gang. As we played in the early July sunshine, we began discussing a group trip to the Texas Rangers game later that night.

The Rangers had moved to Arlington from Washington, DC, in 1972. As the Washington Senators, the franchise had 11 miserable years, producing just one winning season between 1961 and 1971. The 1978 Rangers, who were managed by Billy Hunter and led by a starting pitching rotation that featured Fergie Jenkins and Jon Matlack, were a solid, second-place team. There was definitely an air of excitement at the old Arlington Stadium, especially with the Rangers playing well in early July.

As a lifelong baseball fan and a sucker for all Dallas-area professional teams, I was sold on the Rangers by the mid-1970s and was already well on my way to fanatical-fan status by 1978. I don't think it was my idea to go to the game that night after playing water volleyball, but I certainly didn't argue when the suggestion was made. I also began thinking rather quickly about the attractive young nurse I had met earlier that day. I quickly decided to make my move. I knocked on her door and told her that a group of us were headed to the Texas Rangers game and asked if she wanted to join us.

Naturally, she hesitated. She didn't really know anything about me, and it's not like she could pull out her laptop or her smartphone and research my Facebook page to see my friends, my interests, and my perspectives on current events. (Incidentally, I still don't have a Facebook page, and I doubt I ever will, although I do have a Twitter account so I can tweet with all the teens and twenty-somethings on my roster and any potential recruits.) In 1978, however, social media was still decades away from becoming a reality, but being nosy was still as popular then as it is now. Willetta, who was a former professional dancer, was way ahead of her time in knowing practically everything about everyone—at least everyone who lived in her apartments.

She was quite particular about renters. She was not politically correct, and she simply did not care if she was perceived to be unfair, biased, old fashioned, or a stick-in-the-mud. She called things the way she saw them, and she didn't care if she offended anyone. If you owned a motorcycle, you could not rent an apartment with her. If you owned a van, you were out of luck as well. She allowed renters with good jobs, good reputations, good appearances, and good references. Period. Quite frankly, there's no way she could have run a business the same way today, because she had no problem discriminating against anyone who didn't make a good impression on her. She would simply tell someone that she had no vacancies because she didn't like the person's haircut, personality, or vehicle. End of discussion.

Once you made the cut, though, she was usually in your corner (as long as you paid the rent on time). Fortunately, I paid the rent on time, kept my nose clean, and always treated Willetta with respect. She liked me, and she gave me a ringing endorsement when Nan called her to ask if she should go out with me. It's a damn good thing that I received such a glowing review from Willetta, because by the time I actually went to pick up Nan for our trip to Arlington Stadium for the game, everyone else in the group had backed out.

We sat in the outfield bleachers of the old ballpark, which had been known as "Turnpike Stadium" when it was the minor league home of the Dallas–Fort Worth Spurs. We drank a beer or two, ate a couple hot dogs, and had a great time. We didn't talk much baseball, but I learned plenty about Nan, and I really liked what I learned. She was from Abilene and had attended TCU. Her first nursing job had been in San Antonio, but now she was back in Dallas as a neonatal nurse at Parkland Hospital. I had such a good time talking to her and hanging out that I don't even remember who won the game, which is quite unusual for me. But I do remember that I couldn't wait to ask her out again.

So I didn't wait. I asked her to go out with me the next night. We went to a piano bar near the SMU campus off of Mockingbird Lane and Greenville. It was a great setting because you could enjoy the music and the atmosphere, but it wasn't so loud that you couldn't carry on a conversation. We had a great time and probably talked until 2:30 in the morning. I remember that quite vividly because I had to wake up at 6 a.m. to drive to Ruston, Louisiana, where I was working a camp for head coach Sonja Hogg at Louisiana Tech. I probably talked to Nan every night for a week while I was working that camp, which was a long-distance call that was coming out of my camp paycheck. But it was worth it.

Nan and I just clicked. Once I returned from Ruston at the end of summer camp, Nan and I went out just about every night through mid-December of 1978 when I decided to "pop the question." Actually, I had basically decided that she was "the one" around Thanksgiving when we drove out to Plainview for the big annual tournament held by the Wayland Baptist Flying Queens. In the 1950s, Wayland Baptist had won 131 straight games and became the first dominant power in women's basketball two decades before Title IX. The tournament, which featured eight colleges and eight high schools, was a major event in women's basketball at the time. During the trip to Plainview, which is roughly 45 miles north of Lubbock, we stopped at Jones Jewelry Store, where I had sold my first diamond ring when I was working there as a student at Texas Tech. We were strolling down my memory lane in Lubbock, but I was actually fishing for ideas, trying to determine exactly what kind of engagement ring she might like.

We were engaged at the revolving restaurant atop Reunion Tower in Dallas on December 23, 1978. I didn't really know exactly how I wanted to propose, so I asked the waiter for some advice when I went to the restroom during dinner. He suggested that I give the ring to him and that he would slip it into a champagne glass I could order to celebrate our first Christmas together. It all went perfectly, and the waiter covered up the ring at the bottom of the champagne glass with his hand as he presented the glass to Nan. We raised the glasses to toast, and she started to drink the champagne. Suddenly, she spotted the ring. Her next words—I kid you not—were "Oh shit!"

Always trying to be quick on my feet, I said, "Does that mean yes or no?" She said it meant yes, and everyone around us started clapping and cheering. Later that night, we went to see her parents, who were in town, to tell them the big news and then we drove over to Mama Reeves's home to let her know. She was like a second mother to me, and she was delighted that, at 33, I had finally found "the one." Nan and I were married on July 21, 1979, and we have been happily wed ever since.

One of the funny things about our marriage is that, in a roundabout way, we met because of my addiction and fascination with sports: I was playing water volleyball because I had been playing so much regular volleyball so that I could improve as a volleyball coach. Perhaps Nan and I would have met another time as neighbors even if I had not been playing water volleyball that day. On the other hand, perhaps different circumstances would have produced a different result. Looking back, I'm just thankful it worked out the way it did, and I am thankful I was able to convince Nan to go with me to the Rangers game later that night.

Believe it or not, that's the last baseball game—professional or collegiate—we have seen together in person, aside from games that our son, Matt, or our grandson, Logan, played in Little League. She hates baseball. Imagine that. All I ever wanted to do was play baseball. And then I wanted to coach baseball. And when I envisioned my distant future, I figured I would spend my retirement traveling the country with my wife, visiting one major league ballpark after another.

So perhaps it's a damned good thing I fell in love with a woman who hates baseball. Otherwise, I may have retired at 65 and missed out on Texas A&M making the 2011 run to the national championship.

That just goes to show that things typically have a way of working out for the best, especially if you are willing to go the extra mile and put in the extra hours. I did that a long time ago when I decided to make myself a better volleyball coach by playing the game. My "net gain" was more than I would have ever initially imagined when I first saw nurse Nan from the swimming pool of my apartment complex.

6 Things Are Never as Good— or as Bad—as They Initially Seem

On October 11, 1980, the expansion Dallas Mavericks made their regular-season NBA debut, playing host to the San Antonio Spurs at Reunion Arena in downtown Dallas. As a Dallas native and a basketball junkie, I was absolutely ecstatic about the arrival of the NBA in "Big D." The Rockets had been playing in Houston since 1971, and the Spurs had been playing in San Antonio since 1973 after beginning as the Dallas Chaparrals of the American Basketball Association in 1967. But in 1980, big-time basketball finally came to my hometown.

In the expansion draft, Dallas passed on well-known veteran players from other teams like "Pistol" Pete Maravich, Earl Monroe, Rick Barry, and Doug Collins. Instead, the Mavs chose projects like Jim Spanarkel, Tom LaGarde, Abdul Jeelani, and Winford Boynes, who weren't even household names on their own streets. The only big name the Mavs acquired was with their first-ever first-round draft selection, UCLA forward Kiki Vandeweghe, the 11th overall pick in the 1980 draft. However, Vandeweghe refused to play for the expansion franchise and held out for more than a month until Dallas traded him to Denver for two future first-round picks. With Vandeweghe, the Mavericks were expected to struggle mightily. Without him, the team's chances of competing in the Western Conference seemed as slim as a *Sports Illustrated* swimsuit model's waistline.

Nevertheless, more than 10,000 curious fans showed up at Reunion Arena on a Saturday night in the middle of football season (the Texas–OU game had taken place earlier in the day in the Cotton Bowl) to see the Mavericks play the heavily favored Spurs, who had made the playoffs in each of their first four seasons in the NBA and were led by one of the true stars in the game, George "Ice Man" Gervin.

To the pleasant surprise of those in attendance, Winford Boynes scored 21 points and Tom LaGarde added 19 points and 14 rebounds as the Mavs stunned the Spurs, 103–92. After that night, curious fans across the Dallas area instantly became intrigued. Could the Mavericks possibly be better than everyone anticipated? Could Winford Boynes, who once starred at Oklahoma City's Capitol High School and the University of San Francisco, become the steal of the expansion draft? Could the inaugural season also be a magical and memorable one?

The answer to all three of those questions: not only no, but hell no. After winning the opener and momentarily piquing the interest of local fans, the Mavericks proceeded to lose 27 of their next 29 games en route to an overall record of 15–67. Obviously, the first night was not indicative of how the rest of the season would go. The Mavs were great for a game, but they were predictably pathetic the rest of the season.

Whether it's a basketball team, a new job, a business proposal, or an initial date, we all know that sometimes a first impression can lead to a false assumption. We also know that we shouldn't judge a book by its cover, as virtually nothing—absolutely nothing at all—is as good or as bad as it initially seems. I was reminded of that in October 1980 by the Dallas Mavericks after their first night—and by an event that hit so much closer to home later that month.

The night before I officially began my career as a collegiate coach, I stepped into a rental home in Ruston, Louisiana, with nothing but the clothes on my back and a sleeping bag. A cold front had just blown through north central Louisiana, making temperatures feel more like wintertime in Rochester, New York, than fall in Louisiana. The temperature outside was in the 20s, and the thermostat inside the rental house (owned by local businessman and Louisiana Tech booster Johnny Maxwell) wasn't much higher. The heat wasn't working, and neither was anything else. There was no furniture in the house, and Nan was back in Dallas working at Parkland Hospital. She was going to work and stay in Dallas until at least January, assuming we could sell the historic home that we had recently purchased on Miller Street near Greenville Avenue.

So here I was, all alone in an unfurnished rental home, freezing my butt off with nothing but my sleeping bag. I looked around the empty house and began wondering what the hell I'd gotten myself into and why. Shivering and second-guessing myself, I replayed in my mind the decision I had recently made to temporarily leave my wife behind and to permanently—at least for the foreseeable future—leave my hometown, an incredibly successful athletic program, and a comfortable job at South Oak Cliff to take a shot at the collegiate ranks as an assistant coach at a small school in a small town (Ruston had a population of about 20,000). At that moment, I wondered if my immediate future might be as bleak as the Mavericks.

Fortunately, my pity party ended as I drifted off to sleep. The sun did, indeed, rise the following morning, and as soon as I stepped into my office at the old Memorial Gym on the Louisiana Tech campus, I began feeling better about my decision. And once I made it to the first practice, my second-guessing ceased to exist. Being around the sensational athletes, two other tremendous coaches, and the overall college atmosphere instantly convinced me that I had made the right move. With the exception of that first night in Ruston, I felt at home right away, although I certainly had not been looking to leave South Oak Cliff. After all, when it came to girls' basketball in the Lone Star State, the South Oak Cliff Golden Bears had been rocking and rolling through the 1970s like Deep Purple, Pink Floyd, and Black Sabbath. We were chart toppers and hardwood headliners in every way, and there was no reason to envision our colorful, high-flying triumphant run ending anytime soon. We'd built a tradition of excellence, and every incoming group of underclassmen wanted to continue—or even build upon—the legacy and lineage of championship basketball at SOC.

Don't misunderstand. It's never easy to stay on top. But it is easier to stay at the top of your game when your players enter the program expecting to win and demanding excellence of themselves and their teammates. We had reached that level—and then some—at South Oak Cliff. Entering the 1980–81 high school basketball season, we had won three state championships in a span of four years and had made five consecutive trips to the Final Four in Austin in Class 4A. I loved working with the young ladies in our region in all sports, and I really believed I was making a positive difference in their lives. Besides, my personal life was sensational as well. Nan and I were thoroughly enjoying our young married lives together, and we decided to purchase a home together. Not just any starter home, though. We purchased a grand, beautiful fixer-upper from the early 1920s. We were in the process of remodeling the kitchen when I received an unexpected phone call from Leon Barmore of Louisiana Tech that would ultimately change my life. He made me an offer that I simply couldn't refuse. I would have never left Dallas or South Oak Cliff for "just another job," even at the college level. But in October 1980, Louisiana Tech was certainly not an ordinary job in women's college basketball. Tech had already proven that it was one of the rising powers in women's hoops, and the future looked as big and bright as the Dallas skyline on a clear summer night.

Back in the mid-1970s—before most universities even contemplated making any significant financial investments in women's athletics—Louisiana Tech president F. Jay Taylor didn't just acknowledge or accept Title IX, he fully embraced it. In 1973, Taylor met with a young and stylish physical education teacher named Sonja Hogg, and the result of that discussion was the creation of the Louisiana Tech women's basketball program, with Hogg serving as the head coach, even though she had never previously held that role at any level and had never played the game on an interscholastic or collegiate level. But Hogg, who was barely 30 when she took the head coaching job, was convinced that she could recruit as exceptionally as she dressed, with her suede and leather wardrobe, plentiful jewelry, spiked heels, and fur coats. (Her wardrobe was probably worth more than the $5,000 budget allotted to women's basketball the first year of the program.)

Hogg would eventually prove that she could assemble some sensationally talented rosters at Tech, but there was no immediate indication that she would build anything resembling a dynasty. Tech opened its first-ever season on January 7, 1975, with a home loss to Southeastern Louisiana, one of only four home games that first year. Hogg started a 5-foot-9 post playing her first season and wound up with an 11–7 regular season record before splitting four games at the Louisiana AIAW State Tournament (this was before the NCAA entered women's athletics). Tech's first season ended with a two-point defeat to McNeese State at the state tournament.

During that first season, Hogg's players may have attracted as much attention for how they dressed as they did for how they played. Hogg, with her immense fashion sense and her insistence that the team look and dress like classy young ladies, designed uniform tops unlike any other program in the country, featuring sleeves and collars. Sports bras didn't exist at that time, and Sonja didn't want her young ladies looking like so many other women's teams with bra straps showing during the games. She also balked at the mere thought of being referred to as the "Lady Bulldogs."

"I could just [envision] people saying, 'There comes Coach Hogg and all of her little bitches,'" she said. Instead, they became the Lady Techsters, and President Taylor, who had been a Navy pilot during World War II, circulated a memo among his administrative council making attendance at the early women's home games mandatory. Taylor recognized right away that the women's program could bring the university the kind of national recognition that men's athletics could probably never deliver (even though the school had produced quarterback Terry Bradshaw, who was leading the Pittsburgh Steelers to multiple Super Bowl titles in the 1970s, as well as Baltimore Colts All-Pro quarterback Bert Jones and, later on, NBA All-Pro Karl Malone). "A national championship in football or men's basketball will be difficult," Taylor once wrote to his administrators, "but we can do it in women's basketball." He was right, of course, but it would take more than just good Louisiana players to win at an elite level. In fact, one of Hogg's most valuable high school recruits never played a single second for the Lady Techsters.

In 1975–76, Tech's second year of women's basketball, the Lady Techsters improved to 19–10 overall with a 14-member roster that was composed of all Louisiana athletes who came from hometowns that were all less than 100 miles away from Ruston. Once again, the Lady Techsters earned a bid to the Louisiana AIAW State Tournament, where they won two games before being ousted by LSU. The following year was even better, as Tech posted its first 20-game winning season by going 22–9 and earning the school's first-ever trip to the AIAW Regional Tournament after winning the state championship. Featuring an all-Louisiana roster once again, the Lady Techsters captured the state title by winning four consecutive games at the state tournament. In the regional tournament, Tech opened with a convincing victory over Oklahoma State before falling to Baylor in a tight contest.

Following that season, Hogg made a program-altering decision that proved to be truly brilliant. Hogg had first crossed paths with Leon Barmore when she was in charge of the pompon girls and was a physical education teacher at Ruston High, where Barmore was the boys' basketball coach. Hogg was hired by Tech in 1974. "The first day on the job [at Tech] she was in my office asking what to order [for the basketball team]," Barmore told *Sports Illustrated* in 1983. "I had a free period every afternoon from one to two, and Sonja would come by all that first year to talk." At first, the conversations focused primarily on the fundamentals of basketball, as Hogg would pick Barmore's mind regarding running practices, designing offenses, and so forth. The more they talked, the more Hogg realized that Barmore could be the missing piece to take the Lady Techsters from regional success to national prominence.

Barmore, a former Louisiana Tech men's player, had spent a decade coaching in high schools and was looking for a college job. The only catch was that he absolutely loved living in Ruston. "Let's face it, I'm a northern Louisiana boy," he told the *New York Times* in the early 1980s. So when Hogg convinced President F. Jay Taylor to "pony up" and offer Barmore a contract worth a whopping $13,000 per year, he took the assistant coaching position at his alma mater, thinking, "I'd do it a few years and switch to men's basketball."

Things went much better than Barmore could have ever expected, though. Recognizing her own limitations as a basketball strategist, Hogg turned over all the on-the-court coaching duties to Barmore. Mrs. Hogg (as she preferred to be called by the players) ran the team like a CEO. She handled the television and radio appearances and the print media, worked as the chief recruiter, became a surrogate mother to the players, and served as the face of the program. Barmore was the behind-the-scenes X's and O's wizard. He was the introverted teacher and tactician, and she was the gregarious spokeswoman of the program. When asked once by the *New York Times* what she did during timeouts while Barmore diagrammed plays or dissected in-game situations, Hogg said, "I sit there and watch."

It was obviously an unusual situation, but it worked exceptionally well. From a recruiting standpoint, the affable and energetic Hogg suddenly had the time to broaden her focus well beyond a 100-mile radius of Ruston, Louisiana. Once she looked beyond the borders of Louisiana, she naturally made a trip to the most successful high school program in the Dallas area— South Oak Cliff. Sonja and I quickly became friends, and she caught the attention of my players (as well as all the other students and teachers) when she showed up to SOC in her trademark white Corvette.

The sweet-talking, sharp-dressing Hogg was a natural closer on the recruiting trail (she targeted and landed Debra Rodman from SOC, for example). Meanwhile, the hard-edged, gruff, and ultraintense Barmore, who is a year older than Hogg, developed a systematic approach to everything the Lady Techsters did and brought a defensive mentality to a program that had never really played defense. Barmore was only slightly less edgy than Bobby Knight, and he was so animated on the bench that he sometimes left games more drained than the Louisiana Tech players. Barmore initially tried to be more positive and reserved as a women's coach than he had been as a boys' high school coach, but he quickly went back to his type-A personality traits.

"At first I read all these books on the psychology of women," he recalled in a *Sports Illustrated* article. "But I finally said, 'Enough. I'm just going to be me.' If I'm not being intense, I'm not doing the job. I told [the players]: 'On the court, I treat you as players. Off the court, I treat you as ladies.'" In that same article, Hogg responded: "He's so intense that sometimes I wish he'd take up drinking."

Hogg's style and Barmore's bile paid off. Tech went 20–8 in Barmore's first year on the staff (1977–78) and earned the school's first-ever national ranking (20th) after making its third straight appearance in the AIAW Regional Tournament. In Barmore's second year on staff (1978–79), the Lady Techsters shattered the single-season school record for victories with 34–4 and earned their first trip to the AIAW National Tournament, where Tech ultimately lost to Old Dominion, finishing No. 2 in the country. And in Barmore's third year (1979–80)—the sixth year of the program—Hogg and a bevy of talented players went 40–5 and returned to the AIAW Final Four, losing to Old Dominion (this time in the semifinals) and South Carolina in the consolation game to finish fourth overall.

It was clear to practically everyone involved in women's basketball, including me, that Louisiana Tech was on the cusp of realizing President Taylor's vision of a national championship. After first meeting Hogg when she was on the recruiting trail, I began working the Louisiana Tech camps in the summers, where I also grew to know and appreciate Barmore, who, following the 1979–80 season, had been promoted to associate head coach. Barmore later acknowledged that his promotion helped change the perception that Hogg was doing all the heavy lifting in Ruston. "There was a slight ego problem [in the early years at Louisiana Tech]," Barmore told the *New York Times* in the mid-1980s. "I was doing all the coaching and Sonja was doing most of the recruiting, and she's very good at that because she knows everybody. But she was getting the numbers, and I wasn't."

In other words, Hogg was rolling up the coaching victories, while Barmore's record was still "0–0" in the college ranks. Like most coaches, Barmore wanted credit for the victories he was helping compile. Win-loss records tend to drive and define coaches because they are like a high-profile resume that is printed in the media notes before every game. Imagine if a lawyer's win-loss record was printed and distributed before every trial or a doctor's win-loss record in properly diagnosing illnesses was printed daily in the newspapers. It's difficult not to obsess over win-loss records, and it was probably particularly difficult for Leon to not be receiving any credit for all those wins, since he was leading the on-the-court coaching efforts. The associate head coach title helped address that issue.

Meanwhile, back in Dallas in October 1980, I was focused on taking the South Oak Cliff volleyball team into the playoffs at work and redoing our kitchen at home. I had no illusions of going into the college coaching ranks—at least not immediately. The North Texas State head women's coaching job had opened up after Cherri Rapp left following the 1978–79 season to join Texas A&M, and I had thrown my name into the hat. But the Mean Green decided to stay with a female coach and hired Denise Smith.

By mid-October of 1980, the SOC volleyball team was rolling toward another district championship. Unlike basketball, we were typically derailed in the playoffs, which was possibly the result of my general lack of knowledge regarding the sport. We were pretty athletic, and I knew enough to win district championships, but not state championships. Nevertheless, I was in volleyball mode when Leon called me at home at seven o'clock on a Tuesday morning. Not only had I worked the Louisiana Tech camps, but eight high school teams, headlined by South Oak Cliff, and eight college teams, led by Louisiana Tech, would annually be invited to play in the prestigious Wayland Baptist Tournament in Plainview, Texas, which is just north of Lubbock. So both Sonja and Leon had seen me coach my kids and work their camps.

Still, I was quite surprised when Leon called. He informed me that his close friend, Barry Canterbury, had just decided that he was leaving his role as Louisiana Tech assistant women's basketball coach and head softball coach to enter the sporting goods industry. Canterbury didn't want to start another women's basketball season. He was staying in Ruston, but he was leaving Louisiana Tech right away. When Canterbury broke that news to Sonja and Leon, they decided to offer me the job.

"Gary, we would like for you to come to Ruston to be our assistant coach," Leon said. "We want you to seriously consider it and to come for a visit."

It certainly crossed my mind to tell him "no" right there on the spot because of everything that was happening. There was the historic house in Dallas that Nan and I had purchased, and all our plans to restore and remodel it. Then there was the timing. If he had asked in the summer— before school started—it would have been so much more convenient. But school was well under way—volleyball season was in full swing and basketball season was right around the corner.

In winning the 1980 Class 4A state girls' basketball championship, we had gone 40–0, beating Lubbock Monterey in the title game. And over the past two seasons, we had a combined record of 83–1, with the only loss in 1979 coming to Victoria (43–41) in the state championship game. And if you went back to the end of the '78 season, we were 116–1 in our last 117 games! We had several starters coming back from the 1980 state championship team, and I explained to Leon, "I'm really honored to be considered, but . . ."

"I know the timing isn't great, but what a situation we have here, Gary," he said emphatically. "We have a team that can make a run at the national championship; you already know Sonja and me, and you have already worked with both of us; [former South Oak Cliff star] Debra Rodman is a freshman this year; and you've already done everything you can possibly do in the high school ranks. At least come for a visit."

I told Leon that I'd think about it, and after giving it some discussion and talking it over with Nan, I called him back and agreed to visit. Louisiana Tech officials sent a private plane to Dallas to pick me up and take me to Ruston. It was my first time ever on a private plane, and the pilot told me that since it was such a short flight, he was going to stay relatively close to the ground and follow Interstate 20 all the way to Ruston. Upon arriving, Sonja and Leon wined and dined me, and it was a sensational visit. After that trip, I could suddenly envision making the transition from high school to college, but I still needed a little time to think about it. Two weeks later, Leon called back to say he needed an answer.

"I just don't know if I can do it," I told him.

He said he would call back later in the day. When I hung up the phone and told Nan about the conversation, she made me go back upstairs into our bedroom. "Stay there until you make a decision," she said. "Don't come back down here until you do."

I walked upstairs, slipped back into bed, and began thinking. I loved my life in Dallas. I loved what I was doing, but I had accomplished everything I could as a high school coach, compiling a 238–18 record and winning three state titles. It was probably time for a new challenge at a new level, even though I didn't know too much about college coaching. Nan also knew it was the right move, even though it would uproot us and scuttle our plans for remodeling a home and starting a family in Dallas. I eventually walked back downstairs, told Nan about my decision, and called Leon back, informing him that I would take the job but only after the volleyball team had wrapped up the playoffs. About a week after I made the decision to take the position at Louisiana Tech, the volleyball team advanced to the regional round of the Class 4A playoffs at Sam Houston State University in Huntsville, which is where we were typically eliminated by a team like Conroe or Richardson.

The way things worked out in 1980, our volleyball team was scheduled to participate in a playoff match at nine o'clock on a Saturday morning in Huntsville, and if we won, we would play the next match at some point between 11 o'clock and noon. It just so happened that we were also scheduled to open the 1980–81 basketball season later that same day against Victoria at the University of Houston's Hofheinz Pavilion. Remember, the players on the volleyball team were basically the exact same as the basketball team—they just changed uniforms. If we had won that first volleyball match and advanced to the regional finals, we may not have made the basketball game on time. But we were eliminated in the first match and made it to Hofheinz Pavilion with plenty of time to beat Victoria for my 239th and final win as a high school basketball coach. We returned to Dallas that night; my assistant coach, Detroit McKinney, took over as the head girls' basketball coach at SOC; and I loaded up the car and drove to Ruston the next day, where I spent the coldest and one of the loneliest nights of my life in a rental house with no heating or furniture.

After that first night, though, things were much better and far more fun than I could have possibly envisioned at Louisiana Tech. We didn't even have a senior on the roster in 1980–81, but we were loaded with talent, led by 6-foot junior Pam Kelly, a two-time Kodak All-American, and 5-foot-8 junior Angela Turner, who would go on to earn Kodak All-American honors. We also had a tremendous freshman class that included top recruits from across the nation, such as South Oak Cliff's Debra Rodman, Lyn Anastasio from Virginia, and Janice Lawrence from Mississippi. But the most heralded freshman may have been 5-foot-4 guard Kim Mulkey from right down the road in Hammond, Louisiana. As a star at Hammond High School, Mulkey led the Lady Tornadoes to a combined record of 136–5 and won four state championships. When she graduated in 1980, her 4,075 career points represented a national high school record. She also never missed a day of school—not a single day—from kindergarten through her senior year, as she graduated the valedictorian of her class. Mulkey later said that a big part of why she chose Louisiana Tech was the atmosphere at basketball games, which she compared to a Baptist revival.

That atmosphere was good prior to 1980–81, but it was even better once we started rolling. We opened the season by winning our first six games by an average of 37.5 points per game, and then we slipped past Kansas and Rutgers (at Madison Square Garden) in our two biggest tests of the regular season. As it turned out, those were our biggest challenges of the year. We rolled into the AIAW National Tournament with an unbeaten record, where we opened with a 47-point win over Jackson State and a 33-point win over UCLA. Both of those games were in Ruston, which earned us a trip to Eugene, Oregon, for the AIAW Final Four. After defeating Southern California 66–50 in the semifinals, we faced Tennessee in the title game, which was nationally televised on NBC. We were a heavy favorite against the Lady Vols, and we cruised to a 79–59 victory, marking the 27th time in 34 games that the Lady Techsters had won by 20 or more points. We finished 34–0 and truly established ourselves as one of the elite powers of women's basketball.

Incidentally, I also served as the head coach of Louisiana Tech women's softball team in the spring of 1981, compiling an 18–17 record in my one and only season as head coach. Bill Galloway was hired away from Texas A&M to take over the next year and won 705 games over the next two decades, which is 687 more than me. But at least my one year as softball coach was a winning season.

Obviously, my main focus was women's basketball, and we added further validity to our 1981 AIAW national championship and undefeated record the following season by winning the first-ever NCAA title in women's basketball history in Norfolk, Virginia. At its peak, the AIAW was composed of almost 1,000 member schools. Following the passage of Title IX, however, the NCAA decided to include women's championships. The NCAA's Division II and Division III schools voted to offer championships under the NCAA umbrella in 1980, but Division I members failed to gain a majority vote on this issue until the 1981 national meeting. Even after a decision had been reached, it was quite contentious, as the initial vote on whether to move to the NCAA had ended in a tie, 124–124. The move to the NCAA ultimately passed, but for the 1981–82 academic year, schools were able to compete in either the NCAA or the AIAW championships.

At issue was the fact that the AIAW had fought for women's rights in the midst of the Title IX movement, while the NCAA had initially opposed those efforts. Looking toward the future, however, the NCAA was much better funded and possessed far better access to television contracts. Interestingly, one of the strongest holdouts against the move to the NCAA was the University of Texas, where Donna Lopiano, the previous president of the AIAW, was the women's athletics director. I say "interestingly" because at the time, the University of Texas was more interested in preserving tradition than in leaving for the presumably greener and richer pastures where television contracts could generate far more revenue. Roughly three decades later (2010–11, to be exact), UT's fixation on pushing the envelope of television contracts nearly led to the breakup of the Big 12 and did lead Texas A&M to move to the SEC. But back in the early 1980s, the Lady Longhorns were leading the fight for the underdog AIAW. However, when 17 of the top 20 women's basketball programs, including Louisiana Tech, Tennessee, and Old Dominion, agreed to enter the NCAA Tournament in 1982, it proved to be the beginning of the end for the AIAW.

The NCAA was more established and was able to offer incentives, such as paying transportation costs during the postseason, to participating members, which the AIAW could not match. In other words, the NCAA Tournament was more prestigious right from the start. Case in point: On March 28, 1982, Rutgers defeated Texas, 83–77, in the final AIAW national championship game in Philadelphia. Afterward, Rutgers head coach Theresa Shank Grentz told the *New York Times* that she had withdrawn $500 from her own savings account to pay for a victory dinner for her team.

That same day—March 28, 1982—Louisiana Tech beat Cheyney University of Pennsylvania, 76–62, to win the first women's NCAA national championship. And I can assure you that none of our coaches had to empty their wallets to pay for dinner that evening. The Lady Techsters were rock stars in Ruston in the early 1980s, and we traveled in style. In the April 5, 1982, edition of *Sports Illustrated*, for example, author Barry McDermott noted, "Louisiana Tech's women's basketball budget is more than $100,000, one of the country's biggest, and the school will open a new 8,000-seat field house [Thomas Assembly Center] in May." The article also mentioned that in the third round of the 1982 NCAA Tournament, we packed the old Memorial Gym in Ruston with more than 4,850 people and treated those fans to a convincing 82–60 victory over a University of Kentucky team that was outmanned and overwhelmed.

We had opened the 1981–82 season by winning our first 20 games and running our win streak from the previous year to 54 consecutive victories (the streak was snapped in a 61–58 loss at Old Dominion in the middle of the season). But we bounced back to beat Maryland, Louisiana–Monroe, Baylor, Stephen F. Austin, Alcorn State, and McNeese State before playing host to UCLA in a game that I will absolutely never forget. UCLA was a powerhouse back then, and we ended up beating the Lady Bruins in Ruston by 40 points, 103–63. But that's not why that game and that date—February 20, 1982—will forever be emblazoned in my mind.

My wife was quite pregnant at that time with our first child, but she wasn't due for at least another week when we went to bed the night of February 19, 1982. Nan is so predictable, so practical, so routine-oriented, and so timely that it never really crossed my mind that she might give birth before the due date. And even though she began having labor pains in the middle of the night, she didn't bother telling me until the next morning. Nan has always done things her way on her time schedule, and finally at around 6 a.m. on February 20, she woke me up and told me it was time to go to the hospital. Part of my compensation package at Louisiana Tech was a company car that happened to be a rather hideous brown wood-paneled late-model station wagon. I loved my old sports cars, but I wasn't too proud to drive the family wagon that was provided to me at no cost. We loaded up the wagon that morning and drove the roughly 35-mile trip from Ruston to Monroe at the speed of light—or at least as fast as the ol' Woodie Wagon would go. I know I was going at least 85 miles per hour because I was afraid her water had broken, and I sure didn't want to be the one delivering our baby.

We arrived at the hospital, and Dr. R. Guthrie Jarrell met us to do what he did best. Dr. Jarrell also happened to be the No. 1 supporter of Louisiana Tech basketball in the state. He had arrived at Tech as a freshman in 1945 and played basketball for the Bulldogs that year. After graduating in 1949, he spent the rest of his life delivering babies and supporting Louisiana Tech athletics. Dr. Jarrell was known as "Mr. Tech" in the Monroe area, and he rarely missed any big athletic event involving the Bulldogs or Lady Techsters. Nan also worked at the hospital in Monroe as a neonatal nurse because Ruston was too small to have a neonatal department.

In hindsight, though, we could have taken our sweet time and walked from Ruston to Monroe. Throughout the morning, Dr. Jarrell regularly checked on Nan and talked basketball with me. Morning became afternoon, but nothing was progressing, and our game against UCLA was scheduled for 7:45 that evening.

Finally, at about 3 or 3:30 in the afternoon, Dr. Jarrell came back to check on Nan and informed us that he was going to perform a C-section because the baby wasn't progressing and—these were his exact words—"I'm not going to miss this damn game tonight!" They wheeled Nan into the operating room and our daughter, Paige, was born at about 4:30 that afternoon. Dr. Jarrell examined Paige and Nan, changed his clothes, and took off for Ruston to watch the games. Meanwhile, I stayed with Nan for the next hour until she finally instructed me to go to the game. "You are going to be miserable just sitting here if you miss that game," she said. "So get out of here. And drive a little slower than you did coming to the hospital."

I arrived at the old Memorial Gym, and the public address announcer made an announcement about Paige's arrival. We then proceeded to whip UCLA's butt to continue our dominant run. We were ranked No. 1 in the nation every week of the 1981–82 season for the second straight year, another record, and we once again closed out the season on national television. In a 69–46 victory over Tennessee in the semifinals of the Final Four, we didn't allow a single field goal in the last eight and a half minutes. Two days later, after Cheyney State built an early 16–8 lead in the title game, our players went on a dazzling 22–8 run during an eight-minute stretch. By halftime, we led 40–26, and our giddy fans from Ruston began breaking out their national championship T-shirts.

In winning back-to-back national championships in 1981 and 1982, we compiled an overall record of 69–1. Things were good. Really, really good. But as I noted, things are never quite as good or as bad as they seem. Despite our record and the players' rock-star status, not everyone was completely thrilled with how we were being portrayed.

Leon Barmore was making a huge difference with his tactical knowledge of the game and his intensity. And we were recruiting nationally, just as any national championship–caliber program would do with the kind of success we were having. Our 1981–82 national championship team featured players from seven different states (Louisiana, Georgia, Illinois, Mississippi, Missouri, Texas, and Tennessee). But egos can sometimes derail what opponents cannot. Or, as Charles Caleb Colton once wisely said, "When we fail, our pride supports us, and when we succeed, it betrays us."

It became apparent that Leon was not completely happy with his title of "associate head coach." In an April 1982 issue of *Sports Illustrated*, he was quoted—quite memorably—as saying, "I hit the home runs and Sonja gets to circle the bases." Louisiana Tech's answer to that eyebrow-raising comment was to promote Barmore from associate head coach to "co–head coach" heading into the 1982–83 season. It was a short-term fix to an incurable issue. Leon deserved to be the head coach but certainly not at the expense of Sonja. Leon could have left Louisiana Tech years earlier, as he had been offered a head coaching job elsewhere in Louisiana, but he told the *New York Times*, "I saw the tears in the eyes of my only daughter because she didn't want to move, and I decided moving wasn't worth it." Instead, he accepted the co–head coaching title. Leon and Sonja sometimes fought like brother and sister—or Sonny and Cher—but they were good for each other, and they were outstanding for Louisiana Tech.

"I wouldn't recommend this setup to another school," Barmore said entering the 1982–83 season. "But for our area, for our community, it's worked out well. We get around 5,000 fans a game while other schools get a few hundred."

Once the 1982–83 season began, our crowds actually increased as we opened the home schedule at the brand new Thomas Assembly Center by playing host to a great Southern Cal team led by freshman sensation Cheryl Miller before a raucous, record-setting crowd of 8,700 fans, roughly 700 above capacity. We had been recruiting Miller throughout her glorious high school career at Riverside Polytechnic High in Riverside, California, where she was a four-year letter winner and led her team to a 132–4 record. She was the first player, male or female, to be named an All-American by *Parade* magazine four times. She had a great visit to Louisiana Tech, flying into Shreveport, where we picked her up in a limousine and brought her to Ruston. Cheryl was flamboyant, personable, and lovable. I spent plenty of time with her on the phone, as did Sonja.

She gave us a serious look, but she really wanted to major in communications, which was one of the top majors at USC at the time. I still remember a midnight call from Louisiana Tech President F. Jay Taylor to see how we were doing with Cheryl. I told him we had done everything possible but that the lure of staying close to home at USC and staying close to her brother, Reggie, who was also a "pretty good player," might be too much for us to overcome. Unfortunately, I was right, and we played against Cheryl in one of the first games of her collegiate career.

We actually lost that first game to USC and Miller, but then we rolled off 30 wins in a row to reach the national championship game for a third consecutive year. During our home schedule that year, we beat Alabama, Tennessee, Arkansas, Clemson, South Carolina, Oklahoma, Auburn, and Texas. Imagine trying to schedule those eight programs at Ruston today. Quite frankly, there's no way in hell those schools would come, but back then, Ruston was undeniably one of the marquee destinations in all of women's college basketball. In fact, we were drawing such huge crowds that Sonja agreed to play doubleheaders with the Louisiana Tech men's team. But whenever the women played first, many of the fans would file out of the Thomas Assembly Center while the men warmed up. And consider this: the 1983 men's team featured a future Hall of Famer and 14-time NBA All-Star by the name of Karl Malone who would eventually become the second most popular Louisiana Tech player of that era—behind Kim Mulkey.

That's really not an exaggeration. Mulkey was the Corvette-driving, pigtailed-wearing pride of Louisiana. *Sports Illustrated* referred to her as the Norma Rae of women's basketball, alluding to Sally Field's character in the 1979 American drama film about a petite factory worker in North Carolina who inspired a labor union movement in a small town.

In 1982–83, we ran an "inside-out" offense, playing a double post with 6-foot-3 Janice Lawrence and 6-foot-2 Debra Rodman dominating most opponents on the inside. We controlled the paint with our size, but Mulkey, who was also known as the "Hammond Honey," was the sparkplug who provided tremendous energy and tenacity on the perimeter. Kim was only 5 foot 4, but she was incredibly tough. In fact, no one in the United States took more charges than Kim Mulkey, who once took a charge in an international summer All-Star game against the USSR's 7-foot Uliana Semenova. In that game, the United States dealt the Soviets their first loss in 24 years, which only added to the legend and popularity of Kim Mulkey.

Along with Lawrence and Rodman, Mulkey nearly led us to a third consecutive national title in March 1983. On our way to the NCAA championship, we beat UCLA, UNLV, and Notre Dame on the road. We also avenged the early-season loss to USC by beating the Trojan Women, 58–56, in a neutral-site game, although it was practically a home game for USC, since it was played on the West Coast. Back at home, a television error resulted in Monroe and Shreveport stations cutting to the show *Hee Haw* with three and a half minutes left in the game. According to those stations, they received hundreds of irate phone calls within minutes.

As fate would have it, though, the fans who missed the end of that classic USC–Louisiana Tech game would receive one more chance to watch the Women of Troy and the Lady Techsters battle—this time in the national championship game. In addition to the great Cheryl Miller, USC also featured a lineup that included fellow stars Cynthia Cooper and the McGee twins, Pam and Paula. We took a double-digit lead into the locker room at halftime, but USC stormed back to take the lead late in the contest as we struggled against the full-court press. Nevertheless, we had a chance late in the game, when Mulkey stole the ball and was leading a fast break when she was called for a questionable charging violation. USC held on for a 69–67 win that ended our national title streak and represented only our second loss of the season (both to USC) and only our third loss the last 102 games.

While the end of the 1983 season was tough to take, it was easy to look forward to the following year with the return of three key starters in Mulkey, Lawrence, and Rodman, along with several other experienced reserves. In addition, we would have an early shot at redemption because No. 1–ranked USC was coming to Ruston for our eighth game of the 1983–84 season. Cheryl Miller was even better as a sophomore, but we played a sensational game and defeated the Women of Troy, 75–66, which allowed us to reclaim the No. 1 national ranking. Unfortunately, we didn't save the best for last that season. We were playing well when the 1984 NCAA Tournament began, bringing a 27–2 record into the "Big Dance." We also cruised through the first three rounds of the tournament, whipping Texas Tech, LSU, and Texas before advancing to the Final Four at UCLA.

After arriving on the West Coast, however, we once again ran into a USC team—this time in the national semifinals—that was on a mission and firing on all cylinders. We trailed 40–31 with a little under 14 minutes left to play, but that's when our Janice Lawrence seized control, scoring 16 of her game-high 28 points during an 11-minute span. When Lawrence hit a couple of free throws with a little under three minutes left in the game, it was tied at 57–57, with Louisiana Tech riding a tidal wave of momentum. That's when Miller answered the call, scoring the final five points of the contest to give USC a 62–57 win in the semifinals. Unfortunately for Louisiana Tech, Kim Mulkey played what she later described as "the worst game of her career." She was 0–6 from the field and committed eight turnovers. Not only was Mulkey heartbroken about losing her final game as a collegiate player, but she was also concerned that her performance against USC might cost her a spot on the US Olympic team in the summer of 1984. "It was horrible," Mulkey told *USA Today* many years later, referencing the second consecutive loss to USC in the Final Four. "I was so distraught because (Team USA head coach) Pat Summitt was in the stands watching, and we were getting ready to have the Olympic Trials."

That one subpar performance, however, did not cost Mulkey a spot on the Olympic team, as both she and Lawrence, along with USC's Miller and Pam McGee, helped lead Team USA to the gold medal. After winning gold in Los Angeles, Mulkey returned to Ruston and started to work on an MBA. She had received a $2,000 scholarship, one of only five given to women athletes by the NCAA for postgraduate study. Although she didn't initially envision a career in coaching, she also agreed to serve as our graduate assistant coach for the 1984–85 season. Think about that coaching staff for a moment: all four of us—Sonja Hogg, Leon Barmore, myself, and Kim Mulkey—would eventually be inducted into the Women's Basketball Hall of Fame.

Unfortunately, not even that remarkable collection of coaches could keep the Final Four machine rolling. Louisiana Tech had won two national championships and made it to six consecutive Final Fours from 1978 to 1984. But after compiling a 29–3 record, including easy wins over Illinois State and San Diego State in the first two rounds of the 1985 NCAA Tournament, we were upended one game short of the Final Four by the University of

Louisiana–Monroe, 85–76. The loss ended a string of six consecutive years in which the Lady Techsters had won at least 30 games, and it also marked the end of the Sonja Hogg era in Ruston. Prior to the Louisiana–Monroe loss, Hogg had announced she would be leaving basketball to open a yogurt store in Deer Park, Texas, with one of her longtime friends. The announcement stunned the basketball world, and the timing could not have been worse. Louisiana–Monroe was a tremendous team, and the Lady Indians may have beaten us under any circumstances, but when Sonja decided to make her announcement in the midst of the NCAA Tournament, the attention of our players was at least somewhat diverted.

To most of the administrators and coaches within the Louisiana Tech athletic department, however, Sonja's announcement was not particularly shocking. Ruston was a small community, and it was fairly well known that Sonja's marriage with Ruston attorney Bert Hogg was on the rocks. As the marriage dissolved, it became apparent that Sonja might want a fresh start away from Ruston and away from basketball. Her record at Louisiana Tech, including the co–head coaching seasons with Leon, was 307–55. Hogg eventually returned to coaching at Deer Park High School, where she had plenty of success and helped develop Dena Evans, who was named "Miss High School Basketball" in Texas and became a star at the University of Virginia, where she led her teams to three NCAA Final Four appearances and a 118–17 record during her four-year career. After Deer Park, Hogg also spent six seasons, 1995–2000, at Baylor. Although her final record at Baylor was just 83–91, her 1998 team was the runner-up in the WNIT, and over 10,000 fans watched her last game. She built a foundation for the program that set the table for Mulkey.

Barmore was clearly the natural choice to follow Sonja as the head coach at Louisiana Tech entering the 1985–86 season. And it was assumed by many people in the community and many longtime fans of Louisiana Tech women's basketball that I would become Barmore's first assistant. But it didn't play out the way most people expected; instead, it happened as President F. Jay Taylor instructed.

One of the best high school players in the country in the mid-1980s and one of our prized prospects was Nora Lewis, who led Peoria Richwood (Illinois) High School to a 119–5 record in four years, completing her high school career as the state's all-time leading scorer with 3,314 points. She became the first player in state history to be named All-State all four years, and during her senior year, she was not only voted prom queen but also named *USA Today*'s Player of the Year. As one of the premier programs in the country, it wasn't necessarily a stretch to think that Lewis would play for the Lady Techsters. Just to make sure, though, Barmore and Taylor believed it was a great idea to hire Lewis's high school coach, Mary Kay Hungate, as an assistant at Louisiana Tech. Hungate, who was named the National High School Coach of the Year by *USA Today* in 1985, obviously had the credentials to serve as an assistant at Louisiana Tech. That didn't force my departure from Ruston, but the next move did.

Mulkey had been President Taylor's favorite player, and he was convinced she would eventually make a great head coach. He was right, of course, but I did not envision that her coaching career at Tech would begin just as mine was coming to an abrupt end. According to numerous stories that have been published through the years, Mulkey was studying for her MBA at Louisiana Tech in 1985 when a security guard called her out of class. President Taylor wanted to speak to her. She was worried there may have been a death in the family or some sort of emergency, but instead, Taylor informed Mulkey that he wanted her to become Barmore's assistant. "I listened and respectfully declined because I thought Coach Barmore deserved to be able to choose who would be on his staff," Mulkey told Andy Gardiner of *USA Today*. "But President Taylor went after what he wanted. It became clear that if Leon wanted the job, he was going to have to hire me. So I started out kind of reluctantly and gave it a shot. It was the greatest push from someone that could ever happen. Because this is what I am meant to do, and I didn't know that."

Meanwhile, I didn't know what I was supposed to do. I went to speak with Barmore and President Taylor individually. Taylor told me that they would keep me, but he wasn't very convincing. "You can be a fourth coach," he said, "but you can't recruit." Leon was caught between a rock and a hard place, and he didn't give me much direction. I could tell I was being pushed aside, and I sensed that they hoped I would just disappear.

My wife was livid, I was hurt, and our daughter was just three. We'd built a life and careers in Ruston and Monroe, and I had helped Louisiana Tech become one of the best programs in women's basketball. Deep down, I felt like I deserved to be treated with more respect. I had earned that much, right?

Whatever the case, I now realize it was probably the best thing that could have happened to me. And as I noted at start of this chapter, nothing is ever quite as bad or as good as it initially seems. Being left out—or forced out— was a blow to my ego. But I was 39 years old, and I needed to make a move. If I was ever going to make a name for myself as a college head coach, now was the time. And in April 1985, I received a phone call from Stephen F. Austin State University in Nacogdoches, Texas. Officials from SFA had called the year before to see if I was interested in the job. I'd learned so much from coaching with Leon Barmore and Sonja Hogg and coaching great players in Ruston. Now it was time to take all those lessons and to apply them somewhere else.

7 Building a Winner in the Piney Woods

American history is filled with numerous inspirational stories about men and women who, despite starting fairly late in life in pursuit of their ultimate career aspirations, have achieved their goals and accomplished great things. For example, Henry Ford was 45 when he unveiled the Model T in 1908, Julia Child was 50 when she made her debut on her first television cooking show in 1963, Laura Ingalls Wilder began writing as a columnist in her 40s and didn't publish the popular *Little House* books until she was in her 60s, and Harland Sanders—better known as "Colonel Sanders"—was in his early 60s when he opened his first Kentucky Fried Chicken franchise in 1952.

So while I was certainly no "spring chicken" when I began my career as a collegiate women's basketball head coach in 1985—shortly after my 40th birthday—I also wasn't venturing into unchartered waters. Most well-known, big-time, and successful head coaches began their careers as head coaches in their 20s or 30s, but not all of them. Vince Lombardi, for example, was 46 when he landed his first head coaching job with the Green Bay Packers, Joe Gibbs was in his early 40s when he was first hired as a head coach with the Washington Redskins, Bob Devaney was in his early 40s when he started as the head football coach at Wyoming, and R. C. Slocum was in his mid-40s when he received his first head coaching opportunity at Texas A&M.

All things considered, Stephen F. Austin State University represented an ideal spot for me to begin my collegiate head coaching career. It wasn't necessarily a dream destination, but it was a good place for me to invest my time and efforts for many reasons. First and foremost, it was back in Texas—my home state, my birthplace, my old stomping grounds, and the state where I felt at home. Second, Stephen F. Austin represented a great opportunity to remodel and rebuild something that had already been constructed exceptionally well, as opposed to starting something from scratch. SFA already possessed a strong women's basketball tradition that just needed to be reawakened. The tradition had already been established; all I needed to do was add some fuel to a campfire that was still smoldering.

In 1979 and again in 1980—Sue Gunter's final two years as the head coach in Nacogdoches—SFA had finished fifth in the country in the final national rankings. Think about that for a moment. I'm not talking about fifth in Division I-AA, Division II, or some other lower-level category. Little ol' Stephen F. Austin, located way off the beaten path in the Piney Woods of East Texas, was among the top five women's collegiate basketball programs in the entire country.

In 1978–79, the Ladyjacks went 30–5 with wins over big-name college programs such as Houston, Ole Miss, Tennessee, Maryland, Texas, and UCLA. One year later, Gunter again guided SFA to a top-five finish, with wins over Texas A&M, Baylor, Missouri, Texas, Texas Tech, and Oregon. Behind players like Rosie Walker and Barbara Brown (yes, South Oak Cliff's Barbara Brown, whom I had coached in high school), SFA was ranked as high as No. 2 in the Associated Press poll on January 8, 1980. SFA could have easily won the Southwest Conference title that year, except the SWC didn't exist for women's basketball at the time, and of course, SFA wasn't a member of the league. But rest assured, the 1980 Stephen F. Austin team should have gone to the AIAW Final Four. Unfortunately for them, though, the Ladyjacks were forced to play South Carolina in Columbia for the right to make it to the Final Four. South Carolina protected its home court and advanced.

Under Gunter, SFA was arguably the most dominant women's basketball program in the state of Texas throughout the 1970s (although the University of Texas would argue otherwise), as she built the Ladyjacks into a tremendous national powerhouse. During her 12 years at SFA, Gunter compiled a 266–87 record, leading Stephen F. Austin to four top-10 national rankings. Of course, at that time in the development of women's collegiate athletics and at a school like Stephen F. Austin, Gunter was required to do much more than merely coach the women's basketball team. During her tenure at SFA (1964–80), Gunter coached four sports: women's basketball, softball, tennis, and track. Her basketball teams, however, became her calling card, as the Ladyjacks made five AIAW playoff appearances, won four state titles, and earned a regional crown. Gunter, a 2005 inductee into the Naismith Basketball Hall of Fame, also had a big enough reputation that SFA played host to the biggest powers in women's college basketball during her tenure in Nacogdoches.

After 16 seasons as a coach at SFA, she temporarily moved into the position of Director of Women's Athletics in Nacogdoches, where she served two years before returning to the coaching ranks at LSU. She then coached 22 seasons at LSU and compiled an overall collegiate coaching career record of 708–308, even though she was not credited for her first two years at Middle Tennessee State, when her teams were 44–0, or her first four years at Stephen F. Austin, because official records were never turned over to the NCAA.

Gunter was so respected in her field that she was selected as the head women's basketball coach for the United States Olympic Team in 1980. She guided her team to the title at the Olympic Qualifying Tournament prior to the Olympics, but that team was denied a chance at a gold medal due to the United States' boycott of the Olympic Games, which were being held in Moscow. Gunter, however, had been an assistant coach on the 1976 US Olympic Team that captured the silver medal in Montreal.

Quite simply, Gunter, who died in 2005 at the age of 66 from respiratory failure, was a legendary coach in every sense of the word, and what she accomplished at SFA was remarkable. When she left Nacogdoches, her replacement, Mary Ann Otwell, initially did a fairly solid job as she guided the Ladyjacks to top-20 national finishes in her first two seasons (1980–81 and 1981–82). But Otwell couldn't continually recruit like Gunter had done, and SFA fell out of the national rankings the next two seasons. SFA also began losing the positive aura that Gunter had instilled in the program. Early in the 1983 season, for example, University of Texas head coach Jody Conradt vowed she would never return to the quaint university. Conradt and the Lady Longhorns had just beaten SFA, 95–88, but without Gunter and the respect that SFA had long established, Conradt said after the game that UT would not be back. When the media asked her why, she said, "There's no way to get there."

It's not particularly easy to travel into Nacogdoches—hence the negative nickname "Nac-a-no-where"—but when Gunter was leading the program, it was worth it for top teams to go to SFA for a chance to play against the Ladyjacks in front of what was often a raucous crowd at William R. Johnson Coliseum. Not so with Mary Ann Otwell, who ended up quitting halfway through the 1983–84 season when the Ladyjacks went just 14–12. At the conclusion of that season, SFA school officials contacted me about taking the head coaching job. The timing wasn't right for me at that point, however, and I politely declined.

The next season was absolutely awful for SFA, as the one-time national powerhouse went 3–24 overall under Don Wilhelm, who had been Otwell's assistant and had taken over the program after she quit. In hindsight, it probably wasn't the wisest decision on my part to start my collegiate head coaching career at a school that had just gone 3–24 and was accustomed to winning big under a legendary coach. But I really didn't have any other options. My time was up at Louisiana Tech, and SFA offered me a chance to return to the Lone Star State and to do things my way. Besides, SFA really, really wanted me, which made the job even more attractive.

Interestingly, during this time several other assistants in women's basketball also made the leap to head coach. For example, Wendy Larry, a well-known assistant at Old Dominion under Marianne Stanley, accepted a head coaching job with the University of Arizona in 1985. I was interested in the Arizona vacancy, but the Wildcats' administration had no interest in hiring a man to coach the women's team at the time. After I took the SFA job, Tennessee assistant Nancy Darsch took over at Ohio State, while Virginia assistant coach Geno Auriemma took the head job at Connecticut. Bob Foley, who was assistant at Penn State, also ended up taking over at Providence. In all, five of us received our first head coaching opportunity in 1985–86.

Like the other four well-known assistants in the women's college basketball circles, I believed I was ready for the bigger stage as head coach. I also felt confident that I could recruit to a program with SFA's positive reputation and that I could compile a staff that could return SFA to its former glory. If there is one thing I learned well during my time at Louisiana Tech, it was that great assistants and great players were necessary to make a great program. A good organization was important, but great personnel was vital.

Fortunately for me, I lucked into a great assistant at Stephen F. Austin. When I was offered the job in Nacogdoches by then-SFA vice president Baker Pattillo, school officials asked me to keep assistant coach Candi Harvey on the staff. I didn't know much about her at the time, but it worked out extremely well for both of us. Harvey had played four years of collegiate basketball at Ouachita Baptist University in Arkadelphia, Arkansas, which had produced Dallas Cowboys' star defensive back Cliff Harris. Candi was young, energetic, and eager to prove herself to me. After graduating from Ouachita Baptist, she had served one season (1979) as a graduate assistant at Arkansas State and then became the head coach at Robert E. Lee High School in Tyler. In her first season at Robert E. Lee, Harvey led the Lady Red Raiders to the first winning season in school history and made the state playoffs. She spent four seasons at Lee before accepting the assistant's role at SFA in 1984 under Don Wilhelm.

I still vividly recall my introductory press conference at SFA shortly after the 1985 Women's Final Four in Austin, which featured Old Dominion (the champions), Georgia, Northeast Louisiana, and Western Kentucky. Although times were slowly changing and the bigger schools were beginning to take women's sports more seriously, it was still an era in which the smaller schools could compete on an even footing with the bigger ones in women's basketball, as evidenced by Northeast Louisiana and Western Kentucky in the Final Four. During the introductory press conference, I made note of SFA's glowing tradition and what an honor it would be to coach along the same sideline that Gunter had once strolled. The press conference only lasted about 30 minutes. Any members of the media reading this book right now are probably laughing at the word "only" because I can sometimes go on for 30 minutes on one question. But remember, this was my first collegiate press conference on my own, and my family was still back in Ruston, Louisiana. Besides, I had places to go.

Minutes after the press conference ended, Candi Harvey and I jumped in a car together and drove to Grapeland, Texas, which is roughly 55 miles west of Nacogdoches, about halfway between Palestine and Crockett. Grapeland is the home of the Fightin' Sandies and Sandiettes, and in 1985, it was also the home of a promising point guard by the name of Evelyn Butler, whom I coveted as a play-making passer. We offered Evelyn the chance to be our first-ever scholarship player, and we were so excited and filled with optimism about the role she would play in our vision of the team. It was a huge signing for us in many ways because Evelyn came in right away and led us in assists and minutes played that first season (1985–86). She also opened the door to recruit another big-time player from Grapeland a few years down the road, but more on that later.

Coming off a 3–24 season, Candi and I knew that we needed to recruit a bevy of outstanding basketball players. But at least the cupboard wasn't completely bare. I joked with the media that our roster was a case of good news and bad news. The good news was that we returned all our starters from that 3–24 team. Of course, that was also the bad news.

Obviously, the 1984–85 Ladyjacks didn't have an abundance of stars or marquee players, but they did feature a significant building block in powerful post player Antoinette Norris, who led the squad in scoring (11.3 points per game) and rebounds (11.1) as a true freshman. Antoinette—"Annie" for short—had played her first year at SFA at about 6 feet and 238 pounds. She was effective at that weight but not as versatile or as athletic as I believed she could be at a lighter weight. We challenged her to drop some weight in an effort to keep her on the floor as long as possible.

At about the same time, I was challenged by my doctor to drop some weight as well. The coaching lifestyle—eating fast food at odd hours and working around the clock while watching film, traveling to see recruits, meeting with players, watching more film, and so forth—had taken its toll, and my doctor strongly encouraged me to drop some pounds and lower my cholesterol.

I began pondering how I could transform my team and my own body, and my solution became known as "the Blair Mile." I challenged all my players to run the mile in less than seven minutes. For those who accomplished that feat and also beat me in the competition, the reward would be a T-shirt that proclaimed "I Survived the Blair Mile." To make it even more interesting, we also challenged the women's programs at Louisiana Tech and Sam Houston State to compete in the off-season conditioning program to see which team had the most improved mile time. Guards competed against guards, forwards against forwards, and posts against posts.

Right from the start, I anticipated that Annie Norris would have the most difficult time finishing the mile under seven minutes—and beating me. But I called her into my office and appealed to her competitive nature. Annie had grown up in Kansas with older brothers who had taught her to play multiple sports and had made her tough physically and mentally. After sitting her down in my office, I told Annie that I needed her to be a leader on and off the court. She had already led the team in scoring and rebounding as a true freshman, but what I needed was for her to buy into the off-season conditioning work and inspire others. She embraced the leadership role and went to work, training for the mile, adding muscle, reducing fat, working on her vertical jump by utilizing plyometrics, and doing whatever else was necessary to lead by example.

We trained early in the morning, and it was often arduous for everyone involved in the program. When the big day arrived, however, I still had doubts whether Annie could pass the fitness test. In her training leading up to test day, she had never run a faster mile than 7:02, and halfway through the third lap around the track during the "Blair Mile," I was still ahead of her. As I began the back curve of the third lap, I sensed Annie over my right shoulder, and as she passed me, I shouted, "That a girl!" Not only did she beat me that day, but she also ran a personal best of 6:36. Even before the first game of that first season in Nacogdoches, Annie Norris had helped set a tone for a new beginning at SFA.

She accepted my challenge, and I vowed to step outside of my comfort zone as well, and not just in terms of my physical condition. I knew right away that we could not be successful by simply coaching the way I had at South Oak Cliff or by patterning my style after what we had done under Sonja Hogg and Leon Barmore at Louisiana Tech. This was a different animal altogether.

We featured an abundance of superior athletes at SOC, as well as at Louisiana Tech. We could simply out-run, out-defend, out-pressure, and "out-athletic" opponents at either of my previous coaching positions. That wasn't going to work at Stephen F. Austin, where the talent level had been depleted in the years after Gunter had departed for LSU. I couldn't just run an up-tempo offense or a full-court pressure defense because we simply didn't have the depth. I needed to slow down the pace of the game and to utilize an entirely new plan of attack.

Fortunately, I was blessed to be around coaching greatness at SFA, just as I had been buoyed by great coaching associations at Louisiana Tech. I've always been curious, and I have always tried to learn from the people around me, regardless of whether those people were head coaches, assistant coaches, or athletes. I would strongly recommend that aspiring coaches attempt to learn something from every coaching stop. Never waste an opportunity to learn from those around you. Sometimes you will learn what you should do, and sometimes you will learn what to avoid. But always commit to learning. As the late American philosopher Mortimer Adler once wrote, "The purpose of learning is growth, and our minds—unlike our bodies—can continue growing as we continue to live."

I learned so much from Sonja and Leon when I was at Louisiana Tech, and I learned quite a bit of basketball from the great Harry Miller, who was the SFA men's coach when I arrived in Nacogdoches. Miller was a great X's-and-O's basketball strategist who had first made a big name for himself at Wichita State, where he coached the Shockers from 1971 to 1978. Miller's first team at Wichita State averaged 76.6 points—and remember, that was without a shot clock or three-point arch. The next year, the Shockers averaged 81.5 points per contest.

In 1976, Miller's Shockers won the Missouri Valley Conference title and swept into the NCAA Tournament with 10 wins in their last 11 games entering the "Big Dance." That season ended with a 74–73 loss to a University of Michigan team that finished as the national runner-up to Indiana. Miller's time at WSU, however, ended unceremoniously. He was fired after a 13–14 season in 1977–78, and NCAA violations on his watch contributed to Wichita State's probation in the 1980s. But Miller certainly found a hospitable home at SFA, where he coached the Lumberjacks from 1978 to 1988.

In Nacogdoches, Miller guided Stephen F. Austin from the NAIA to the NCAA Division II and into Division I. He went to the NAIA and Division II national tournaments before putting the Lumberjacks in the 1987 NIT in SFA's first season at the highest level. Miller also adjusted his offense at SFA, playing more patiently to compensate for his talent. Even at a much slower and methodical pace, it worked.

The bottom line was that Miller could flat-out coach. Former Stephen F. Austin athletic director Robert Hill, who was the school's radio play-by-play announcer when Miller arrived, once told the *Wichita Eagle*, "[Miller] was such a great floor coach. In tight games, I would just chuckle because I knew he would out-coach the other guy on the bench."

Miller could be gruff at times, but he and his wife, Tillie, who sold us our home in Nacogdoches, could also be extremely inviting, especially if anybody wanted to talk basketball. After Miller died in 2013, one of his sons, Gary, told a reporter for the *Tyler Morning Telegraph*: "I always remember my parents' front door being open to anyone. Whether it was competing coaches, his own assistants, athletic directors, players, managers, sports writers, trainers, etc. . . . our home was always a place that people gathered and were welcome. My folks made everyone feel at home and special. It wouldn't be long before our mother would whip up a meal and everyone would eat throughout our home and enjoy conversation, as well as time together."

I personally experienced that hospitality, and I learned a tremendous amount about basketball from Coach Miller. I will never forget the first time he invited me into his house, because it was the night I killed his plant. Miller thought watching women's basketball was only slightly more entertaining than watching paint dry. Nevertheless, he welcomed me over for steaks one night, and I happily accepted. His wife was out of town, and my wife and daughter had not yet moved to town, so it was just the two of us grilling steaks and talking basketball.

Actually, he talked basketball—I listened to every word he said and pretended to enjoy a drink with him. As soon as I entered his home, Miller told me that he was going to fix me a drink. He pulled out a big tumbler and a bottle of scotch, filled my tumbler almost to the top of the glass—as if it was iced tea or Diet Coke—and mixed in just a little bit of water. Then he poured himself a tall scotch and water, and we began talking hoops.

The problem was, I hate scotch—absolutely abhor it—but I was trying to impress a legendary men's basketball coach, and I sure didn't want him to think I was anything less than a man's man, so I faked drinking the scotch. Every time he would go to check the steaks, run to the restroom, answer the phone, or anything else that took him out of my sight, I would pour more of my scotch into the plant next to my chair. I never took a single sip, but I certainly learned plenty that night. Harry ran a triple post offense, and we discussed the intricacies of the strategy. Ultimately, I ran the triple post most of the time because I had several guards who couldn't shoot, and I had post players—like Annie Norris—who could make things happen close to the basket.

Norris worked extremely hard during the off-season, and she played her second season at 208 pounds—30 pounds lighter than the previous year. We also received a big lift from Chris Joseph, a 6-foot forward/center, giving us a strong punch in the paint. Our first official practice of my first season as a collegiate head coach started at 12:01 a.m. on October 15, 1985, because I wanted to start as soon as the NCAA would permit it.

Ironically, we opened the 1985–86 season by playing host to Texas A&M, where both Candi Harvey and I would eventually become head coaches. At the time, the Lady Aggies were led by head coach Lynn Hickey, and I thought it was a great opportunity for us to begin reestablishing SFA as one of the premier women's basketball teams in the region. A&M was coming off a 14–14 season in Hickey's first year as head coach, and I really believed we could be competitive right away.

I was wrong. Despite "Purple Fever Night," where we passed out flash cards to the first 1,000 fans and held a pep rally before the game, A&M beat us by 24 points in the season opener. Four days later, we traveled to Lubbock, a homecoming of sorts for me, to play Texas Tech, which was in its fourth season under Marsha Sharp. I had the upper hand on Marsha at the high school level when I was at South Oak Cliff and she was at Lockney High School, but our first meeting at the college level was not even remotely close, as the Lady Red Raiders beat us by 20 points. In fact, we opened that first season 0–4 before finally beating Lamar, 76–58, in the Oklahoma

City Classic for our first win. Once we picked up that first win, we started a little roll. During the course of the season, we compiled two three-game winning streaks and one five-game winning streak late in the year. Two of those winning streaks were halted by Leon Barmore, Kim Mulkey, and the rest of the Lady Techsters. Louisiana Tech beat us 73–55 and 75–49, but all things considered, that first season was a really good one for us. We went 16–12 overall and 7–3 in the Gulf Star Conference, which placed us second in the league, one game behind Northwestern State (Louisiana), where my wife had earned her master's degree.

I've always joked that my wife can handle so many things going on at once that I should also find her a newspaper route to give her something else to tackle long before dawn. She does more with time than Rolex or TAG Heuer, and she can juggle tasks like a circus performer with a bag full of rings. Following the birth of our daughter, Paige, Nan not only continued her work as a neonatal nurse but also started on her master's so she could fulfill her dream of teaching college. Stephen F. Austin provided the perfect opportunity for her transition to teaching. After we sold the house in Ruston and moved to Nacogdoches, Nan began as an instructor in SFA's Division of Nursing in 1985. It was a perfect move for Nan, and it benefitted Paige as well.

In 1975, SFA had opened the Early Childhood Laboratory (ECHL) to serve infants through five-year-olds. The ECHL was established for the education of SFA's students preparing to work with young children and their families, and it was designed to facilitate the total development of young children. The curriculum is intended to develop intellectual and personal competence rather than to train children in performing a limited set of academic skills. It was run by the wife of the university's vice president, Dr. Janice Pattillo, and it was fabulous for Paige as well as for our second child, Matthew, who was born on June 18, 1986 (at least we avoided basketball season with the birth of one of our kids).

Beginning with Matt's birth in the summer of '86, the year that followed was an absolute blessing for me in so many ways. During my first year at SFA, Candi Harvey and I were a two-person staff. Prior to the 1986–87 season, however, I was permitted to bring on Nell Fortner, who was once a *Parade* All-American at New Braunfels High School in Central Texas, where she averaged 40 points as a senior and once scored 72 points in a single game. After her brilliant high school career, she signed to play volleyball and basketball at the University of Texas from 1978 to 1982. In volleyball, she led the Longhorns to the 1981 AIAW national championship, and she also scored 1,466 career points in basketball to help Jody Conradt compile a 127–26 record over the course of four seasons. After graduating from Texas, Fortner began coaching at Killeen High School, where she stayed from 1983 to 1986. At that point, she realized she needed to earn her master's degree to eventually coach at the collegiate level, and we welcomed her with open arms as a graduate assistant. With the addition of Nell—first as a graduate assistant and later as a full-time assistant—we had a staff that could contend with the coaches at Texas, Louisiana Tech, and virtually anywhere else. Nell was a natural coach, as she later proved as the head coach at Purdue. She coached the USA women to a gold medal at the 2000 Olympics and coached in the WNBA with the Indiana Fever before taking over head coaching duties at Auburn.

Along with adding Fortner to our staff, we recruited point guard Carmen Alvarez from Odessa Junior College to help us cut down on our turnovers, and we witnessed the growth of younger players on our returning roster like Evelyn Butler and Trina Williams. Meanwhile, Annie Norris continued to improve her physical conditioning and her consistency around the basket. Norris, who played her junior season at about 198 pounds, spent the summer of '86 playing with the Athletes in Action European team, touring Germany, Switzerland, Austria, and Yugoslavia. The daughter of a preacher, Norris also took her faith seriously. As a sports ministry, the Athletes in Action team would play international opponents and then provide their Christian witness to fans at halftime.

Norris had always been a solid shooter from about 15 feet, and in her own mind, she envisioned herself as a smooth-shooting small forward. But that's not what we needed from her. In order for us to be successful, especially in those early years, we needed Norris near the basket on both ends of the floor. Despite the fact that she was only 6 foot, Norris possessed a knack for rebounding that made her a force in the paint. Off the court, she wore dresses practically everywhere she went, and she was the epitome of a preacher's daughter—a sensitive, compassionate, and caring young woman. On the court, though, she featured a stallion's mentality that made her a rebounding machine. Much to her chagrin, I told her to envision that she had a 3-foot chain around her neck that was attached to each basket because I wanted her near the paint on both ends. During the 1986–87 season, Norris increased her scoring average to 18.3 per game to lead the team for a third consecutive year and also averaged a team high of 10.5 rebounds per contest.

Most important, Norris's leadership helped SFA return to the postseason, as we went 25–6 overall and 9–1 in the Gulf Star Conference to earn a bid into the 1987 WNIT, where we won our first two games before losing in the third round to Creighton. During the course of the season, we compiled a 14-game winning streak and also recorded victories over Southwest Conference foes Baylor, Houston, and SMU. We were again manhandled by Louisiana Tech, 76–42, but the 1986–87 season was a huge step in the right direction.

The one thing that really disappointed me during those first couple of years at SFA, however, was the low turnout for home games at Johnson Coliseum. I didn't expect to magically attract huge crowds like we had in Ruston, Louisiana, but I was hoping for bigger and more enthusiastic crowds as our team improved. During those early years in Nacogdoches, I came to the conclusion that part of my job as head coach—a really big part of my job—would be taking on the role of marketing coordinator. There was really no budget for marketing women's or men's basketball at Stephen F. Austin. Nor was there an athletic marketing department or even a single employee devoted to athletic marketing. Quite frankly, I realized that if marketing was meant to be, it was up to me. And if it was up to me, it would also have to be done inexpensively, as I was earning $45,000 a year at the time.

The good news for me was that any marketing was probably going to be well-received, since it had never really been done previously. Up to that point, marketing basketball games to the students and the citizens in Nacogdoches and Lufkin basically involved opening the ticket booth windows before games. That's it. We didn't even feature halftime shows. At halftime, the cheerleaders would leave the floor to grab something to drink at the concession stands. A janitor who weighed about 360 pounds and answered to the nickname "Stick" would then sweep the floor with a push broom. Once he was finished sweeping, he'd roll out a rack of balls and start shooting half-court shots. When—or if—he made one, the fans went wild, but that was the extent of our halftime shows. I don't even remember having any canned music to entertain the fans.

Once we started doing a few things from a marketing and entertainment standpoint, people were entertained, although one of my first ideas didn't turn out so well. In the 1950s, stuffing as many people as possible into a telephone booth was quite the rage across the country and internationally. That evolved into car cramming in the 1960s, and I figured that I could attract plenty of fraternity and sorority members to come to the women's game to participate in—or at least view—a mattress-stuffing contest at halftime.

As hoped, we attracted plenty of participants and curious onlookers, as the winning team managed to stuff 27 people onto the mattress in two minutes. The problem was that the guy at the bottom nearly suffocated, and we had to call the medics onto the floor because he had lost his breath. As I watched the medical staff attend to him, I saw my career flash before my eyes as I prayed for his prompt recovery. My career could have ended at that moment.

Fortunately, the student was fine and the crowd was entertained, but we never pulled that stunt again. After that near disaster, I went back to grass-roots tactics and began holding luncheons for fans and speaking at booster clubs. Under the direction of Sue Gunter, SFA had developed and nurtured a fan following for women's basketball, but I had to rekindle that following and find creative ways to increase it. I started running co-op newspaper ads in the *Nacogdoches Daily Sentinel*, visiting local businesses and encouraging business leaders to take their employees to games, meeting with principals of elementary schools and inviting young children to attend the games at discounted rates, calling high school and junior college coaches to invite them to games, and organizing groups of SFA students to attend the games and compete for prizes against other organizations.

At Louisiana Tech, I had overseen the organization and the implantation of youth camps that drew interest among younger fans. Youth camps were practically nonexistent at SFA when I first arrived, but we built them up to the point where we were attracting more than 300 kids per session who left the camps in purple T-shirts and as dyed-in-the-wool Ladyjacks fans.

At one time or another, we also hired the high-flying, trampoline-utilizing, and thunder-dunking Bud Light Daredevils; we utilized several jugglers and jump rope specialist; we recruited members of the SFA football team to play basketball during halftime or in between the men's game and the women's game; and we used a variety of other acts and entertainers. There was one promotion I didn't try that was a big hit at Sam Houston, one of our big rivals in the Lone Star State. I was sitting with several SFA administrators, including university president Dr. Baker Pattillo and athletics director Steve McCarty following our women's game against Sam Houston State in Huntsville, and prior to the men's game, the coeds at Sam Houston started strutting onto the court for a lingerie show. The crowd went wild, but before I could even utter a word, Dr. Pattillo and McCarty both looked at me and shook their heads emphatically. I was never permitted to duplicate that promotion, which was probably a good thing, but I was always looking for ideas to help put butts in the seats and improve the game-day environment in Nacogdoches.

All our efforts to improve the team and enhance the atmosphere inside Johnson Coliseum really began to pay off following our second year. My first two years, we had a combined record of 41–18, and we had begun to turn the heads of some impressive recruits with the way we played on the court and the way we hustled on the recruiting trail. We also moved into a more prestigious league, going from the Gulf Star into the Southland Conference (SLC) for the 1987–88 school year. The big draw with the SLC was that the winner of the league was assured an automatic bid into the NCAA Tournament. The goal for our first season in the SLC was to win the league and return to the NCAA Tournament, and thanks to the leadership of veterans like Annie Norris, Trina Williams, and Evelyn Butler, along with the development of play-making guard Ylondia Douglas and the outside shooting of Mozell Brooks, we accomplished that feat in rather remarkable fashion.

I knew going into our third year that we had a chance to be a good basketball team, and I wasn't afraid to match us up against anyone in nonconference play, including the Australian National Olympic team. We lost to the Australians, 74–70, in early November, but playing against a team like that—the average age of the women on that team was 26 or 27—really toughened us up. In fact, I made a habit of scheduling national teams throughout my tenure at SFA.

Back to the 1987–88 season, which we opened with a 10-point victory over UCLA and then lost to Texas, 94–71. Following the loss to Jody Conradt and the Longhorns, we went on a sensational run, starting with a win over Hawaii. Overall, we won 18 of our next 19 games, including wins over SMU, Baylor, Kansas State, and Arkansas. Our victorious run came to an end with an 18-point loss to—you guessed it—Louisiana Tech, but we bounced right back to win nine of our last 10 games, finishing the regular season at 28–4 and 13–1 in the SLC. We won the conference title in our inaugural year in the SLC and earned a bid to the NCAA Tournament, where we opened with an 84–62 win over LSU. Our season ended with a second-round loss to Iowa, but we finished with a No. 11 national ranking, and we were probably the second-best women's program in the Lone Star State behind Texas.

With the departure of Annie Norris, the 1987–88 SLC Player of the Year and the second-leading scorer in SFA history (2,062), we couldn't afford to pat ourselves on the back. Replacing Norris, who went on to play professionally in Spain, was not going to be an easy task. But to elevate the program, we had to go win a head-to-head recruiting battle against Texas, Louisiana Tech, and other top schools in the region, which is exactly what we did following that third season. Trinity Valley Junior College in Athens, Texas, featured one of the prized prospects in the country in six-foot-three post player Portia Hill, who was the 1988 Junior College Player of the Year. Hill could dominate a game, as she proved by scoring 50 points and grabbing 29 rebounds in a game against Blinn Junior College. Every program in the country could have used Hill, but we beat Texas for the right to sign her, and she immediately paid huge dividends.

Hill, the SLC Player of the Year in 1988–89, averaged 23.9 points and 12.4 rebounds in her first year as we repeated as SLC champions. Even though we once again lost to Louisiana Tech, we went 13–1 in SLC play and won 30 games for the first time at SFA since 1978–79, when Sue Gunter's team finished fifth nationally. Most important, we went back to the NCAA Tournament, where we defeated Washington in the first round before being eliminated in the second round for a second consecutive season, this time by Maryland. Hill definitely led the way, but we also received plenty of great contributions from veterans like Evelyn Butler, Connie Cole, and Ylondia Douglas, as well as from younger players like Dayna Reed, Stacy Brown, and Melissa Peay. It was a key year for us in many ways because we were beginning to prove that we were an elite national program that was not just dependent on one or two elite players. We wanted to prove that we were a program to be reckoned with every year.

We took another big step in proving that the following season—Portia Hill's senior year—when she was again named the SLC Player of the Year after leading our team in points (23.2 per game), rebounds (10.4 per contest), shooting percentage (60.1), steals (76), and blocks (24). But once again, we were so much more than a one-person team. Connie Cole, Dayna Reed, Melissa Peay, Stacy Brown, Stacy Jackson, and a freshman by the name of Trenia Tillis were outstanding players throughout the season as we rolled to our third consecutive SLC championship—this time with a perfect 14–0 record. In some ways, Tillis was an even bigger recruiting victory for us than Hill, because as a freshman, she was able to play for four years instead of two. Trenia had been a *Parade* high school All-American at Grapeland, which is the same school we recruited Evelyn Butler from. Evelyn's success at SFA is a big reason we were able to convince Trenia to bypass the University of Texas, Louisiana Tech, and others to follow in Evelyn's footsteps. In my eight years at SFA, the biggest recruiting victories where we went head-to-head with the superpowers in our region were for Portia Hill and Trenia Tillis.

The one year (1989–90) that we had them both on the roster together was special, as we went 28–3 overall (one of the losses again came against

Louisiana Tech) and finished the year ranked sixth nationally. We again advanced to the second round of the NCAA Tournament before losing to Arkansas. Following that season, we not only lost Hill to professional basketball overseas, but we also lost Candi Harvey, who accepted the head coaching job at Tulane. It was a good move for Candi, and I planned to promote Nell Fortner, but she was also leaving for Louisiana Tech. It was tough replacing two coaches, but we hired Sue Donohoe and Julie Thomas to keep the train rolling.

We continued to win at an impressive rate, and we began attracting such large crowds for our women's games in Nacogdoches that we flip-flopped with the men for doubleheaders. At most schools, the men played the nightcap of doubleheaders, but at SFA, the women became the main attraction. We really had things rolling, and we expected to win every game. In fact, I recall that after one of our big games, I invited about 20 or so of our biggest boosters to my house. Nan had prepared some appetizers and such, and everybody was patting me on the back while I was loving all the attention. At some point, Nan had heard so much talk about how great I was doing from all the boosters that she finally looked at me and said, "Let's put things in perspective. You save games in your work; I save lives. What's more important in the real world?" I nodded and smiled. She wasn't putting me down or anything; she was just bringing some perspective to the party. She has also had an amazing way of bringing perspective to my life.

While it's never easy to stay on top, it is true that success breeds success. Even though it's extremely difficult to replace players like Annie Norris and Portia Hill, we were recruiting good players who expected to come to Stephen F. Austin and win. And year after year, our returning players demanded excellence of themselves and our newcomers. Led by Dayna Reed, Lori Davis, Stacy Brown, Shannon Lawson, and Trenia Tillis, we again went 14–0 in the SLC in 1990–91, earned a trip to the NCAA Tournament, won an opening-round game, and finished the year ranked in the national top 20. But the 1990–91 season—we went 26–5 overall—will always be especially meaningful to me because we finally beat Leon Barmore, Kim Mulkey, and the Lady Techsters. And we did it in Ruston.

We led by as many as 12 points in the second half of the game, but Louisiana Tech made a great comeback and was in position to win the game in regulation. But one of our sophomore guards, Deneen Parker, hit a beautiful three-pointer to send the game into overtime. Dayna Reed scored 21 points, and Stacy Brown put the finishing touches on the game with some clutch free throws in the final five seconds of regulation for a 77–74 win. About 100

SFA fans made the trip from Nacogdoches to Ruston, and they were seated at the top of the Thomas Assembly Center. But within seconds of the game ending, nearly all the purple-clad fans made it to midcourt to celebrate with our team. Even our bus driver ended up in the middle of that celebration. I was so elated to have finally beaten Louisiana Tech that I surprised my team and stunned my family by shaving off my mustache on the bus after the game. I first grew the mustache in 1975 while traveling in Europe, so Nan and my kids had never seen me clean-shaven.

We played plenty of close games that year. Early in the conference season, for example, we beat Sam Houston State, 68–67, in a game that we had no business winning. Our girls entered that game lacking focus, and Sam Houston played exceptionally well under the direction of first-year head coach Vic Schaefer. They outplayed us, but fortunately, we were vastly superior in terms of overall talent. That was my first encounter with Vic Schaefer, and I was impressed with his intensity and how tough his team played. As the years went along, Vic impressed me with what he was able to accomplish with Sam Houston's limited budget. Vic never beat me during my time at SFA, but he did a great job at Sam Houston and we became really good friends.

Meanwhile, we continued to build great teams at Stephen F. Austin, as our 1991–92 Ladyjacks went 28–3 overall and won the Southland Conference for the fifth straight year. That was certainly one of our best teams in my time at SFA, as we started that season by whipping Arkansas, 83–57, and we ended the season with a heartbreaking 61–57 loss to Southern Cal and the great Lisa Leslie in the Sweet Sixteen of the NCAA Tournament. We finished that year—my seventh in Nacogdoches—ranked fourth nationally.

Entering my eighth season at SFA in 1992–93, I wasn't necessarily looking for another job, but it was apparent that other programs were looking at me. We'd built a consistent winner in Nacogdoches, and our 1992–93 team won the SLC for the sixth straight year. We finished the season at 28–5 overall, whipped Clemson in the opening round of the NCAA Tournament and lost another heartbreaker to end our season, falling to No. 1–ranked Vanderbilt, 59–56, in a game that was played in Nacogdoches before a sellout crowd. It was the first time a No. 1–ranked team had ever played in Nacogdoches, and I remember the T-shirts we had made for our fans that featured our slogan—"The Best Little Basketball Town in Texas"—across the front of the shirt, a play on the musical *The Best Little Whorehouse in Texas*.

What I remember most vividly, however, is the heartbreaking nature of that loss. We were up by one point in the second half, and we had the momentum and the crowd fully on our side. I sensed that Vandy was gassed and could be in trouble, but then the shot clock went out. It took 15 minutes to replace it, which gave Vanderbilt a great chance to regroup. When play resumed, the Lady Commodores hit two quick three-pointers to change the complexion of the game.

Our team that year could have easily made it to the Final Four, but I was beginning to wonder what it would take to get SFA to that level, especially since some of the bigger schools in the Southwest Conference and other power conferences were putting much more emphasis and more money into women's athletics. It was going to be harder and harder to win consistently at places like SFA and Louisiana Tech if bigger schools were going to invest big money in women's athletics.

Timing is everything in life, and following the 1992–93 season, I saw that my friend John Sutherland had decided to leave Arkansas following back-to-back losing seasons. Sutherland had produced several really good seasons, but the Razorbacks were moving into the sparkling new Bud Walton Arena for the 1993–94 season, and Arkansas wanted a fresh start with its women's head coach. It just so happens that I had enjoyed some success against Arkansas during my time at SFA, and so they offered me Sutherland's job. We had accomplished so much at SFA, and we loved our time in Nacogdoches, but it was time for a change.

8 Early Years in Arkansas: Hog Heaven and Frustration-ville

Question: What do Paul "Bear" Bryant, Barry Switzer, Lou Holtz, Jimmy Johnson, Hayden Fry, Tommy Tuberville, Frank Broyles, Joe Gibbs, Gus Malzahn, Johnny Majors, Butch Davis, Ken Hatfield, Jerry Jones, and Fred Akers all have in common?

Answer: Arkansas.

Some of the aforementioned legendary coaches, like Bryant, Switzer, and Akers, were born in Texas. Others played at the University of Arkansas (Johnson, Malzahn, Jones, and Hatfield), and the rest of the coaching icons served as either head coach or an assistant with the Razorbacks at one time or another. But the bottom line is that those men are some of the most prominent names in coaching history, and they are a big reason Arkansas proudly claims to be the most influential football coach–producing state in America.

Quite honestly, the list of big-time women's basketball coaches with Arkansas roots is not nearly as distinguished or lengthy. But when I received a phone call following the 1992–93 basketball season from Bev Lewis, who was then the director of women's athletics at the University of Arkansas, I was intrigued enough to listen and take a visit to Fayetteville. Highly acclaimed author John Grisham had lived throughout northeast Arkansas before his writing career took off, selling over 225 million copies of his books. I figured if Grisham could sell that many books coming out of northeast Arkansas, I could at least write an interesting chapter on my career in the Ozarks.

Arkansas was a big-time athletic program that had made the leap from the Southwest Conference (SWC) to the Southeast Conference (SEC) for the 1991–92 calendar year. The switch in conferences was one sign of Arkansas' commitment to developing an elite athletic program. The more significant sign to me, however, was the construction of Bud Walton Arena, commonly referred to as the "Eighth Wonder of the World" by Arkansas fans.

Arkansas' women's basketball program had enjoyed a moderate level of success in the 1980s and early 1990s under the direction of Matilda Willis and John Southerland, who combined to string together nine 20-win seasons from 1981 to 1991. The Lady Razorbacks went to the AIAW Sweet Sixteen in 1982 under Willis, Arkansas then won the 1987 NWIT under Southerland, and Southerland's teams went to the NCAA's Elite Eight in 1990 and won the 1991 Southwest Conference outright title by going 28–4 overall and advancing to the Sweet Sixteen of the "Big Dance."

Southerland's biggest claim to fame, however, came on February 23, 1990, when Arkansas ended the longest conference winning streak in NCAA history by defeating the Texas Lady Longhorns, 82–77, in Austin. The win broke UT's 183-game winning streak against Southwest Conference foes and allowed Arkansas to share the SWC title with Texas. It also ended the nation's longest active home winning streak at 47 games. Senior guard Juliet Jackson, who hit six free throws in the closing minute to clinch the game, said afterward, "We messed up all their streaks." The following year, they messed up another one, as the Lady Razorbacks became the first team other than Texas to win an outright SWC title.

When the Razorbacks made the move to the SEC, however, they were unable to continue their success in women's basketball. In fact, it came screeching to a halt. Southerland's Lady Razorbacks went 11–14 in 1991–92 and 13–14 the following season. Those were not up to the University of Arkansas' basketball standards under any circumstances, especially not with the men's and women's programs set to move into the new state-of-the-art arena. Prior to the 1993–94 basketball season, the Razorbacks' men's and women's basketball programs had played in the 9,000-seat Barnhill Arena, an older (opened in 1954) but decent facility that was typically filled to capacity and loud as a rock concert for men's games. In fact, it was nicknamed

"Barnhell Arena" because Arkansas students often made it hellacious on opposing teams.

With Arkansas moving to the SEC, though, athletic director Frank Broyles recognized the need to dramatically improve facilities. Bud Walton, cofounder of Walmart and the brother of Sam Walton, visited Broyles, who informed the entrepreneur of a proposed $37 million facility that would make Arkansas the envy of the college basketball universe in the early 1990s. Walton volunteered to donate half the necessary funds, and from that visit, Bud Walton Arena was born. Ground breaking to grand opening in November 1993 was accomplished in a remarkable 18 months. When it opened in 1993, it had more seats (capacity is 19,200) in less space than any other similar facility in the world.

The first women's game ever played in Bud Walton Arena—known affectionately as the "Basketball Palace of Mid-America"—was an 80–68 win over DePaul on December 8, 1993. That also marked my first home victory as the head coach of the University of Arkansas.

Arkansas women's athletic director Bev Lewis called me out of the blue after the 1992–93 basketball season and asked if I was interested in coming to take a look at what the school had to offer. It didn't take me long to answer and emphatic "yes." It's not that I didn't love my time at Stephen F. Austin—I absolutely did—but the future of women's basketball at SFA was not as bright as its past. Bigger schools in bigger conferences were beginning to invest significant money into upgrading women's athletic programs in the early 1990s to comply with Title IX requirements and improve the overall image of the athletic programs. Throughout much of the 1970s and 1980s, smaller schools like Stephen F. Austin, Louisiana Tech, Old Dominion, Wayland Baptist, Delta State, Cheyney State, Western Kentucky, Long Beach State, and Montclair State could compete at the highest levels because so many of the bigger schools—universities that today belong to the "power conferences"—simply didn't place much of a priority on women's facilities or paying competitive salaries to coaches.

During my final season at Stephen F. Austin, for example, I earned an annual salary of $105,000, with some bonus incentives. That salary made me the highest-paid women's coach in the Southland Conference. When Arkansas offered me the head women's job, the base salary was roughly $20,000 more, and the bonus incentives were far more attractive. The biggest difference, though, was the investment that Arkansas was making in its basketball facilities. At Arkansas, I had the opportunity to recruit to the most magnificent basketball facility in Middle America, if not the entire country. In Nacogdoches, I had tried and tried and begged the administration just to remodel the locker rooms. The administrators wanted to help, but the funds just weren't there. And significant dollars weren't likely to ever come flowing. Bud Walton wasn't visiting with me daily at SFA, asking me what he could do to help the program—but he was at Arkansas. Clearly, Arkansas was prepared to invest heavily in its athletic department, including the women's programs.

That alone made it an extremely attractive job offer, and once I visited Fayetteville, I was completely sold on the job. Not only did Arkansas feature fantastic facilities and a big-time conference affiliation, but Fayetteville, situated on the outskirts of the Boston Mountains in the midst of the Ozarks, is absolutely breathtaking. Partly because of its scenic beauty and its 4,000 acres of parkland and beautiful lakes and rivers, *U.S. News* ranked Fayetteville as one of the best places in the country to retire. And *Forbes* rated it the eighth-best city in the country for business and careers because of major employers like the University of Arkansas, Walmart (based in nearby Bentonville), J. B. Hunt Transport (in nearby Lowell), and Tyson Foods (in nearby Springdale), which is the world's largest processor and marketer of chicken, beef, and pork. The university, along with those corporations and others, made Fayetteville practically recession-proof, which meant selling tickets would never be a major concern.

Without a doubt, I was sold on my first visit. All I had to do was go back to Nacogdoches and break the news to Nan. Nan was extremely supportive of the move, as she had been with so many other moves and changes in my career. Not only was she teaching at Stephen F. Austin, but she also had become the director of nursing at the largest hospital in the area. Even though I was the highest-paid coach in the SLC, I was neither the highest-paid nor the smartest member of our household. Nevertheless, Nan was ready to make the move, and we both knew that with her medical experience, educational background, and skill set, she would have no problem whatsoever landing a great job in Fayetteville, Arkansas, or practically anywhere else in the country. Our children were still young enough—Paige was about nine and Matt was about six—that pulling them out of their existing schools wouldn't be a big deal either.

It was just good timing all the way around for just about everyone. I really liked Bev Lewis, as well as Dan Ferritor, who was the chancellor at Arkansas from 1986 to 1997. It was the perfect opportunity to move to the next level—as long as I could also convince Sue Donohoe to come to Arkansas. Donohoe was a remarkably sharp young woman who had graduated summa cum laude from Louisiana Tech University in 1981 and had earned her master's degree in physiology in 1983 while serving for two seasons as a graduate assistant coach for the Lady Techsters, which is where I first grew to admire and appreciate her. After Tech, she served as the head coach at Carthage and Lake Highlands (she compiled a 124–24 record in the high school ranks) and then joined Stephen F. Austin as an assistant for my final three years. But she wasn't just any assistant. She became my right-hand staff member, especially after Candi Harvey left for Tulane following the 1989–90 season.

One of the best pieces of advice I could possibly offer to any young person, whether he or she is an aspiring coach, an entrepreneur, or practically anything else, is to surround yourself with good people. That applies to athletic teams or multifaceted corporations. It applies to professional endeavors and personal matters. Quite frankly, it applies to everything you do. Think about it: Who you hire, who you work for, who you work with, who you marry, who you befriend, who you choose as a partner, who you choose as a client, and who you choose not to spend time with will all ultimately play a huge role in what you achieve or fail to achieve in life. Legendary coach John Wooden said it this way: "Whatever you do in life, surround yourself with smart people who'll argue with you."

Legendary leader Ronald Reagan stated, "Surround yourself with the best people you can find, delegate authority and don't interfere as long as the policy you've decided upon is being carried out." Andrew Mason, the founder of Groupon, said, "Hire great people and give them the freedom to be awesome." Entrepreneur, author, and motivational speaker Jim Rohn wrote, "You are the average of the five people you spend the most time with." And in the Bible, Proverbs 13:20 states, "Whoever walks with the wise becomes wise, but the companion of fools will suffer harm."

I can't emphasize that enough. And unfortunately, I have seen too many coaches self-destruct or fail to reach their full potential because they do not fully embrace that principle on multiple levels. Practically every coach I know eventually realizes that you need great players to become a consistently great team. If you surround yourself with mediocre players and expect to be great, you'll eventually be looking for a new job. On the other hand, if you surround yourself with great players who possess great attitudes, you'll dramatically improve your chances of success.

Unfortunately, there's no guarantee that assembling, recruiting, or drafting the best players will ensure success, because in team sports, the players are only part of the equation. As a head coach, CEO, or leader of any sort, you better also surround yourself with great assistants, great managers, and great people who share your vision and work to bring everyone together. This is where many coaches ultimately fail. Perhaps it's a matter of pride, ego, overconfidence, short-sightedness, or something else, but coaches sometimes have such a belief in themselves that they mistakenly believe they can do it all alone.

That line of thinking is a recipe for disaster. No matter how great of a strategist, recruiter, motivator, communicator, planner, or visionary you may think you are, you cannot be all these things to everyone on your team, regardless of whether you're coaching 100 football players, 12 basketball players, or five golfers. No matter how hard you try, you can't possibly relate or connect consistently with every player on your roster. Nor does any head coach have the time to promote the program, scout the next opponent, work individually with specific players, evaluate the previous game tape, plan the next practice, assess the academic progress of the squad, answer calls from parents, recruit future players, attend booster club events, make travel arrangements, organize future schedules, and handle the inevitable personal issues and squabbles that arise in the locker room during the course of a season. It's impossible for one person to do it all, so you better make sure you surround yourself with great assistants and staff members who are not afraid to voice their opinions. You do not want to hire yes-men or yes-women that are afraid to disagree with you. If you are craving positive affirmations or just need someone to obey your every command, get a Labrador—don't hire people who are just going to agree with you or submit to your every command.

I don't need an assistant coach who is going to compliment me or sing my praises; I need assistants who are going to complement me, especially when I am off-key. When I'm looking for assistants or key staff personnel, I'm seeking people who are smarter than me, who are strong in my areas of weakness, and who are motivated enough to be capable of replacing me. Seriously, if I am not hiring an assistant who could replace me, I am hiring the wrong person.

Fortunately, I learned that lesson early in my coaching career watching Sonja Hogg and Leon Barmore at Louisiana Tech. The Lady Techsters would have never become one of the dynasties in women's college basketball in the 1980s if Hogg hadn't recognized her weakness as an on-the-floor strategist and hired Barmore, who was an X's-and-O's genius. Being part of that Louisiana Tech staff was a blessing to me in so many ways, especially in seeing firsthand the importance of hiring great people who were capable of eventually succeeding—and even surpassing—Sonja Hogg.

I've tried to follow Sonja's lead everywhere I've gone, which is why it was especially important to me to convince Sue Donohoe to join me at

Arkansas. Ultimately, I knew that Sue wanted to leave coaching to enter into athletic administration, and I told her that if she came with me to Arkansas, I would help her transition into an administrative position when the time was right. When she agreed, one huge piece of the staff puzzle was firmly in place.

I didn't keep any of John Southerland's full-time assistants when I took the job at Arkansas, but fortunately, I did keep one of the graduate assistants, Amber Nicholas (now Amber Nicholas-Shirey). Nicholas was an All-SWC and Academic All-American player for the Lady Razorbacks in the late 1980s and early 1990s. During her playing career, Nicholas's teams won 86 games and two SWC titles and made three NCAA appearances. She played in all 117 games of her career and started a school-record 87 consecutive games. And she was the MVP of the 1991 SWC Tournament, leading Arkansas to the first non-Texas title. Her presence on that coaching staff gave us some continuity and a tie to the returning players, as well as Arkansas' past. Beyond that, Nicholas was a brilliant young mind. A kinesiology major, she graduated with a 3.9 GPA and was twice voted to the College Sports Information Directors of America's Academic All-America Team. She was a perfect fit along with Donohoe, which left me with one more glaring need on the staff: a national recruiter.

I knew from the start that I could recruit Texas and attract some good players from the Lone Star State to Northwest Arkansas. I also knew that as the head coach of the Lady'Backs, I could convince practically every kid in Arkansas to come to the school. Coaching in Arkansas is so much different than coaching in Texas. As of 2016, the state of Texas featured three NBA teams (Mavericks, Rockets, and Spurs), two WNBA teams (Dallas and San Antonio), two NFL teams (Cowboys and Texans), two MLB franchises (Rangers and Astros), one NHL team (Dallas Stars), one SEC school (Texas A&M), four Big 12 schools (Baylor, Texas, TCU, and Texas Tech), four Conference USA programs (Rice, North Texas, UTSA, and UTEP), and two American Conference schools (Houston and SMU). And that doesn't even include the Southland, SWAC, and Sun Belt Conference members, who are too numerous to mention.

In Arkansas, by comparison, the Razorbacks and Lady'Backs have no athletic competition. University of Arkansas' athletic teams are the showstoppers and headliners in "The Natural State." As such, the head coach at Arkansas in practically any sport can expect to attract the state's best athletes to Fayetteville. Unfortunately, the state just isn't big enough or deep enough talentwise (especially in basketball) to build a national program by simply recruiting in-state student athletes. Even on the men's side, coaches often had to look beyond the state's boundary lines to build a powerful team. For example, Sidney Moncrief, Marvin Delph, Ron Brewer, Ronnie Brewer, and Corliss Williamson were all born and raised in Arkansas. But so many of the Razorbacks' other stellar players through the years—guys like Scott Hastings, Alvin Robertson, Darrell Walker, Joe Klein, Todd Day, Scotty Thurman, Cory Beck, and Lee Mayberry—attended high schools outside of Arkansas. You must be able to recruit nationally at a place like Arkansas to compete at the national level.

Ditto with the women's program, which is why I targeted one of the best national recruiters in the business at that time: Tom Collen of Purdue. Collen began his collegiate coaching career in the early 1980s as an assistant with Miami of Ohio and then went to Utah in the mid-1980s. His final recruiting class at Utah ranked 19th nationally, starting an eight-year run of the top-20 national recruiting classes. At Purdue from 1986 to 1993, Collen's recruiting paved the way for the Boilermakers to earn the school's first-ever trip to the Final Four in 1994. Collen had worked at Purdue under the direction of head coach Lin Dunn and had teamed at one point with fellow Purdue assistant Gail Goestenkors, who would go on to build Duke into a national power. In women's basketball circles, though, Collen was known as one of the premier national recruiters in the game, and I also learned that his relationship with Lin Dunn was strained at the time. Collen was a bright coach in many areas, but his greatest gift—and my greatest staff need— was his proven dependability in identifying, cultivating, and signing prized recruits. I made my case to Bev Lewis and other Arkansas officials about the need to pursue Collen and, unlike any of the financial-based requests I had made at Stephen F. Austin, Bev gave me blessing—along with the financial resources—to sell Collen on leaving West Lafayette, Indiana, for Fayetteville, Arkansas.

Fortunately, Collen bought into my vision for the Arkansas program and the potential of the Lady'Backs becoming one of the prominent powers in the SEC. That wasn't going to be easy, since the SEC had sent six teams— more than any other conference—to the 1993 NCAA Tournament. And remember, the NCAA Women's Tournament was still just 48 teams in '93. One-eighth of the schools in the '93 Big Dance were from the SEC, and half of those schools—Tennessee, Vanderbilt, and Auburn—advanced to the Sweet Sixteen. Meanwhile, Arkansas had finished in the bottom third of the SEC women's standings in '93 at 4–7 in league play, which was actually an improvement from the year before when the Lady'Backs finished 11th in the 12-team conference at 3–8 in league play. Obviously, the roster we inherited from John Southerland wasn't overflowing with elite SEC talent. But fortunately, the cupboard wasn't completely bare either.

We returned some solid players like Stephanie Bloomer, Shea Henderson, Allyson Twiggs, and Shannon Jones. We also inherited Southerland's final recruiting class, which included Carrie Parker, Taqueta Roberson, and Kimberly Wilson, an outside sharpshooter from Class AA Hampton High School, located in a small community (her graduating class consisted of 56 students) about 110 miles southeast of Texarkana. Wilson would eventually prove to be a tremendous player for us (a four-year All-SEC honoree), and she was such a good shooter from the three-point range that she ultimately earned an invitation to the inaugural WNBA training camps in 1997.

Even with a solid nucleus in place, Sue Donohoe, Tom Collen, Amber Nicholas, and I all knew that our long-term future at Arkansas depended on how we recruited in the present. We needed to sign an impact class in November 1993, and so we hit the recruiting trail at a full sprint in that spring and summer.

Speaking of that time of year, one of the things I will never forget is my first-ever trip to the Sandestin Hilton in Destin, Florida, for the annual SEC spring meetings in late May. The spring meetings are a monstrous deal today, as coaches, school officials, and media from all SEC locations converge on Destin. Back in 1993, it wasn't quite the media event it is now, but it was still an anticipated event that was close to marking its 10th anniversary.

My first major revelation of the SEC spring meetings was that it is practically impossible to travel from Fayetteville to Destin in one morning and arrive on time for a 2 p.m. meeting. To make a long story short, I was running extremely late when my plane landed in Fort Walton Beach, Florida. I then rented a car and made the 50-mile drive to Destin. When I arrived at the hotel, the meeting was about to start, and I was practically ready to burst with excitement—and so was my bladder. I was running so late when I landed that I figured I wouldn't have time to stop at an airport bathroom or along the way to the hotel. By the time I'd arrived at the Sandestin Hilton, however, the situation was dire. I hurried into the men's room before the dam burst and was going about my business when I glanced up from the urinal and noticed to the right of me was none other than legendary Georgia football coach and athletic director Vince Dooley, while the gentleman to my left was legendary men's basketball coach Rick Pitino, who had just guided Kentucky to the 1993 Final Four a couple months earlier. Now, you have to understand that I am a total sports fanatic who loves talking sports with anyone, especially legendary figures like Vince Dooley and Rick Pitino, neither of whom knew me from Adam. As you can imagine, it took every ounce of will power and restraint to keep from extending my hand over the urinal divider to introduce myself. I am so glad I resisted the urge, because there is nothing quite as awkward as trying to shake another man's hand in the men's room.

My other major revelation was meeting then-SEC Commissioner Roy Kramer. Long before Mike Slive became the SEC commissioner and the most powerful man in collegiate sports, there was Roy Kramer, who first oversaw the expansion of the SEC in the early 1990s with the addition of Arkansas and South Carolina. Kramer then divided the league into two six-team divisions for football, added an eighth conference football game for each school, and organized the first Division I-A conference football championship game. Early on, the SEC Championship Game—sarcastically dubbed the "Kramer Bowl" by many skeptics—was unpopular among the league's coaches. For example, when Alabama head football coach Gene Stallings first learned of the extra game, he was adamantly opposed and predicted it would negatively affect the league for generations to come. "The SEC will never win another national championship," Stallings said, as documented in Ray Glier and Phil Savage's book, *How the SEC Became Goliath: The Making of College Football's Most Dominant Conference*.

Stallings, however, immediately proved himself wrong. Alabama defeated Florida in the 1992 SEC Championship Game at Legion Field in Birmingham, Alabama, and the Tide went on to whip Miami in the Sugar Bowl, winning the national championship. From then on, the nationally televised "Kramer Bowl" became a showcase for the SEC. "The SEC Championship Game was one last audition for voters before the final polls, and it came when many teams had finished their regular seasons," Glier wrote. "More than that, the SEC Championship Game and the eight-game schedule were booster rockets for the conference schools. . . . Until the Big 12, then the Atlantic Coast Conference and the Big 10, and the Pac-12, added their own conference championship games, the SEC was on the national stage by itself with the SEC Championship Game in early December. When the game was moved to the Georgia Dome in 1994, it became a spectacle."

Moving the game to the Georgia Dome in '94 was one of the big topics of the 1993 spring meetings, and I could sense that I was part of a movement in the SEC that was not only historic for the league but also seismic for national television. While other "power" conferences partnered to broadcast

football games with ABC/ESPN, which would typically broadcast different games depending on the region, the SEC's deal with CBS called for a
national game of the week each Saturday during the fall. "[Because of CBS],
the SEC went from a very strong regional brand to a national brand," said
Tony Barnhart, SEC columnist and CBS analyst, as reported by Dirk Chat-
elain of the *Omaha World-Herald* on December 31, 2011.

Football was the driving force, but the SEC's national brand earned the
league higher revenues than other conferences, which benefitted all sports
programs in the league, including women's basketball. I just remember listening to Kramer and feeling like I was a part of something extremely special. I also remember sitting in the meeting room with the other women's
coaches in the SEC, looking around the table and feeling like I had just
been accepted into the most prestigious and elite club. Seated around the
table were some of the true legends of women's basketball—Tennessee's Pat
Summitt, Jim Foster of Vanderbilt, Ole Miss's Van Chancellor, Joe Ciampi
of Auburn, Georgia's Andy Landers, and LSU's Sue Gunter, who was the
first person to build SFA into a powerhouse program. Everyone knew me,
and I was welcomed at the table, but I was undeniably in awe of the mag-
nificence of the SEC, especially compared to the Southland Conference. We
were all sitting in that room like 12 gunslingers that had money to spend
and ammunition to fire.

I left the meetings on cloud nine, but I also realized that I would not be
returning unless we signed a recruiting class that allowed us to compete with
the powers of the SEC—which is exactly what we did. Among our many
long-term needs was a play-making point guard, and Collen had mentioned
a young woman named Christy Smith from West Lafayette, Indiana, that
might suit our needs nicely. She was raised 10 minutes from the Purdue
campus but wasn't quite good enough to play for her hometown collegiate
program. At that point in her career, she wasn't a great offensive player, but
she was smart, intense, and an outstanding defender. We immediately began
recruiting her, and although she was a little reserved, she eventually warmed
to the idea of playing at Arkansas.

Smith was the key to our first recruiting class, but we also went after
Karen Jones from Corpus Christi, Tiffany Wright from San Antonio, and
Treva Christensen from Joplin, Missouri. We really wanted those four play-
ers, and I really wanted to show off Arkansas' big-time football program.
After recruiting for many years to Stephen F. Austin and Louisiana Tech—
two programs that didn't traditionally draw big football crowds (and that's

putting it nicely)—I was champing at the bit to use the Razorbacks' football team to show off the school's overall athletic prowess.

Although the '93 Razorbacks were certainly not a great team (they finished 5–5–1), I picked what I thought to be a great game on October 30, 1993. It was Arkansas' homecoming game against Terry Bowden's unbeaten Auburn Tigers. We really wanted to put on a great show for our recruits, and—as fate would have it—the weather turned downright awful. It was 31 degrees and snowed throughout the game, and the game was about as dreary as the weather. The Razorbacks lost the game, 31–21, and I was scared to death that we were also going to lose all four recruits.

Thankfully, all four recruits committed to playing for us, and they ultimately served as the foundation of what would become a truly special team. Long before that "fabulous foursome" could steer the program into unchartered waters, however, we first needed to navigate through some stormy conditions. We knew going into the 1993–94 season that our first year could be a difficult one, but I never anticipated just how difficult it would start.

Practically everyone in the state was buzzing with excitement about the opening of Bud Walton Arena, but it had yet to be completed as the men's and women's programs prepared for the start of the 1993–94 season. As a result, both teams were conducting preseason practices inside old Barnhill Arena. In fact, my predecessor, John Southerland, had actually planned to keep the women's team playing in the smaller Barnhill Arena because he thought it would be a more intimate and intimidating venue than playing before thousands of empty seats in the 19,200-seat Bud Walton Arena. As a result, my office that first year was in Barnhill. I used Eddie Sutton's old desk and Nolan Richardson's old office space, and even though I didn't have a brand new office, I felt like a king. I even had my first office window.

Of course, I was an anxious king the night of our public debut for our preseason Red–White intrasquad game. The women were going to play at 6 p.m., and Richardson's men would play afterward. The Arkansas men were coming off a strong season in which the Razorbacks went 22–9 overall, 10–6 in the SEC and advanced to the Sweet Sixteen. The Arkansas men were the preseason favorites to win the SEC in 1994, and we were expecting a packed house for the scrimmage (at least for the men's game) as fans clamored for a glimpse of a team that possessed legitimate Final Four expectations.

Hours before our scrimmage, as our girls were going through warm-up drills, one of our sports information directors pulled me aside and informed me that the mother of one of our players, Michelle Thacker, had been killed in an automobile accident. Thacker, one of our senior captains, was a 6-foot-3 post player from Coweta, Oklahoma, and her mother was practically our team mom. All the girls on our team knew and loved Mrs. Thacker.

No college course or self-help book adequately prepares you for breaking the news to a young person that his or her parent has unexpectedly passed away. There's no right way or painless process. It's gut-wrenching and heartbreaking. Unfortunately, I've had to do it several times during my career, but I most vividly recall pulling Michelle aside as the rest of the team ran out of the basketball locker room and onto the floor for pregame warm-ups. My pregame anxiousness immediately turned to anguish as I looked into Michelle's eyes. She instantly knew something was terribly wrong when I pulled her into the volleyball locker room. In fact, her first question was, "Is it my daddy?" I shook my head no. Tears were already streaming down her cheeks as she asked the next question, "Is it Momma?"

I asked Sue Donohoe to travel back to Oklahoma with Michelle because I didn't want her driving and I didn't want her to be alone. Coaching women's sports can be difficult even in the best of times because women are often far more emotional than men. That's not stereotyping; that's just my assessment after decades of coaching women. If a young couple breaks up after dating for a while, the young man might go to basketball practice to forget about the situation for a couple of hours, and he certainly isn't going to tell the entire locker room about it. But women are just different. Practices can be completely derailed by a breakup, and the locker room can become a bit of a circus as the other girls discover the details and form opinions on how the breakup occurred. There are also many other factors—like menstrual cycles, bad hair days, swimsuit season, fashion, social media, and so forth—that affect the emotional well-being of a women's team that do not typically impact a men's team. Bottom line: emotions play a huge role in coaching women under normal circumstances. This is especially true in the aftermath of a tragedy like the death of Michelle Thacker's mother.

That was a difficult way to begin any season, especially our first at Arkansas, but we weathered the storms and produced a pretty good 1993–94 season. We opened with a loss at Kent State in Ohio and then went 2–1 at the Rainbow Wahine Classic in early December in Honolulu, Hawaii. All things considered, spending early December in Hawaii is not a bad plan. The sun must have been good for us because we returned to Fayetteville and won our first four games at the new Bud Walton Arena, beating DePaul in the women's debut at the new facility and rolling past New Orleans and Northwestern State before Southwest Missouri came to town on

December 29. The Lady'Backs had lost to SMSU the previous two years, and the Lady Bears came to Walton ranked No. 23 nationally. It was a great game that was locked in a 63–63 tie in the closing seconds when I called a timeout and drew up a play for our outside shooting specialist, Kimberly Wilson, who promptly drained a three-pointer to give us a 66–63 victory, our first win over a top-25 opponent. At that point in the season, we were 7–3 and ranked No. 15 nationally in one poll. Then reality hit. Really hard.

We opened SEC play by traveling to Tennessee to face the No. 1–ranked Lady Vols, who manhandled us, 89–67. That was a foreshadowing of things to come, as we finished 3–8 in the SEC. We lost to every ranked SEC opponent on our schedule with the exception of No. 15 Alabama. We beat the Tide, 82–75, at home on February 2, 1994, for what was probably the biggest win of our first season. We also did a nice job of protecting our home court throughout the year, going 9–4 at Bud Walton and averaging 3,806 fans per game. That obviously doesn't sound like much in a 19,200-seat arena, but it was actually 1,300 more fans per game than the Lady'Backs had averaged the previous year. And the best sign of progress was that we finished the season with an overall winning record at 15–14. I'd never endured a losing season at that point in my career (I'm not counting the 1972–73 golf season at South Oak Cliff), and I was pleased with the fact that the streak had continued. Overall, the first year had not been easy for me at work or for my family as they adjusted to their new home.

One of the more heartbreaking moments for me as a father in those early years at Arkansas was watching my daughter, Paige, fail to reach one of her goals. In Nacogdoches, Paige was always one of the best athletes and a really popular kid in elementary school. After we moved to Fayetteville, Paige tried out for cheerleader going into the eighth grade. Parents weren't allowed to watch the tryouts, which took place in the morning. After they were done, Nan, Paige, and I went to lunch and returned to the school at 1 p.m. when the results would be posted. Paige ran up to the door with all her friends to check the list, and Nan and I could instantly tell she had not made it by the dejected way she was walking back to the car. That just tore us up. It was the first time Paige hadn't made a team, and it really broke my heart because I knew that she would have made the cheerleading squad if we hadn't moved to a new town. When you coach, your whole family ends up making sacrifices, but things eventually improved for all of us, both personally and professionally.

Our basketball program had established a foundation for Arkansas' future success in our first year. We competed well throughout the season, Kimberly

Wilson was selected to the Freshman All-SEC team, we had a great recruiting class coming in the following season, and we were all inspired by what Nolan Richardson's men's team accomplished in 1993–94. Led by power forward Corliss Williamson and sharp-shooting wing Scotty Thurman, the Razorbacks went 14–2 in the SEC, won the league title, and stormed into the Final Four in Charlotte, North Carolina. Playing Richardson's famed full-court defensive style of "40 minutes of hell," the Razorbacks pounded Arizona in the national semifinals and outlasted Duke, 76–72, to win the national championship.

My future athletic director at Texas A&M, Bill Byrne, used to often say that "a rising tide lifts all ships." To Byrne, that meant that if one of the programs at a school won the national title, it would affect all the programs because, among other things, it would make other sports teams realize that they too could win it all. The men's national championship certainly inspired us and enhanced the school's image. During the 1993–94 season, we practiced before the men, and for the last 30 minutes of practice, we'd have 500 people or more in the stands waiting for the men's practice. Practicing under the scrutiny of fans and media helped us, and we all saw the excitement generated by the men's run to the Final Four. Memorabilia tents were set up all over the state of Arkansas just to sell national championship gear after the Razorbacks' triumphant run.

Our girls fed on that energy, and we entered our second season with a definitive goal to reach the postseason. We opened the season at the 7Up Desert Classic in Las Vegas, and our first game of the season was most definitely a sign of things to come as we nipped Pittsburgh, 76–75, in the closing seconds on a Kimberly Wilson shot. I turned 50 the summer of '95, but I am convinced it was the 1994–95 season—not my age—that turned my hair grey. Over the course of posting a 23–7 overall record and earning Arkansas' first-ever bid to the women's NCAA Tournament as a member of the SEC, we won nine games in the closing minute, including three on the final shots of the game.

On December 10, 1994, for example, we faced Southwest Missouri State in Springfield in a game that came down to the closing seconds once again. We trailed by 10 early in the game, but we took our first lead with less than three minutes left in the game on a driving layup by Allyson Twiggs, and Stephanie Bloomer hit the game-winning free throws with 16.5 seconds to play for the 61–60 win (that team also set a school record for free-throw percentage at .770). That may have been the highlight of the nonconference season, but then we opened SEC play at 1–3 following a one-point loss to No. 17 Ole Miss.

Fortunately we were so young—that team was loaded with freshmen and sophomores—that we didn't stay down for long. We showed great resiliency by bouncing back with wins over ranked foes Oklahoma State and Florida, and then we came up with probably the biggest win of the season—a signature victory that propelled us into the NCAA Tournament as a sixth seed—against No. 8 Vanderbilt at Bud Walton. Kelly Johnson buried a 15-foot baseline jumper as time expired in overtime to give us our first-ever victory over Vanderbilt, 73–71. During our final seven conference games, we went 6–1 to tie for fourth place overall. Not only did we earn a trip to the "Big Dance," but we also opened the NCAA Tournament with a 67–58 win over San Francisco in the opening round of play in Seattle. We lost the next game, 54–50, to the host team, Washington, but making the NCAA Tournament was a great experience for our team, and it was an overall great year for our program.

Our success also helped us continue recruiting at an exceptionally high level. In the aftermath of our run to the NCAA Tournament, we signed *Parade* All-Americans Tennille Adams and Shaka Massey, as well as All-State guard Sytia Messer from Waldo, Arkansas, who would go on to earn Freshmen All-SEC honors the following year.

Looking back on that team, we had so many contributors step up in so many ways, as both Kimberly Wilson and Stephanie Bloomer were chosen as second-team All-SEC representatives. But undoubtedly, the breakthrough star was Christy Smith, who led the nation in free-throw percentage (.899) and led the SEC with 3.0 steals per game. I don't think I've ever had a true freshman who was so reliable, dependable, and unflappable. She was so valuable that I never wanted to take her out of a game—so I didn't. Literally. Beginning with a December 6, 1994, start at No. 6 Alabama, Smith played every minute of every regular season conference game, as well as both of our games in the SEC Tournament. Overall, she played 525 consecutive minutes of conference games—setting an SEC record for men and women—en route to becoming the 1995 SEC Freshman of the Year and the first Arkansas woman to ever earn Associated Press All-America honors. Beyond all that, she was just an absolute pleasure to coach.

Case in point: When we lost by one point to Ole Miss on January 14, 1995, not only did we fall to 1–3 in conference play, but it could have been an especially demoralizing loss for our team because we made an absolutely remarkable comeback in the final few seconds of the game to even have a chance to win. With just 2.5 seconds left, Ole Miss hit two free throws to go up by five points. For all intents and purposes, it looked rather hopeless. But Treva Christensen then executed the perfect Christian Laettner-like length-of-the-court pass, which was caught by Kimberly Wilson, who turned in one motion and fired a perfect three-pointer that cut the lead to 75–73. We called timeout and said to our team that we had to have a charge. Then Christy Smith—the nation's best free-throw shooter—made a terrific defense play to draw a charge with 0.03 seconds left, and she went to the line with us trailing by two points.

She had a golden opportunity to tie the game and send it into overtime, and there's no person in America I would have rather had on the line than Christy. She had this routine on the free-throw line where she would bounce the ball twice, give the ball a half spin, and say to herself, "nothing but net" before shooting it, typically hitting nothing but net.

She drained the first free-throw to cut the Ole Miss lead to 75–74, and I had a crisscross play called to hopefully give us a chance to tip the ball in for the winning basket if Smith missed the second free throw. But I was worried that the official who had made the charging call, Doug Cloud, might have a quick whistle on us if we were too aggressive in going for the rebound, so I called the play off. Besides, I was pretty certain that Smith would drain the second free throw to send us to overtime. Unfortunately, even Miss Dependability sometimes misses. The ball was practically in the net when it rimmed out and we lost the game, 75–74. It was the kind of loss that can linger with a team and derail the confidence of a young player like Christy.

That's not what happened, though. I didn't find this out until much later, but Christy's roommate was a fellow freshman guard named Tiffany Wright, who later shared with me the story of the morning after the Saturday loss to Ole Miss. Tiffany and Christy always went to church on Sunday, but Christy's alarm clock went off particularly early on January 15, 1995. As Christy slid out of bed, Tiffany asked her why she was waking up so early. Christy said, "I'm going to the gym to shoot free throws. I will not let this team down again with the game on the line."

Unbeknownst to anyone at the time, she would have a chance to redeem herself on a much bigger stage with so much more on the line. But the point of that story is that Christy went right back to work, and we turned our season around the next game with a big win at nationally ranked Auburn. Even as a freshman, Christy had such a presence and possessed that rare ability to make everyone around her better. She even had this subtle way of earning the respect—and perhaps also gaining the favor—of officials. During a timeout fairly early in the 1995–96 season—Smith's sophomore year—an official walked up to me and said that she wished every player could be more like Christy. I asked her what she meant, and she began raving about how she had never seen a player like Christy who literally thanked the officials every time they handed her the ball to shoot a free throw or to throw the ball in from out of bounds. I hadn't even noticed it, but obviously it had made a positive impression on many officials. Wouldn't it be refreshing if NBA stars did the same thing?

Like Christy was making a difference with the officials, we were making a positive impression on basketball fans throughout the state, as we started the year ranked in the Top 10 and then bolted to a school-best 13–1 start on January 2, 1996. At that point, we had an even better record than the men's team, which was 11–2 in early January and eventually went back to the Final Four for a second consecutive season before losing in the championship game.

Our women were on quite an impressive roll until an overtime loss to Alabama sent us on a five-game losing skid. We seemed to get back on track with a pair of wins over South Carolina and LSU, but on January 28 at Kentucky, Smith's season ended with a torn ACL. Beginning with that game, we lost five of our final 10 games, which resulted in us being a bubble team for the NCAA Tournament at 20–11. Unfortunately, our bubble burst, and we ended up traveling to Amarillo, Texas, for what proved to be the final NWIT—not to be confused with the WNIT—instead of going to the NCAA Tournament for a second consecutive year. We won our first game over Princeton but then lost our next two games, bringing what had been an extremely promising season to a bitter end.

The next season was equally as disappointing—if not more. We once again began the year with great expectations and a No. 18 national pre-season ranking. We had more of a veteran team, as Kimberly Wilson was entering her senior season and the members of my first Arkansas recruiting class—Smith, Karen Jones, Tiffany Wright, and Treva Christensen—were entering their junior seasons. We also started just as strong as I could have possibly envisioned, building a 9–1 record before the Christmas break. Then we came back and played host to No. 6 Tennessee on December 29 in our SEC opener. In a truly great defensive effort, Sytia Messer, a 6-foot-8 guard from Waldo, Arkansas, held Tennessee star and All-American Chamique Holdsclaw to a single field goal and only seven points.

Meanwhile, Christy Smith and Kimberly Wilson each scored 21 points. At one point, we built a 48–36 lead, but the Lady Vols rallied to win, 76–75, with less than a minute left to play. Tennessee had one last chance to win the game, but the Lady Vols missed an inside shot and Karen Jones pulled down the rebound of her life and was fouled by Tennessee. Jones hit one free throw in the final seconds to give us the 77–75 win, the first ever for Arkansas over Tennessee. We also won our next two games to improve to 12–1, but then we hit another tailspin.

Beginning with a 100–81 loss at Illinois (a team that featured my future assistant coach Kelly Bond as point guard), we dropped nine of our final 15 games. We struggled miserably on the road, going 1–5 in the SEC away from Bud Walton. We went to the 1997 SEC Tournament in Chattanooga, Tennessee, needing an impressive run to secure a bid in the NCAA Tournament. We started well with a 71–60 win over Kentucky but then were rolled by No. 7 Alabama for the second time during the 1996–97 season. "Final Four" Alabama handed us our most lopsided loss of the season, 102–61, on February 6 in Tuscaloosa. We were almost twice as good a month later in the SEC Tournament, but we still lost by 22 points and were eliminated from the conference tourney.

At 18–10 overall and 5–7 in the SEC, we were once again on the NCAA bubble. This time, ESPN sent its cameras to Fayetteville to film us in the locker room as we watched the NCAA Tournament Selection Show. We felt pretty good about our chances, because we had been ranked in the top 25 every week of the season except for the early March poll. I was wired with a microphone during the Selection Show, but our name was never called, and with no NWIT (Triple Crown Sports revived the tournament in 1998 and changed the name to the WNIT), we were done for the year.

It was a disappointing, demoralizing, and bitterly frustrating finish, especially for Kimberly Wilson, who had to finish her brilliant career in such an inglorious and exasperating fashion. And to add insult to injury, Colorado State came after my top assistant coach, Tom Collen, after that season and offered him the head job. My backup point guard, Roxanne McCrory, also decided to follow Tom to Colorado State, and Shaka Massey, perhaps the most high-profile recruit I had signed in my four years at Arkansas, was also unhappy. Massey's brooding had become an issue in the locker room, and it was for the best that she transferred to Louisiana Tech, where Leon Barmore could try to make the most of her massive amount of talent.

Still, losing players, losing my top assistant, and losing out on a chance to make a run in the NCAA Tournament made for a particularly gloomy spring in 1997. I was obviously happy for Tom, who would ultimately lead the Rams to five consecutive 20-win seasons and four NCAA Tournament berths, but now I needed to find my next lead assistant, and I needed some-one who could make a difference.

Sue Donohoe had decided to go into administration at Arkansas and then went on to the Southland Conference and the NCAA as an admin-istrator. When Donohoe left the staff, we hired Trenia Tillis, who had been a star player for me at Stephen F. Austin. We also promoted Amber Nicholas-Shirey to full-time assistant coach. Trenia and Amber were won-derful coaches who related well to the players because they had recently been players themselves. But I still needed another top-flight assistant coach, and there was at least some self-imposed pressure to find the right person and return to the NCAA Tournament.

In my first four years at Arkansas, we'd produced four consecutive win-ning seasons and made one trip to the NCAA Tournament. But after all the postseason success I had previously tasted at South Oak Cliff, Louisiana Tech, and Stephen F. Austin, I had a rather bitter taste in my mouth in March 1997 after being left completely out of the postseason for the second time in four years.

I certainly had not lost confidence in myself or in our team, but I was beginning to question our luck. We'd been ranked in the top 10 in 1996 and again in 1997, and yet we had failed to make the Big Dance either year. Injuries to Christy Smith and Treva Christensen really hurt us in 1996, and we had really just collapsed in 1997. As I assessed our program and the immediate future, it was critical to make the right hire right away, and it would certainly be beneficial if we could catch a positive break or two in the ensuing season.

Fortunately, the right man for the job was right under my nose. An old friend delivered an old-school mentality to our defensive attack, and the big break we needed would ultimately be gift-wrapped by the oldest school in the United States.

9 *Good Morning America's* Team, and Good-Bye

One of the most magnificent things about sports is the unpredictability of games. Computer programs can calculate the odds of one team winning or losing and experts can break down the most miniscule details of a team's tendencies to help predict outcomes, but once the ball is actually tossed into the air, kicked to the other team, or pitched toward an opposing batter, scientific calculations, mathematical equations, and statistical propensities become anything but foolproof. The sports we love aren't decided by computer programmers, and the outcomes are not predetermined by finite architectural designs or an engineer's feasibility assessment. Even in our high-tech, smartphone-obsessed, high-def society, the sports we most love and admire aren't determined on paper, computer screens, or social media platforms.

In sports, the improbable is not just possible—it's well documented and celebrated because it reminds us that farfetched dreams really can come true as the result of intangible qualities like determination, focus, toughness, and self-confidence. From a business standpoint, Goliath typically squashes David on Wall Street or Main Street, and the political longshot doesn't often stand a chance against deep-pocketed candidates. But in sports, we fondly recall the 1980 US Olympic Hockey Team that stunned the mighty Russians and made us scream a triumphant "YES!" to Al Michaels's celebrated question, "Do you believe in miracles?"

The 1969 New York Mets were also miraculous, while the 2004 Red Sox overcame a Ruthian-sized curse and a 3–0 deficit in the American League Championship Series to win it all; Buster Douglas shook 42-to-1 odds to take down heavyweight champion "Iron Mike" Tyson; fur coat–wearing Joe Namath made the boldest Super Bowl prediction of all time and backed it up by leading the underdog New York Jets past the heavily favored Baltimore Colts; and Jim Valvano guided North Carolina State to the national title and past mighty Houston in the game of the century at the 1983 men's NCAA Tournament, while Villanova's Rollie Massimino orchestrated an even bigger upset just two years later in slaying the beasts from Georgetown. Strange, bizarre, unpredictable, incalculable, memorable, and miraculous things can happen in sports.

I obviously knew that, but I was reminded and uplifted by that realization—and actually lived it—in the spring of '98 when we made the most unexpected and unprecedented run to the Final Four ever at that point in the history of the women's basketball tournament. Prior to 1998, Missouri State had been the lowest-seeded team (eighth) to reach the Final Four when it advanced to Los Angeles in 1992. We took it a step further in '98, becoming the first No. 9 seed to ever reach the Final Four, and we made it to Kansas City for the Final Four by beating three higher seeds than us: No. 8 Hawaii, No. 5 Kansas, and No. 2 Duke in the West region. We also caught a bit of a break as a result of the most unexpected upset in the history of the NCAA Tournament, but I am jumping ahead of myself.

Our memorable 1997–98 season and run to the Final Four actually began with me making one of the best hires I could have ever possibly made. In replacing Tom Collen following the 1996–97 season, I contemplated going in many directions, including trying to find another national recruiting expert from a big-name basketball school. That recipe had worked well in landing Collen from Purdue, but quite honestly, the name that kept coming to mind wasn't from a big-name program and wasn't known for recruiting nationally. Regardless, there was just something special about Vic Schaefer, who had served as the head women's coach at Sam Houston State from 1990 to 1997. In 1995–96, Schaefer was named the Southland Conference Coach of the Year after leading the Ladykats to their most wins in a decade (18). And he'd done that on a shoestring budget with extremely limited resources. We'd also become close friends and golf buddies while I was coaching at Stephen F. Austin and stayed in close contact. Hiring a friend is risky. If things don't work out, you don't just lose an employee; you risk jeopardizing a friendship.

Nevertheless, I sensed that Schaefer was worth the risk. Even though he was a head coach at Sam Houston, I knew that they were not paying him particularly well, and I also knew that Schaefer and his wife, Holly, recently had twins. In fact, I was quite humbled by the fact that the Schaefers named their twins Logan and Blair. When he told me that he'd named his daughter Blair, I was practically speechless, which everyone knows is rare, indeed.

At Arkansas, we could offer Vic considerably more money than he was making at Sam Houston, and Holly had played collegiate basketball at Arkansas State in Jonesboro, so I hoped that she would be receptive to the move as well. To make a long story short, I offered Vic the job, he accepted, and so began an outstanding coaching relationship that spanned some 15 years and benefitted us both tremendously. Vic and I were great together because we complemented each other's strengths and detected the minutest details, although my family might disagree. At one point in our coaching careers at Arkansas, Vic and I took a weekend trip to Little Rock along with Paige, who was about 16 at the time. She spent the night at a friend's house, and Vic and I played golf the next morning and then went to pick up Paige. We were talking basketball on the drive back to Fayetteville, and when we reached Clarksville, I noticed that I needed gas. Paige was in the backseat, basically asleep. I told her that if she needed to go to the bathroom she had to do it now, because I was not going to stop again until we were back in Fayetteville, which was still an hour and a half away. Paige said she was fine.

Well, I went into the gas station, purchased my Diet Coke, and went to the restroom. We hopped back in the car and started back home. Five to seven minutes later, my phone rang: "Dad, did you forget something?" We had left her in the convenience store! She had gone to the bathroom without me noticing and had to borrow the clerk's phone to call. I'm sure the clerk was wondering, "What kind of man would leave his daughter in a convenience store?" My wife still talks about that one. It wasn't one of my finer moments as a father, but it was one of many unforgettable moments that I can recall with Vic Schaefer.

Vic is the personification of intensity and is also fiercely competitive. In addition to being a good recruiter and technician, Vic was also passionate about coaching defense. Ultimately, I turned the defense at Arkansas completely over to Vic, whose nickname became the "Secretary of Defense."

He provided us a shot in the arm, and our first season of coaching together was certainly memorable as we welcomed back Christy Smith, Tiffany Wright, and Karen Jones for their senior seasons in 1997–98. We also had a solid collection of veterans like juniors Sytia Messer, Tennille

Adams, Brandi Whitehead, and Treva Christensen, along with JUCO All-American Kamara Stancle, sophomore post Karyn Karlin, and a sharpshooting, 5-foot-8 freshman guard from Fort Cobb, Oklahoma, named Wendi Willits. Wendi was a sensational outside shooter who once hit 11 three-pointers in a high school game in which she didn't even play the fourth quarter. She had first attracted the attention of some college recruiters in her home state when she was in sixth grade—yes, sixth grade—following her team's 39–38 victory. What was so remarkable about her performance in that game is that she scored all 39 points.

Entering that 1997–98 season, I liked our team, our coaching staff, our chemistry, and our chances of returning to the NCAA Tournament. We once again started the season in strong fashion, going 7–0 through early December with an impressive win over No. 11 Iowa in the Reebok Classic in Boston (at Boston Garden, where my beloved Celtics played), and we had an emotional win at Louisville in which Christy Smith hit a half-court shot just before the buzzer at halftime. We stumbled a couple of times in December, but we had another big win at Valparaiso in overtime and wrapped up non-conference play at 10–2 as we prepared to open SEC play at No. 1 Tennessee on New Year's Day 1998. That's when things turned really tough really quickly. We'd beaten Tennessee the year before, and the Lady Vols had gone on to win the national championship. The 1996–97 Lady Vols were obviously good, but they also lost 10 regular-season games and four conference games en route to winning the national title.

The 1997–98 Lady Vols, however, were a destructive force on a mission. Entering our game on New Year's Day, Tennessee was unbeaten behind the strength of the "three Meeks": Semeka Randall, a freshman guard from Cleveland; Tamika Catchings, a 6-foot-1 freshman forward and the daughter of the former NBA player Harvey Catchings, from Duncanville, Texas; and Chamique Holdsclaw, a 6-foot-2 junior from Astoria, Queens, who was the leading candidate to win SEC and National Player of the Year honors. During the course of the 1997–98 season, Tennessee averaged 14,952 fans for home games, an attendance figure that was greater than five NBA teams that year. The Lady Vols also led the nation in scoring (89.1 points a game) and average margin of victory (31.2 points) during the regular season. In a particularly dominant 125–46 destruction of DePaul, Tennessee did not allow a single shot, much less a point, in the first four minutes of the game while steamrolling ahead by 21–0. Think about that—DePaul didn't even take a shot in the first four minutes. Quite frankly, the Lady Vols were a menacing machine, and they had obviously not forgotten the previous year's loss to us. We were annihilated, 88–58, on New Year's Day.

Fortunately, we still had the rest of the conference schedule to regroup and refocus. Perhaps even more fortunately, the schedule makers didn't make us face Tennessee again in the regular season. We won our next three games, including an overtime victory over Alabama, one of three overtime games we played in the SEC.

In all three overtime games, we gave up a three-point shot to our opponent that sent the game into overtime. We lost two of those three games by not fouling and sending the other team to the line. The two losses were to Vanderbilt and Georgia, and all three games were at home.

In early February, we beat Auburn at home, 71–63, to improve to 7–4 in the SEC and 17–6 overall with three games left to play in the regular season. Barring a complete collapse to close the regular season, we looked to be well on our way toward reaching our goal of earning a bid into the NCAA Tournament.

At least until we completely collapsed. In our next game, we lost by 22 at LSU and then by 18 at Ole Miss on Valentine's Day, dropping us to 17–8 for the year and 7–6 in conference play. That set up a regular-season home finale against Georgia that we really needed to win.

Instead, we lost in overtime. At 7–7 and tied for sixth place in the SEC, we were certainly not locks for the postseason. In fact, we went to Columbus, Georgia, for the SEC Tournament in late February knowing that we needed at least one win—and maybe more—to have a good shot at reaching the NCAA Tournament. Fortunately, we beat Auburn, 59–43, in our first game before being routed and ousted by No. 10–ranked Florida, 63–49. We then went back to Fayetteville and waited hopefully for the NCAA Selection Show—this time without the ESPN camera crew.

That year, however, we erupted in celebration when our name was revealed as the No. 9 seed in the West Region. Fortunately, the SEC was so strong that year—led by unbeaten Tennessee—that we received more bids (six) than any other conference in America. Our road would not be an easy one, as we were scheduled to face No. 8 seed Hawaii in the opening round at Stanford University's Maples Pavilion. And if we beat Hawaii, the No. 20–ranked team in the nation, our reward would likely be to face No. 1 seed Stanford—a program that had appeared in three consecutive Final Fours and had won 59 consecutive home games—on its home floor. Or so we thought.

Following our game with Hawaii—a game in which we rallied from a five-point halftime deficit to win, 76–70, behind Karyn Karlin's 24-point effort, Wendi Willits's long-range shooting, and a near flawless game by Christy Smith—Harvard became the first 16th-seeded team to ever win an NCAA Tournament game, men's or women's, by upending Stanford, 71–67, behind Allison Feaster's 35 points and 13 rebounds. Prior to Harvard's victory, top seeds were 75–0 against 16th seeds in the women's and men's tournaments. "I guess this means my name is going to go into some book now," Harvard coach Kathy Delaney-Smith said after the game. Asked if she had ever had a bigger day, Delaney-Smith said, "My wedding day, maybe. I'm not even sure if that measures up."

More than 5,000 fans had packed the Maples Pavilion on March 14—a Saturday night—to watch the Stanford–Harvard game. It was a late game—even by West Coast standards—so I'm not sure how many of our fans back in Arkansas even realized that Harvard had won and that we had a great opportunity to advance to the Sweet Sixteen until Sunday, or even Monday morning, when the results actually appeared in newspapers there. And because we were in the West Regional, our game against Harvard on March 16 also started late (9 p.m. PST, 11 p.m. CST) for a weeknight. An announced crowd of 2,013 (although there weren't nearly that many) showed up on the Monday night, with most of the fans pulling for the underdogs from Harvard, now Chelsea Clinton's alma mater. Among the attendees at the game were Stanford head coach Tara VanDerveer and several of her players, who sat several rows behind our bench.

Fortunately, we never gave the pro-Harvard crowd reason to cheer. Wendi Willits, who had made the first start of her collegiate career against Hawaii, was making her second start against Harvard and hit five three-pointers in the first half. The combination of Willits's shooting and Schaefer's full-court press propelled us to a 45–32 halftime lead. We didn't play Nolan Richardson's 40 minutes of hell, but our superior quickness and tenacious defense forced the Crimson into 18 turnovers. Christy Smith also added 19 points and 11 assists, and in the two games at Stanford, Smith did not have a single turnover.

It was during the press conference following our win over Harvard that I first coined the phrase "*Good Morning America*'s Team," because our fans back in Arkansas probably weren't discovering that we were moving on to the Sweet Sixteen until the morning after our game.

The great thing about the timing of the NCAA Tournament's opening rounds was that it coincided with the beginning of our spring break.

Advancing to the Sweet Sixteen in the West Region meant that we'd go from Palo Alto, California, for the opening two games to the New Arena in Oakland for our Sweet Sixteen matchup against Kansas. So instead of flying back to Arkansas for a couple days, we stayed on the West Coast for 13 days and enjoyed a sight-seeing vacation of sorts in California. In the days after beating Harvard, we toured Alcatraz Island, visited San Francisco's Pier 39, rode the trolleys, and genuinely had a great time as we prepared for the Sweet Sixteen. But it was also a business trip, and we were focused on continuing our unlikely run into the postseason. To do that, we needed to play extremely well in defending Kansas All-American Lynn Pride, who had been a *Parade* All-American at Sam Houston High School in Arlington, Texas. Kansas also possessed a significant overall size advantage, as the Jayhawks had seven players who were 6 feet or taller.

Once again, Vic Schaefer devised a great defensive game plan, and we held the 6-foot-2 Pride without a single field goal in the game, which started very late, at 11:37 p.m. central time. We played a solid first half, but we shot only 36 percent from the field, which was a big reason Kansas led 32–28 at the half. I don't remember saying anything particularly magical during halftime, but we caught fire in the second half. Sytia Messer scored 17 of her 23 points in the second-half effort as we dominated Kansas, 51–31, in the final 20 minutes. In the course of winning the game, 79–63, we shot 63 percent from the field in the second half. It was probably our best half of the year, and it came at a terrific time. The win placed us in the Elite Eight for just the second time in school history. The only other time Arkansas had advanced that deeply into the NCAA Tournament was in 1990, when the Lady'Backs beat my higher-seeded team at Stephen F. Austin in the Sweet Sixteen and then lost to Stanford in the Elite Eight.

This time, we faced Duke, the regular season champions of the Atlantic Coast Conference (ACC), for the right to go to the Final Four. Duke featured outstanding guards in Nicole Erickson and Peppi Browne, and the Blue Devils also had a force in the paint in 6-foot-6 center Michele Van Gorp. Duke also led the ACC in three-point shooting during the course of the season. It was going to be a big-time challenge to beat Duke, but I liked our chances, and I certainly loved the chemistry of our team. We believed in ourselves even if no one else did.

While I have often been guilty of overanalyzing things and saying too much in pregame speeches, I had decided on the trip from the hotel to the New Arena in Oakland that, for the sake of emphasis, I would keep my pregame comments short and to the point. When the bus stopped at the loading docks of the arena, I stood up and addressed the entire team. "Don't get off the bus if you don't expect to win," I said, and then exited the bus.

Fortunately, my entire team followed me. I don't know what we would have done if Christy Smith, Sytia Messer, or anyone else had stayed seated. Once the game started—again late at night on the West Coast—it was a terrific contest to watch, at least for any night owls. Both teams seemed a little nervous from the start, as Duke missed its first seven shots and we missed six of our first seven. We finally got on track with a 14–6 run, giving us a 24–16 lead following a three-pointer by Treva Christensen, who scored nine of her 12 first-half points during that early run. But Duke didn't fade, and we only took a 32–31 lead at halftime.

The second half was truly sensational to watch and absolutely stressful to coach. The lead changed hands 14 times in the second half, and at one point, Duke's Michele Van Gorp was really beginning to take control in the paint. We had a backup freshman post player named Celia Anderson, who really hadn't played much at all throughout the regular season. Celia has gone on to be a tremendous inspiration to young people as a published novelist who earned a master's at Arkansas and also a PhD. Coupling her love for basketball and education, Celia travels to schools throughout the United States to deliver her original presentation, "GAMETIME" (Gaining a Meaningful Education to Insure Maximum Elevation), which motivates students to "get in the game of life." One of the stories I am sure she enjoys telling is about getting into that Duke game. With Duke ahead, I turned to her and told her that I wanted her to go into the game and put her elbow into Van Gorp as hard as she could while going up for a layup. She did exactly as I said, and Duke coach Gail Goestenkors was so livid that our freshman backup post had outmuscled Van Gorp that she pulled her from the game and didn't put her back in. That was a real turning point for us.

We also did a great job defending the perimeter and not allowing Duke to beat us from the outside. While the Blue Devils led the ACC in three-point shooting, they made just one of 11 treys against us. Down the stretch, every possession was a war, and we went up 73–72 on Tennille Adams's offensive rebound and follow shot with 1:38 to play. A minute later, Duke's Nicole Erickson missed another three-point shot and the 5-foot-6 Christy Smith grabbed the rebound and was fouled. As she stepped to the line, I couldn't help but think back to when Smith—the nation's best free-throw shooter—missed the second free throw, with 0.03 seconds left, that would have sent us to overtime against Ole Miss. Instead of letting that memory demoralize her, she woke early the next morning—before attending church—to shoot free throws, telling her roommate, Tiffany Wright, "I will not let this team down again with the game on the line."

She didn't. She drilled those two free throws against Duke to put us up, 75–72. Then, with 16 seconds remaining, she was fouled again. "When she went back to the line, I thought, thank you, Jesus," said Sytia Messer, who was voted the regional's most outstanding player, in the postgame press conference.

I was thanking Jesus too. One of the game announcers that night, Beth Mowins, had a memorable call that can still be heard in the Arkansas Razorbacks' Athletic Museum: "Do you believe in fairy tales?" Mowins asked. "Christy Smith does!" To accomplish great things in this sport, you must want the ball at the end of the game, and Christy Smith wanted the ball. Christy looked so calm and composed at the line. It wasn't until many years later—after she had become a coach—that she acknowledged what was really going through her mind as she stepped to the line:

> I remember growing up and shooting free throws out in my driveway, pretending like if I made them that my team would go to the Final Four or win the national championship. You do it and miss them and pretend to grab an amazing rebound or you just start over. I had pretended to be in that situation thousands of time, but when I was actually there, I was thinking, "You have to knock these down. There is no second chance." Honestly—and I would have said this back then—but I couldn't feel my arms. There was no body part that I could feel. I was thinking, "Hope I don't airball it, and I hope this sucker goes in." Fortunately, it was a fairy book–type ending for me personally and for my team. To be able to be fouled and go to the line and make four free throws in the final 31 seconds to get us to the Final Four was a dream scenario.

Duke's last two shots in the final seconds were air balls, and the celebration was on for our team, as the players flooded the court around Smith, who dropped to her knees as time expired. The celebration was kind of a blur, but I still remember going onto the loading dock and waiting for the bus. It was the wee hours of the morning, but all the girls were dancing, and they circled around me as I joined them in their celebration. It was such a great feeling of exhilaration and satisfaction, and probably only a handful of people back in Arkansas had stayed up that late on a Monday night/ Tuesday morning to see us make history. We caught a commercial flight out that morning—after 13 days away from Arkansas—and boarded a bus for the two-hour ride from Tulsa to Fayetteville. As we approached Fayetteville at roughly 6 p.m., I told the girls to be prepared, because there might be a small group of fans at the arena to welcome us back. We were tired and our dirty laundry stank from our nonstop trip, but when we rounded the corner and Bud Walton Arena came into focus, the small group that I had hoped would greet us turned out to be 3,000 people, including then-Arkansas head football coach Houston Nutt and the entire football team. We even picked up a police escort. It was a really special homecoming, but we didn't have much time to bask in the glow of our accomplishment.

We washed our clothes that night, and the following day, on Wednesday, the girls attended classes, worked out from about 1 to 3 p.m., and then boarded a plane for Kansas City by 4 p.m. It was a whirlwind time, and my only regret is that we didn't have more time in Kansas City to enjoy the moment. Kansas City is one of the great basketball cities in America, even though Kemper Arena—the site of the 1998 Final Four—was well past its prime. But Kansas City residents and fans treated us so well, and the restaurants were fabulous. As soon as we landed, we enjoyed a big Italian meal and then checked into the hotel. Looking back, that Thursday was a complete blur: we worked out in the morning, attended a press conference that afternoon, and went to a party for the teams in the evening—all the day before the two national semifinal games. It's a good thing I won the press conference on Thursday, which also included Louisiana Tech's Leon Barmore, North Carolina State's Kay Yow, and Tennessee's Pat Summitt, because Friday was not a particularly good one for me or the Lady'Backs.

We played the second game on Friday—Louisiana Tech cruised past North Carolina State in the opening game—and we were confident that we could play with Tennessee and force the Lady Vols into a tough game, despite the fact that we had lost by 30 to Tennessee in Knoxville on New Year's Day. In fact, I was so confident in the way our team was playing that I refused to let my coaching staff stay in the hotel on Thursday night to watch film. We all went to the big party—no other team's coaches did—and thoroughly enjoyed ourselves. I wanted all my coaches to experience the celebration of the Final Four, and we'd take our chances against the best team in Tennessee history the next day.

Prior to the game, I told my team that we were not going to sit back in a two-three zone. We are going to attack, run, and press to do anything in our power to make it an ugly game. We accomplished our goal of making it ugly and physical right from the start, but the officials were making it impossible for us to continue that style of play. We were whistled for seven team fouls before Tennessee was called for its first with 11:56 remaining in the first half. One of the officials, Karen Wilhite, was calling her first Final Four, and at one point, I pointed toward Pat Summitt and told Karen, "That woman does not need your help. This is my first Final Four just like it's your first Final Four. Let's enjoy it together." When the officials finally called Tennessee for a foul, I bowed toward them.

Despite the lopsided amount of fouls called early in the contest, we grabbed a 5–4 lead on Christy Smith's three-point shot three minutes into the game. Tennessee's National Player of the Year, Chamique Holdsclaw, didn't score for the first nine minutes, and the Lady Vols didn't shoot particularly well in the first half. We pressed, trapped, and slowed Tennessee's transition game, which seemed to frustrate the Vols. We had a number of chances in the first half, but Tennessee played well on the defensive end. Semeka Randall scored 22 points, and she did a great job pressuring Christy Smith. Uncharacteristically, we committed 17 turnovers in the first half, which was about 15 more than we could afford against a team as good as Tennessee. Still, we had a great chance after Treva Christensen hit two threes in the final four minutes of the first half, and we cut the lead to eight. We had another chance to trim the lead even further when Christy Smith rebounded a Tennessee miss with about 25 seconds left in the half.

I was hollering for one shot, but with a crowd of 17,976 inside Kemper Arena, Christy Smith couldn't hear me. Instead, she missed a quick three, and Tennessee started a fast break the other way. As I watched the fast break unfold, I was thinking Holdsclaw would go in for a layup, and I yelled at Wendi Willits to double-team her. Instead, Holdsclaw dished off to Kelly Jolly, who drilled a three-pointer that just beat the buzzer. Instead of being down by five or even eight and riding a wave of momentum, we were down by 11 at the break.

I was cussing myself out as Leon Barmore came running alongside press row yelling words of encouragement toward me. "Blair, your team is playing great," he was saying. "Keep it up." But that whole time I was thinking to myself, "I'm the dumbass coach that let Jolly get wide open like that." I walked with my head down toward the tunnel, and just as I entered, I realized was in the wrong tunnel. I was in the press tunnel, while both teams and the officials had gone the other way.

Well, I wasn't going to go back into the arena and let everyone see the idiot coach who made all the wrong moves and then went into the wrong tunnel at the half, so I just kept walking in the underbelly of the arena.

Finally, I ran into a security guard, who stopped me and said, "Only coaches and players can go beyond this point." I then had to have my assistants come help me convince him that I was actually the Arkansas coach.

If that wasn't bad enough, Tennessee outscored us 13–1 in the first three minutes of the second half, padding the spread to 52–29. Ten minutes into the second half, Kemper Arena began to empty and our Cinderella-like run came to an abrupt halt. When it was all said and done, we actually played Tennessee to a closer game in the Final Four than we had on New Year's Day, but only by two points. Our 86–58 loss established a new Final Four record for the largest margin of victory at that point in history at 28. Two nights later, Tennessee completed its masterful season with a 93–75 win over Louisiana Tech to run the Lady Vols' record to 39–0.

For us, it certainly wasn't an ideal ending to the season, but it had been a magical run, and we returned to Arkansas feeling like rock stars. I received a modest raise of about $22,000 following our trip to the Final Four, and with how well Nan was doing, we were ultimately able to build our dream house on two acres of a cul-de-sac near where Eddie Sutton had lived when he was coaching the Arkansas men's team. It's a two-story, 3,800-square-foot house with a wraparound porch that we absolutely loved. We also loved our neighbors, which included Vic and Holly Schaefer not too far down the road, and felt like we had found a permanent home in Fayetteville.

The fans in Arkansas really embraced me because I was constantly out shaking hands, kissing babies, and promoting Arkansas basketball. We started a basketball tailgate at Arkansas football games so that recruits could visit and soak up the atmosphere of Arkansas athletics, whether the football team was playing in Fayetteville or Little Rock. The NCAA allowed us to hold the tailgates as long as we charged a $5 entry fee, if recruits were on an unofficial visit. We'd cook great food and mingle with the fans and prospects. Throughout the year, I'd also host fan luncheons to promote the Lady'Backs. My agenda was to promote Arkansas women's basketball. Period.

In that regard, I was probably more well received by fans than men's coach Nolan Richardson, who led the Razorbacks to the 1994 national championship, was the national runner-up in 1995, and opened doors for the next wave of black coaches. But his legacy also includes his tumultuous relationship with former Arkansas athletic director Frank Broyles. Richardson was outspoken about his frustration with Broyles over his support for the football program and Houston Nutt, a consistent backing that Richardson believed he never got from Broyles. "There was a time when I wouldn't give [Broyles] the spit if he was dying," Richardson told ESPN staff writer

Myron Medcalf in 2015. "That anger. When you've got that kind of an anger in you, it takes away from living because you're so angry." Richardson often came across as angry—angry about Nutt's compensation and bonuses, angry about racial injustices, angry about the way he was portrayed by the media, just angry. The anger led to his firing in 2002 after he dared Broyles to fire him during a postgame news conference. Following his firing, Richardson filed an $8 million lawsuit against the university, alleging racism and bias in his termination after the school gave Nutt bonuses and extensions for what Richardson believed were lesser achievements. But US District Judge William R. Wilson, who reasoned that the lawsuit centered on "wounded pride," dismissed the case in 2004.

Years later, Richardson let go of the anger and he is once again beloved in Arkansas, where he lives on a 155-acre ranch in Fayetteville. But during the late 1990s and early 2000s, Richardson was often brash, bold, and combative. Fortunately, he was not that way toward me. Nolan and his staff treated me great. His wife, Rose, came to a number of our games and befriended our players, even inviting them out to the Richardson ranch from time to time. Nolan had a huge heart, and he was beloved in Arkansas for all the work he did for charities. He was misunderstood by many people because he had no filter. His players loved him because he taught them life lessons and how to be men first. Nolan was a trailblazer, and he often said things that ruffled feathers.

I was just looking to make friends and influence fans to also buy season tickets to women's basketball games. In the aftermath of our magical run to the 1998 Final Four, sports fans in Arkansas were willing to listen to my sales pitch—and so were recruits.

Following our '98 postseason run, All-American point guard Christy Smith was a second-round draft pick of the WNBA's Charlotte Sting, where she led the franchise into the playoffs as a rookie. While it was nearly impossible to replace a player of Smith's caliber, we were extremely fortunate to find another superstar point guard and clutch performer in Amy Wright, who was also from Indiana (Northeastern High School). Wright averaged 22.3 points, 6.9 rebounds, and 4 assists per game while leading her team to a 16–5 record and the sectional championship. We all sensed that she was going to be really good. We just never envisioned how good she would be and how quickly she would assert herself.

Wright would eventually break Amber Nicholas's Arkansas career assist record, and she became the first point guard in school history to lead the Lady'Backs to four straight postseason appearances. She stepped into a good situation as a true freshman, as she joined a team that featured some really good veterans like Sytia Messer, Tennille Adams, Karyn Karlin, and Kamara Stancle, along with some promising younger players like Wendi Willits, Celia Anderson, and Lonniya Bragg. We were ranked 18th in the preseason polls and started our season opener at the "Four in the Fall" Tournament in San Jose, California, where promoters brought together what they considered the four best teams in the country. They invited Stanford, Connecticut, Virginia, and us, and we agreed to play Stanford in our opening ball game. The game was billed as a chance for Stanford to gain a measure of revenge, since we had advanced to the Sweet Sixteen the previous year on Stanford's home court. But on Friday the 13th, in 1999, we again made the Cardinal live through some misery as we beat No. 19–ranked Stanford, 76–71. Wright had an interesting double-double in her collegiate debut, scoring 10 points and also getting 10 turnovers.

Unfortunately, that game was one of the high points of what was truly a roller coaster regular season. We played No. 3 UConn in our next game, and the Huskies dominated every aspect of the contest in a rather humbling 100–64 beatdown. However, we bounced right back to win our next five games, winning the championship of the Arkansas Classic on our home floor and beating a Baylor team that was coached by my former boss, Sonja Hogg. We climbed as high as No. 13 in the national polls by early December but then lost four games in a row, including a 20-point home loss to No. 2 Tennessee in our SEC opener.

The SEC was once again the strongest conference in the country, as eight schools (Tennessee, Georgia, Alabama, Auburn, Florida, Georgia, Kentucky, LSU, and Mississippi State) would eventually earn bids. We were at 13–10, riding the roller coaster, when we traveled to No. 19 Auburn in early February for a key contest. Not only did we lose the game, but we also scored our lowest number of points for the entire season (46) and lost our leading scorer, Karyn Karlin, for the rest of the season. Karyn was averaging 16 points and 6.3 rebounds per game, but she tore her ACL against Auburn. That demoralizing loss sealed our fate, as we finished 11th out of 12 teams in the SEC at 5–9 in conference play and limped to a 15–14 overall record after we were eliminated by Mississippi State in the first round of the SEC Tournament in Chattanooga, Tennessee. It was quite a disappointing season following the run to the Final Four the previous year.

But the late, great John Wooden once said, "Things turn out best for the people who make the best of the way things turn out." In other words, we all have a choice to let a bad situation make us or break us, and I was especially proud to watch how that 1999 team continued to strive for the best even when things seemed rather bleak. Injuries and circumstance threw us to the wolves a couple times, but we emerged as the leaders of the pack.

Even though we didn't earn a bid to the NCAA Tournament, we accepted a bid to the 1999 WNIT and then opened the first round by defeating Southland Conference champion Northwestern (Louisiana) State, 78–60, at Bud Walton Arena, which set up an interesting "Border War" against Oklahoma, led by head coach Sherri Coale, junior forward Phylesha Whaley, and Canadian guard Stacey Dales, who went on to be an All-Star in the WNBA and has enjoyed a great career as a sports broadcaster. It was also interesting because an arena conflict in Norman, Oklahoma, moved the game to Arkansas, and two of our players (Wendi Willits from Fort Cobb and Kamara Stancle from Muskogee) were from the state of Oklahoma. Adding further intrigue to the matchup was a heavy snowstorm in mid-March that almost prevented us from playing the game. While we had averaged 4,000 fans per game, an announced crowd of only 890 showed up on Sunday, March 14, 1999. The Arkansas band wasn't even in attendance.

Those who braved the elements were rewarded, though. It turned into a showdown between Oklahoma's Whaley and Wendi Willits. Despite the fact that the three of the Sooners' players fouled out, Whaley gave Oklahoma an 83–81 lead with 12 seconds left. But we answered with a big follow shot with 3.7 seconds left to send the game in overtime. Willits hit two three-pointers in overtime to help lead us to a 97–93 win, despite 40 points from Whaley.

Starting with the third round against Rice, Arkansas fans began pouring back into Bud Walton Arena, while we were doing everything possible to market to local fans and businesses. I was calling businesses throughout Northwest Arkansas, trying to convince owners and managers to purchase group tickets for their employees. We defeated Rice, 76–70, to reach the national semifinal game. Behind a career-high 23 from Lonniya Bragg, we then pounded the MVC runner-up Drake Bulldogs, 80–56. And thanks to 9,041 fans at the Drake game, we earned the privilege of hosting the 1999 WNIT championship game against Wisconsin. The title game against Wisconsin was scheduled for March 23. The night before the game, Sytia Messer's mother suffered a heart attack in Waldo, Arkansas. Messer left Fayetteville to be with her mother, who passed away around 2 a.m. on game day.

Without Messer, who averaged 12.2 points per game and was our third-leading scorer, we played inspired basketball before an all-time record crowd of 14,163 fans (still the largest to see a women's sporting event in Arkansas). We stormed to a 10-point halftime lead and increased the lead to 14 points in the second half before Wisconsin made a run. The Badgers cut the deficit to one point with 7:44 left in the game and only trailed by three when we called a timeout to set up a three-point shot from Willits. We set up the shot, and it bounced around the rim a few times before falling through the net to give us a six-point lead. Bud Walton Arena erupted after that shot, and we went on to win the WNIT championship with a 76–64 victory. I was especially proud of Kamara Stancle, a junior college All-American who started in Messer's place and tied Willits for the team lead with 15 points. It was also quite rewarding that Messer was still named to the all-tournament team. Some say that winning the WNIT is like taking 65th place (following the 64 teams that make the NCAA Tournament), but winning a championship sure feels better than 65th place, even though you'd obviously rather be in the NCAA Tournament every year.

I was quite proud of that title and proud of how we had transformed the women's basketball program at Arkansas. But perhaps my proudest moment during my time at Arkansas was watching my son and daughter excel. Paige became a solid tennis player during high school, and Matt became a very good cross country runner and soccer player. As a huge baseball fan, however, I also vividly recall Matt's successes on the diamond. When I was playing youth baseball in Dallas—it was called Boys Baseball Incorporated—I was skinny and had no power, and there was never a fence. It wasn't like today's Little League parks. When my son started playing Little League baseball in Fayetteville, I remember being so proud of him when he slammed a ball off the right-centerfield fence for a double, which is something I never accomplished. I remember beaming with pride as I looked out there and saw Matt standing at second base. I take great pride in developing collegiate athletes, but there is nothing like watching your own kids—and now my own grandkids—reach their goals.

Unfortunately, as a women's basketball program, we failed to reach our goals the year after winning the WNIT. We started the 1999–2000 season at 8–0, but then we lost seven of our next eight games. We seemed to right the ship with five straight wins in January and early February, but then we stumbled down the stretch, losing our final six regular-season games and then losing to Florida in the opening round of the SEC Tournament. At 14–14 overall and 4–10 in the SEC, we were once again bound for the WNIT. And once again, we came alive and made a great run before big home crowds.

I was on the phone at one time or another with upper-level executives from Tyson, J. B. Hunt Transport Services, and Walmart, as well as practically every mom-and-pop franchise in the area. We once again played well, beating Wichita State, 83–63, in the opening round at home and surviving a thrilling 89–88 overtime win against Missouri. The Lady Tigers sent the game into overtime tied at 77 on a shot by Amanda Lassiter with a half-second left. Mizzou then jumped ahead 86–81 with 2:20 remaining in overtime, and things were looking bleak. But Willits and Brandi Whitehead combined for the next six points, and Lonniya Bragg scored on a short jumper off a pass from Wendi Willits to put us ahead, 89–88. Lakishia Harper then made the defensive play of the night, blocking Kerensa Barr's 10-footer at the buzzer and sending us on to the next round, where we beat Georgia Tech, 78–67.

That set up a rematch against Florida, which had already beaten us twice that year. The third time was not the charm, though, as we hit only one field goal in the first nine and a half minutes. We were down 23–2 before Wendy Willits hit a three-pointer. As a result, Florida advanced to the Women's NIT final Saturday with an 83–62 semifinal victory in front of 3,862 spectators at Walton Arena, which prevented us from facing Wisconsin again in the WNIT championship game.

Despite all our success in the WNIT—where we'd gone 8–1 the previous two years and played in front of some large, enthusiastic, and boisterous crowds in Fayetteville—I, along with the rest of the coaching staff, believed it was extremely important to return to the NCAA Tournament as we entered the 2000–2001 season. As a staff, we lost Trenia Tillis, who left Fayetteville to take the head coaching job at Tyler Junior College. But we had made a positive addition in hiring Kelly Bond, who had played point guard for the University of Illinois and led the Illini to back-to-back Sweet Sixteen appearances as a player before taking a coaching position at Providence College. Kelly brought some new energy to the team, as did freshman Shameka Christon from Hot Springs, Arkansas, the highest recruit from the state. In high school, the 6-foot-1 Christon helped lead the Hot Springs Lady Trojans to consecutive state championships in 1997 and 1998, and as a senior in 2000, she was named Gatorade Circle of Champions Arkansas Player of the Year, as well as Arkansas Miss Basketball.

We didn't start the season particularly well, losing three of our first four games, and we didn't start conference play in strong fashion either, as we opened SEC action at 0–3. But senior veterans like Wendi Willits and Lonniya Bragg, along with junior point guard Amy Wright, kept us steady and kept the chemistry together in the locker room. And as youngsters like Christon and sophomore India Lewis began to mature, we really started playing well. Beginning in mid-January 2001, we strung together five consecutive SEC wins, including consecutive victories over ranked foes Mississippi State and Vanderbilt, to turn the season around. We finished the regular season at 17–11 and 6–8 in the SEC. We then traveled to the SEC Tournament in Memphis knowing that we needed to perform well to secure an NCAA Tournament bid.

And we played really well in Memphis, opening with an impressive 94–76 victory over Mississippi State. That earned us the opportunity to play Florida once again. Not only had the Gators ended our season in the WNIT the year before, but they had also beaten us at home earlier in 2001, 75–64, for their 10th consecutive win over Arkansas. It was becoming a mental issue with some of our older players, but fortunately, that wasn't the case for Shameka Christon, who made it clear that she belonged on the All-SEC Freshman team by scoring 22 points and grabbing 11 rebounds in our 78–69 win. We led by as many as 20 before Christon departed the game with a busted lip that required four stitches. Florida closed to within 7, but we went on a 7–0 run late to advance to the SEC Tournament semifinals for the first time in school history.

We lost in the semifinals to Georgia, but we had done enough in Memphis to earn a return bid to the NCAA Tournament, where we were a No. 9 playing Baylor, a No. 8, at Duke. Interestingly, I would face Kim Mulkey Robertson, one of my former players at Louisiana Tech, in that game for the first time as the Baylor head coach. We made just 10 of 35 shots in the first half, including 10 straight misses before halftime, but we stayed close thanks to 10 steals and 15 turnovers. Baylor led 33–28 at halftime, but we went on a 21–10 run to take a second-half lead we would never give back. Lonniya Bragg led the way with 16 points and 14 rebounds, and Amy Wright finished with 13 points, 7 rebounds, and 4 assists. Our NCAA Tournament run ended the following game when Duke hammered us, 75–54, in the second round, but it had been a successful bounce-back season. We finished the year with 20 wins; Wendi Willits finished her career as the school's best three-point shooter; Shameka Christon finished her freshman year in style; and, most important, we finished the season back in the NCAA Tournament. And we didn't just show up once we made it to March Madness; we won a game and represented the SEC well.

It was a good year, and we went on do some really good things the next two years as well. In 2001–2, for example, we rallied from a 1–5 start in conference play and hit our stride in late January when we beat No. 7 South Carolina and No. 8 Vanderbilt to defeat top-10 teams in consecutive games at Fayetteville for the first time in school history. The 74–46 win over South Carolina was particularly sweet, since USC had beaten us three weeks earlier, 91–66, in Columbia. In the win, we forced 26 turnovers, while India Lewis and Dana Cherry had 17 each as we took out our frustrations. Four days later, Shameka Christon poured in 21 to lead us past Vanderbilt, 67–57, as we controlled the game start to finish.

After our horrendous start in conference play, we finished at 7–7 and beat South Carolina again—this time by 18 points—in the SEC Tournament in Nashville. We lost in the next round to the hometown team, Vanderbilt, 81–78, but even in the loss we were impressive. Shameka Christon had the greatest game at Arkansas in over a generation, but her 40 points in 37 minutes played were not enough to overcome Vanderbilt at the Gaylord Entertainment Center. At the start of the second half, it looked like there wouldn't be much drama as Vandy extended its 44–26 halftime lead to 22 points, 52–30, with 17 minutes left. Then Christon took over, scoring a school-record of 28 points for a half. We cut the lead to one, 79–78, with 22 seconds left and had the last shot. But with nine seconds to play, Christon was called for a questionable charge that allowed Vandy to shoot free throws for the margin of victory. Of course I called it a flop.

We earned a six seed in the NCAA Tournament and opened the Big Dance with a 78–68 win over Clemson when Shameka Christon scored 36 points in 33 minutes. That loss was the first ever for Clemson under Jim Davis in the first round. We lost to an outstanding Kansas State in the second round, but we finished with 20 wins for the sixth time in my nine years at Arkansas, as Amy Wright finished her collegiate career with a school-record 717 assists. Wright's court awareness and passing skills also allowed the 2001–2 team to set a school record for the fewest turnovers in a single season (433).

The next year was even better, as we became the third team in school history to start and finish the season ranked in the Associated Press Top 25. We started the year 10–1 with the only loss coming against No. 1 Duke, 74–72, in overtime. While we didn't beat the No. 1 team, we did stun No. 2 LSU, 82–72, on January 19, 2003. Before the largest regular-season crowd in school history (11,486) and an ESPN television audience, Shameka Christon (25 points, 7 boards), India Lewis (19 points), and Dana Cherry (13 points, 12 rebounds) led us to a convincing win. The victory over LSU gave us a 16–2 overall record.

We struggled down the stretch, but we again played well in the SEC Tournament, as it was held in Little Rock and west of the Mississippi River for the first time. We beat Alabama in the first round, which was a difficult task since we had beaten the Tide in the final game of the regular season four days earlier. We lost to eventual SEC Tournament champion LSU, 78–72, in the closest game the Tigers played en route to winning the title.

During that 2003 SEC Tournament, I also fielded a phone call that changed my life. Throughout that season, I had been lobbying for a new contract, as I only had one more year left on my contract, which paid me $175,000 annually, one of the lowest salaries in the SEC at that time. We were on our way to our seventh 20-win season in 10 years at Arkansas and our fifth appearance in the NCAA Tournament during that time. But I was becoming frustrated because we weren't making any progress on my contract. I was happy at Arkansas, and I believed we could continue winning for the foreseeable future if the administration made a serious commitment to me. I had gone to Bev Lewis, the director of women's athletics, asking for a four- or five-year contract valued at $300,000 a year, which was reasonable offer for coaches with my track record and who had taken teams to the Final Four. But I sensed that Lewis had her hands tied, and my suspicion was that Arkansas Chancellor John White, who had succeeded Daniel Ferritor in 1997, wanted a woman to coach the women's basketball team. I didn't want to go into the last year of my contract without an extension or deal in place because I sensed that unless we went back to the Final Four, White would simply choose not to renew my contract and I would be out of a job.

So when I received a phone call from Bill Byrne at the 2003 SEC Tournament, my interest was piqued. Byrne was the new athletic director at Texas A&M, and he wanted to meet in Dallas to discuss bringing me on as the Aggies' new women's basketball head coach. I wouldn't have even thought twice about meeting with an A&M athletic director in the past because A&M had not been committed to winning in basketball under previous regimes, which is why Kim Mulkey Robertson had turned down the A&M job several times previously. But I knew Bill Byrne's reputation for building programs at Nebraska, and I knew that he had been attracted to Texas A&M because the new administration was committed to winning in multiple sports in the Big 12.

I flew from Little Rock to Dallas to meet Bill Byrne at the Renaissance Hotel. We had breakfast, and Bill was honest and to the point with me. He told me about his vision, his plans, and what he planned to pay me if I accepted the job. He'd done his homework on me and was prepared to offer me the job. Bill said, "Gary, I'm offering you five years at $350,000. I'm not offering you a dime more. Do you know why I'm not going to offer you anymore? Because that is exactly what I'm making, and I'm not going to pay you more than me." We laughed and talked some more. Quite frankly, I was extremely impressed with Bill and the prospect of resurrecting the sleeping giant at Texas A&M.

I flew back to Little Rock, met with Bev Lewis, and told her what A&M was offering me, hoping still that she would make me a counter offer that would keep me at Arkansas. Instead, she told me, "Gary, you need to go ahead and take it. That is a great contract situation. I don't think we can do that." They wanted me to coach that next year at Arkansas—my final year of the contract—for $175,000, and then could discuss a new contract. Taking the job at A&M was a total no-brainer, but I waited until after the season to make a final decision.

We earned a No. 7 seed and opened the NCAA Tournament with a 71–57 win over Cincinnati. We then were eliminated by a great Texas team that made it to the Final Four. But the bottom line for us was that for the third consecutive year, we were beaten in the second round of the NCAA Tournament.

I then went back to Arkansas and discussed the entire situation with Nan. She absolutely knew that taking the A&M job was the right move for me. She also knew that moving to College Station, Texas, wasn't the right move for our family. She had a great career in Arkansas, my Paige was a junior at the University of Arkansas, and Matt was a junior at Fayetteville High School. My family was very supportive of me making the move to Aggieland, but it was going to be a unique situation because I was making the move by myself and we were going to try a long-distance family relationship. It was a tough move to make for numerous reasons, but it would also eventually prove to be the right move.

10 One Direction: Starting to Write the Story of My Coaching Life

On the afternoon of December 19, 2002, the Texas A&M women's basketball team checked out of a hotel in South Florida and boarded a charter bus bound for that night's game against the University of Miami. At that point in the young season, the Aggies were 6–1 and riding a six-game winning streak, their longest such streak in two years. But the Hurricanes easily represented the biggest and toughest challenge of the season for Texas A&M, which had recorded all its wins against small schools like Prairie View A&M, Arkansas–Pine Bluff, and UT–Arlington. The game also represented a homecoming of sorts for Texas A&M's best player, Toccara Williams, who had played at South Broward High School in Hollywood, Florida, roughly 20 miles north of downtown Miami. A large group of Williams's childhood friends and family members planned to attend the game to celebrate Williams's return to the Sunshine State.

On many levels, Miami represented a big early-season game for the Aggies, and as the driver pulled into the loading docks area of Miami Arena, the venue that served as the home of the NBA's Miami Heat from 1988 to 1999, an air of anticipation filled the bus. According to members of the traveling party, however, nobody had paid too much attention to where the team was going until the driver turned into the loading docks and noticed an unusually quiet and empty setting for being less than two hours away from tip-off on game day. In fact, only one security guard was at the entrance of the loading docks, and he graciously informed the team and coaching staff that no games were scheduled for Miami Arena that night and that the University of Miami women played at a much smaller arena on campus. That arena—the Knight Sports Complex—is located in Coral Gables, about 45 minutes to an hour south with traffic. Fortunately, the Aggies made it to the arena in time for tip-off, but the Hurricanes rolled to an 84–58 blowout victory.

The outcome of the game provided a more accurate depiction of where the 2002–3 team stood, as the Aggies lost 16 of their final 20 games to finish the season at 10–18 overall and 3–13 in the Big 12. But perhaps it was the story of the team showing up at the wrong arena on game night that best symbolized the bigger picture of Texas A&M women's basketball at that time. In the midst of its seventh consecutive losing season, Texas A&M was a program that seemed to lack a sense of direction.

Following the Aggies' last loss of the 2002–3 season—an 81–60 setback against Baylor in the Big 12 Tournament at Reunion Arena in Dallas—Texas A&M athletic director Bill Byrne fired women's head coach Peggie Gillom, who had compiled an overall record of 53–76 in five seasons in College Station. Obviously, that wasn't good, but the record against Big 12 Conference foes was even more discouraging: 15–65, which equates to a .188 winning percentage. Even the 1962 New York Mets—the worst baseball team in MLB history—had a .250 winning percentage.

In five seasons, the Aggies had finished last in the Big 12 standings three times, 11th once, and ninth once. And it wasn't just the losses that were mounting; embarrassing losses were becoming quite common. In the final two months of the 2003 season, for example, A&M lost four times to conference opponents by at least 38 points or more. And in in her last four years at A&M, Gillom's teams lost a whopping 15 conference games in which the Aggies failed to score at least 50 points, including two games in her final season when the team did not surpass 39 points in the losses. After five futile years, it was really no surprise to anyone in the coaching industry that Gillom was fired. What surprised me after finally accepting the job offer was the perception—even in College Station—that it wasn't possible for anyone to consistently win in men's or women's basketball at Texas A&M.

Texas A&M sports fans were so beaten down by bad basketball that most of them simply chose to ignore the sport. The fans in Aggieland, who were so sensational and passionate in football season and even baseball season, often went into sports hibernations during basketball season. From 1982, when women's basketball first became an official sport in the Southwest Conference, until the conclusion of the 2002–3 season, A&M had never won a regular-season conference title. Never! Furthermore, the Aggies had only made two appearances in the NCAA Tournament. And throughout the 1990s and into the early 2000s, the men's program may have been even worse. Beginning with a last-place Southwest Conference team in 1990–91, the A&M men produced an overall conference record (SWC and Big 12 combined) of 54–138 through the end of the 2002–3 season. During that 13-year stretch of stench, the Aggies made a postseason appearance in one NIT. That also represented the only winning season for the men's program during that time frame.

Texas A&M, with all its resources and athletic traditions, may have been the worst basketball program in the entire country when factoring in both the men's and women's continued futility. Under Melvin Watkins, who arrived in Aggieland to direct the men's program in 1998–99, A&M never produced a winning record and never finished in the upper half of the Big 12 standings. A&M produced plenty of rank teams, but no ranked ones. And like the women, the men endured some humiliatingly lopsided defeats.

Throughout most of the 1990s, the Aggies—at least in terms of media coverage for basketball—were more regional than an area code. All those humbling losses and all the negative publicity that surrounded both the women's and men's basketball programs made Reed Arena a great place to study or to read a book on game nights. Reed Arena, which opened as the home for Texas A&M men's and women's basketball in 1998–99 (the first season for both Watkins and Gillom), was already woefully outdated and underdeveloped the day it first opened. Due to budgetary cuts and bad luck, the facility was built with no luxury suites, no video boards, and no real attention to detail in terms of making it a showplace for basketball fans or recruits. Construction on the $36.8 million facility began in the summer of 1995, and roughly 40 percent of the steel skeleton was in place in October 1996 when the roof came crumbling down. A 20-foot-tall, 120-foot-long section of crisscrossed beams that was lifted about six stories by two cranes came loose, crashing into a tower that was supporting three other massive steel webs. Beams, bolts, and metal pieces weighing 250 tons tumbled, smashing 16 rows of concrete where seats were to be installed. Fortunately, no one was killed or seriously injured, but the accident resulted in further cutbacks and delayed the opening of the arena by more than a year. It also served as a bad omen of things to come.

When it finally opened in November 1998, Reed Arena was practically a mausoleum. The locker rooms for the teams were unimpressive and small, the practice gym was tiny, the concourses were barren and antiseptic, there was no hanging scoreboard above the basketball court, and there was no real indication—aside from the removable basketball court with A&M logos painted on it—that Reed Arena was the home of Aggie basketball. The combination of a sterile environment and bad teams meant that Reed Arena often featured no atmosphere, no energy, and no home-court advantage.

The real problem, however, was that there was no serious commitment or long-term vision for basketball from the Texas A&M administration. That had been the case, according to many long-term observers, at A&M for many years. However, with the arrival of former CIA director Robert M. Gates as president of the university in the summer of 2002 and then with the hiring of Bill Byrne as athletic director in January 2003, Texas A&M was becoming far more aggressive in its commitment to across-the-board excellence in all sports. Gates earned high marks for his bold vision, sharp intellect, and ability to attract top scholars and administrators, including Byrne, to College Station. And when I met with Byrne in Dallas shortly after he had fired Gillom, he assured me that he was 100 percent committed toward building a top-10 athletic program that featured basketball programs that would consistently participate in NCAA Tournaments and contend for conference championships. As long as I knew that the athletic director was 100 percent committed—financially, strategically, philosophically, and so forth—I believed Texas A&M, even without a great basketball tradition or a great basketball facility, could be a golden opportunity because of the passion of the fans I'd seen on display at Aggie football games. I also knew how much my brother, Steve, admired the university after the year he had spent there as well as the pride that Texas A&M former students possessed for their school. It never crossed my mind that I couldn't win at Texas A&M.

In all honesty, though, when I left that meeting with Bill Byrne, moving to College Station to become the head coach at Texas A&M was not my first choice, just as I had not been Bill Byrne's first choice to follow Gillom as A&M's head coach. As soon as he fired Gillom, Byrne initially offered the job to Leon Barmore, who had retired as Louisiana Tech's head coach following the 2001–2 season. Barmore eventually came out of retirement to join Kim Mulkey's staff at Baylor in 2008, but he turned down Byrne's offer in 2003. Mulkey had turned down A&M numerous times previously, because—before Byrne—she knew the administration was not seriously committed to women's basketball.

Nan and I sat down together, weighed the pros and cons of accepting the A&M opportunity, and discussed the logistics of maintaining a marriage while residing roughly 500 miles apart from each other for much of the year. Quite frankly, it probably wouldn't have worked if we were younger, and it definitely wouldn't work for many couples at any age. But Nan and I have always had a unique relationship, and we both knew that we could make it work for as long as it was necessary. We also knew that if we were miserable or if the distance threatened our marriage, we could do something different.

The bottom line, however, is that both of us are extremely driven, career-oriented, and independent. Other than those shared qualities, we are probably the perfect example of "opposites attracting." I love so many aspects of coaching at the collegiate level, including attending the fundraising and social events that require mingling with donors, entertaining fans, engaging with media members, networking with colleagues, and speaking to large audiences. My wife, on the other hand, is not particularly comfortable in those types of environments. She can easily lead a lecture, write a grant, or develop a strong nursing curriculum. In contrast, I am a gregarious, outgoing, long-winded social butterfly who is the living, breathing personification of a run-on sentence or an infomercial spokesman. While my wife loves quiet time at home and being with our family, I enjoy the media spotlight and being in the public eye. She likes intimate conversations; I love working crowded rooms. We're just different that way, although she accompanied me in plenty of those situations throughout my coaching career. In fact, I cannot adequately thank her enough for stepping outside her comfort zone so many times through the years as she moved our family and her thriving career to follow me from South Oak Cliff to Louisiana Tech and then from Stephen F. Austin to Arkansas.

When the A&M opportunity was presented, however, Nan didn't want to move again for numerous reasons. When we had moved to Arkansas from Nacogdoches a decade earlier, both of our children were young enough that leaving friends and established connections wasn't that big of a deal, but that was no longer the case. Their roots were firmly entrenched in Fayetteville. Besides, we were quite secure in our commitment to each other and our trust in one another after 24 years of marriage. Furthermore, Nan's career as an associate professor and the director of the University of Arkansas Eleanor Mann School of Nursing was thriving, and we'd already built our dream house in Fayetteville, where we planned to eventually retire and host our grandchildren. (Paige married Beau Thompson, a high school basketball coach in Arkansas, in 2006, and they now have three children: Logan, 13; Lola, 6; and Landry, 4.)

My family was far too established in Fayetteville to make a move to College Station, which is why I had hoped for a contract extension at Arkansas. But when that didn't happen, I realized that at 57, this might be my last chance to coach in one of the "power conferences" and also likely my last chance to return to the Lone Star State, where Kim Mulkey was rocking-and-rolling at Baylor and Texas Tech's Marsha Sharp and Texas' Jody Conradt had established their respective programs as national powers. I'm from Texas, and my entire coaching career has been in the South. I wasn't ever going to be comfortable going to another region of the country, and I couldn't even envision being recruited to a school on the West Coast or the Northeast.

I essentially had only two options: either roll the dice and take a major gamble by coaching at Arkansas during the last year of my contract with the hope of somehow convincing the chancellor that I was, indeed, the right man for the job or go to Texas A&M where I would make significantly more money and have the security of a multiyear contract. A&M wasn't a perfect situation because it required moving away from my family, but with my wife's support, I decided to go for it. I left a talented program at Arkansas that had become a prominent postseason player for a school with a depleted roster and an unhealthy self-image in terms of its overall basketball reputation and potential.

On the women's front, A&M certainly didn't have much history on its side. After all, the school was founded as an all-male military institution in 1876, and school officials waited another 87 years before reluctantly admitting female students in 1963. More than a decade later, when the decision was made to sanction women's athletics as part of the athletic department on June 15, 1975, 10 full scholarships were shared among 53 of the 120 athletes who competed in eight sports in the Association for Intercollegiate Athletics for Women. Under the direction of Kay Don, the first women's basketball coach and assistant athletic director for women, the total women's athletic budget for the first year was $91,000 and encompassed salaries, uniforms, equipment, and travel expenses. Out of necessity, though, almost all the female athletes used their own equipment and the women also helped raise funds by cleaning debris and concession items left in the stands at Kyle Field after football games. By 1977, the women's basketball team finally was given its own locker room, a converted men's dressing room at G. Rollie White Coliseum. They dressed up the facility by placing silk flowers in the urinals.

Female athletes weren't even allowed to eat at the old athletic dormitory, Cain Hall, where the men dined, until 1980. And it wasn't until 1984—Lynn Hickey's first year as the head basketball coach—that tickets were sold for women's basketball games. Hickey, who was hired as the women's athletic director and head basketball coach for an annual salary of $40,000, helped transition A&M women's athletics into the modern era. But she still had to deal with plenty of obstacles. "I had just come from Kansas State, where we had our own band, our games were on television, we had our own set of cheerleaders and I came to A&M and there were no yell leaders and no band," Hickey told Richard Croome of the *Bryan-College Station Eagle* in 2015. "I went to see the band director at that time and he just said, 'Lynn we just don't have time, we can't do this,' so he gave me a copy of their eight-track tapes and said, 'You can play this during your game.' I went 'Oh my God,' and I left his office in tears."

A&M eventually produced some decent teams under Hickey (1985–94) and my former assistant at Stephen F. Austin, Candi Harvey (1994–98). During a three-year span that covered Hickey's last season as head coach and Harvey's first two years, the Aggies went to the Sweet Sixteen of the NCAA Tournament (1994), won the NWIT championship (1995), and won the last Southwest Conference Tournament title (1996) to earn a return trip to the NCAA Tournament. But that was the entire extent of A&M's postseason history, and the program fell on hard times as soon as the Aggies moved into the Big 12 in 1996–97. Toward the end of the Peggie Gillom era, attendance at women's games in the 12,900-seat Reed Arena was so miniscule that the handful of fans that attended games could often hear what the coaches were saying during timeouts in the team huddles—and even in the locker rooms if coaches were particularly loud.

Nevertheless, I was excited about the possibilities at Texas A&M, even though it had been extremely difficult to say good-bye to my players at Arkansas. While the chancellor was not in my corner, the players meant the world to me. In fact, I literally broke into tears during a 35-minute meeting with the Arkansas team on March 31, 2003, and I had to fight back tears while addressing the media later that day. The 10 years at Arkansas had been so good for me and my family, and I was bitter about the chancellor's desire to replace me with a woman. Not any particular woman, just a woman. In fact, I let some of that bitterness leak out in my final Arkansas press conference when asked about not having my contract renewed, saying "Maybe Bev's hands were tied." I stopped short of saying that it was Chancellor

John White who did the tying, but it didn't take much creativity to connect the dots.

Upon my departure, the rumors began circulating about possible replacements. Some of the names mentioned included my top assistant at Arkansas, Vic Schaefer, and then-TCU head coach Jeff Mittie. But I knew neither of them had a real chance because they both had hair on their chests.

Not surprisingly, Arkansas did hire a woman, as former Georgia player and Austin Peay head coach Susie Gardner was introduced as the Lady'Backs' head coach after guiding Austin Peay to three consecutive Ohio Valley Conference titles. Unfortunately for Arkansas, Gardner did not enjoy similar success in Fayetteville. While she compiled an overall four-year record of 64–54, Gardner's teams never made it to the NCAA Tournament and never produced a winning record in SEC play. Arkansas was 16–40 during her tenure in conference play. She resigned at the conclusion of the 2006–7 season following a 10-game losing streak to close the year. That streak broke the record of nine straight losses set by the previous year's team.

Fortunately for me, Arkansas' decision to hire Gardner allowed me bring two of my assistants, Schaefer and Kelly Bond, to College Station, while Amber Shirey elected to stay at her alma mater. Schaefer undoubtedly would have stayed at Arkansas if he had been given an opportunity to be head coach, but since that wasn't the case, he interviewed for the head coaching job at New Mexico State. He believed it was time for him to be a head coach, and there's no question that he could have been a great one right then. But New Mexico State was not an ideal destination, and I did not give up on luring Vic and his family to College Station because I had one major thing going for me: his roots. Schaefer, an All-State player at Houston Lutheran High School before going on to play two seasons at Alvin Community College, graduated from Texas A&M in 1984. The opportunity to return to College Station to raise his twins was certainly enticing, and he ultimately decided it was the best choice.

By that time, Kelly Bond had also proven to be a sensational coach who could relate to the players exceptionally well because she had been in their shoes. Bond played point guard—a natural leadership position—for the University of Illinois and helped the Illini to back-to-back NCAA Sweet Sixteen appearances. She also led the squad to the 1997 Big 10 Championship. And her Chicago roots helped us expand our recruiting reach. She played high school basketball for the legendary Chicagoland coach Arthur Penny at Whitney Young High School. We also hired another point guard in Amy Tennison, who had once starred at Duncanville High School and then went on to become the Southland Conference Freshman of the Year at Sam Houston State. Before joining our staff, Tennison, a 1999 graduate of Sam Houston, was the head coach at Cedar Hill High School and had also been an AAU coach.

As I've mentioned before, you must surround yourself with great people if you want to accomplish great things. It's a necessity at any school, business, or organization. But I believed it was especially important to hire a great staff at Texas A&M because our task was not just to rebuild a program but to completely change the basketball culture. We had to convince the student body that attending women's basketball games was more fun than going to the library. We had to sell a community that wasn't accustomed to attending basketball games that sitting courtside could be far more entertaining that sitting at home and watching *The Bachelorette*, *Survivor*, or *American Idol*—some of the most popular reality television shows in 2003. And most important, we absolutely had to find a way to connect with our prospective fan base. I knew it wasn't going to be easy to win games right away, but if we could win the hearts of prospective fans, we could generate some excitement that we could then sell to recruits and to everyone else. Doing that required some serious grassroots marketing efforts. I was determined to walk from store to store and from door to door to introduce myself to business owners, homeowners, and students in an effort to persuade them—or beg them, if necessary—to give us a chance. And to do that, I absolutely had to rely on my assistants. I am not the brightest or best coach in the country, but I have learned to lean on my assistants and delegate as well as any coach in the game. And in looking back on where we started and how much we've accomplished at Texas A&M, I am ever so thankful to Vic, Kelly, and Amy, along with Erich Birch, Johnnie Harris, Bob Starkey, Amy Wright, and all my other assistants.

I am also forever thankful to my family for allowing me to totally immerse myself in Aggieland. With my wife and kids back in Fayetteville, I was on the job full time, all the time, doing everything possible to make friends in the community, recruit players, and win the favor of fans. Right away, I began studying the people of Bryan–College Station and committed myself to learning what being an Aggie was all about. I knew some facts, but I didn't know the real history of the university and its evolution. That was a big part of my job that first year as I began drinking the maroon Kool-Aid and embracing the traditions of Texas A&M. I learned right away, for example, that Texas A&M graduates loathe being referred to as ex-Aggies or alumni. There's no such thing, I quickly learned, because once an Aggie, you're always an Aggie. Graduates of Texas A&M are "former students," not exes. There's a big difference. I read books about Texas A&M's military heritage and the great leaders the school had produced: Medal of Honor recipient Horace C. Carswell, Class of 1938 and the namesake for Carswell Air Force Base in Fort Worth; General James E. Rudder, Class of '32, commander of World War II's historic Pointe du Hoc battle (part of the Invasion of Normandy), and the 16th president of Texas A&M; Henry Cisneros, Class of '68 and the first Hispanic mayor of a US city (San Antonio); George P. Mitchell, Class of '40, the former CEO of Mitchell Energy, pioneer of fracking technologies, and a real estate developer who is essentially the father of The Woodlands; Rick Perry, a former yell leader from the class of '72 and the 47th governor of Texas from 2000 until 2015; and so many other remarkable leaders.

I also studied the school's football heroes: 1940 Heisman Trophy runner-up John Kimbrough, who was the star of the 1939 national championship team; 1957 Heisman Trophy winner John David Crow; All-Americans like Joe Boyd, Jack Pardee, Dave Elmendorf, Lester Hayes, Jacob Green, Ray Childress, and Kevin Smith; 1998 Lombardi and Chuck Bednarik Award winner Dat Nguyen; and legendary coaches like D. X. Bible, Homer Norton, Bear Bryant, Jackie Sherrill, and R. C. Slocum. I also learned the story of the 12th Man tradition, which dates back to the Dixie Classic—the predecessor to the Cotton Bowl—on January 2, 1922. With injuries mounting on his beleaguered team and powerful Centre College out to a 7–3 lead, head coach D. X. Bible recalled that one of his former players, E. King Gill, was working in the press box, serving as a spotter for Jinx Tucker of the *Waco News-Tribune*. Bible called A&M head yell leader Harry "Red" Thompson to the bench and sent Thompson to the press box to retrieve Gill. Once Gill made it to the sidelines, Bible asked him to dress in the uniform of an injured player. Gill never played, but Thompson was so excited about the Aggies' comeback victory and so impressed by Gill's willingness to answer the Aggies' call that he scheduled a yell practice on the steps of the YMCA as soon as the team and students returned to campus. At that yell practice, Thompson first used the words "12th man" in reference to Gill. Ever since, Texas A&M has been known nationally as "the home of the 12th Man." From one generation to the next, students at A&M have stood throughout games as a symbol of their willingness to follow Gill's lead and answer the Aggies' call, if necessary.

The more I studied, the more impressed I was with Texas A&M, and I became convinced that we could build a tradition of excellence at A&M in women's basketball. I was also determined to start right away by building up our players and coaching them up. Everybody knew that Texas A&M had struggled and that the roster was not loaded with McDonald's All-Americans. Quite frankly, I wouldn't have been hired if everything had been peachy. Things were in disarray, but as a staff, we were not going to throw the players that we inherited under the bus. If we treated them right and showed them the respect they deserved, they would serve as ambassadors to help recruit others. I wanted our current players to believe that being part of Blair's first team was special. That was so important to me because I have heard many coaches blame their predecessor, the current roster, or the administration for not marketing them. We weren't going to blame anyone, and we were going to embrace our players and the building process.

I took that message to the 12th Man Foundation's 2003 summer board meeting at the picturesque Keystone Resort, some 70 miles west of Denver. The 12th Man Foundation is the fundraising organization of Texas A&M athletics, and the attendees at that meeting included many of the most significant, powerful, and affluent supporters of Texas A&M athletics. Two new coaches were invited to speak at those meetings: new football coach Dennis Franchione and me. Obviously, Franchione was the headliner of the meetings, but I was thankful for the opportunity to speak to the group at a luncheon on the final day of meetings. I recall how my coauthor, Rusty Burson, then of the *12th Man Magazine*, introduced me before my speech. As we waited for everyone to be seated and served, we had a short but memorable conversation in which he asked me, "Coach, have you ever heard of Huey Lewis and the News?" I was puzzled but acknowledged that I was familiar with the San Francisco–based rock band that had produced one hit after another in the 1980s. Then I asked him the meaning behind that question.

"Well, I'm pretty sure that 'Bad Is Bad' could be the theme song for Aggie women's basketball," he said. "Look, don't take this the wrong way, but why in the world would you leave a place like Arkansas—where you took a team to the Final Four—to come to a place like Texas A&M? Do you realize what you are getting yourself into? I know you have seen the records, but do you realize just how bad this program really is?"

I smiled and pointed out the window toward the largest mountain in Summit County and told him that I would not be at A&M if I didn't think we were capable of climbing mountains to reach unprecedented heights. That was also my message to the donors, many of whom had probably never been to a women's basketball game at A&M. Even Rusty—a reporter who covered A&M athletics—acknowledged that the only reason he had gone to a handful of games in recent years was because his kids were intrigued by the five-pound candy bar the marketing staff gave away to one lucky fan each game. With so few fans in the stands, his kids were sure they could win the candy bar, which they occasionally did. As I addressed the donors, I talked about winning much more than a candy bar. I had all the women in the audience stand up and I deputized them. I told them all it was up to them to go back to their homes to begin promoting Texas A&M women's basketball and help us recruit players. I talked about attracting the top high school players in Texas to Reed Arena, building a fan base, and competing in the Big 12, where Texas, Texas Tech, Kansas State, and Oklahoma had all been nationally ranked in '03 and where Baylor was clearly on the rise. I encouraged the donors to embrace my vision, to fill the empty seats at Reed Arena, to take ownership in our program, and to send their tallest daughters and granddaughters to me immediately. People laughed, although most of them probably thought I was suffering from altitude sickness in the thin Keystone air as I talked about my vision. But that was the start of our campaign to win the hearts of former A&M students and fans, and I think my message at least intrigued some people.

When I returned to College Station, I continued that message everywhere I went. As the summer turned into fall, I went to every A&M sporting event—football games, volleyball games, and soccer games—to meet students and fans and to encourage them to attend women's basketball games. And then once we were close enough to the season to print tickets, I began passing out tickets to anyone who would listen to me and take them. My first home in Aggieland was in the Park Meadow subdivision in Bryan, and I began walking the streets with tickets in hand, knocking on one door after another.

I remember one Baptist pastor invited me into his home, many people engaged me in lengthy conversations, and I began building relationships one person at a time. People didn't know me, but they could tell I cared about Texas A&M, and few people rejected free tickets. Word began to spread about the head coach who was pitching his team door-to-door, and KBTX News 3 sports director Darryl Bruffett followed me with his television crew one day to spread the news. I also called in to local sports talk radio shows and offered tickets to listeners. I once called in to a show hosted by Robert Cessna, the sports editor of the *Eagle*, to tell listeners that I was on my way home and gave out my home address in case anyone was interested in tickets. I had barely been home a few minutes before heard a knock on the door. I opened it to find a barefoot young man with long hair and shorts standing on my front porch. Before I could say a word, he said, "Coach, I am here for some tickets." I suppose I could've been murdered at that moment, and once my wife heard what I had done, she told me to never give out my home address again. I learned my lesson, but maybe he came to a game.

In addition to my door-to-door efforts, I joined the Rotary Club, just as I had done at Arkansas and Stephen F. Austin. I spoke to civic clubs, Aggie Mothers' Clubs, campus clubs, women's clubs, and anyone else who was interested in me—or at least pretended to be. I'd take tickets to the donut stores on Saturday mornings, pizza buffets in the afternoons, and restaurants at night. We also introduced "Kids' Court" inside the practice gym before games, allowing children to shoot baskets, make crafts, play on the inflatables, and participate in other activities before tip-off. If you can entertain the kids, the parents will follow.

In the midst of all the promotions and talks I was making, we also managed to recruit a few players and prepare our team for our first season. We signed a couple of junior college players, landing guard Erica Roy from Little Rock, Arkansas, and Fort Smith Junior College, and guard Charlette Castile from Duncanville and Paris Junior College. Erica, a sophomore, immediately started in the backcourt with senior guard Toccara Williams, while the starting frontcourt included senior center Lynn Classen, senior forward Janae Derrick, and sophomore Tamea Scales.

To say that we experienced growing pains that first year would be a huge understatement. We struggled, stumbled, and stammered our way to an overall record of 9–19, which represented the first losing season in my entire career as a basketball coach. We also tied Kansas for last place in the Big 12 standings at 2–14 in league play, a mere 12 games behind Texas and Kansas State, which tied for the conference title at 14–2. Statistically, we were last in the Big 12 Conference in free-throw percentage, field goal percentage, field goal percentage defense, three-point field goal percentage defense, rebounding offense, rebounding defense, rebounding margin, and assists. We were also next to last in scoring offense. We obviously didn't do many things particularly well in the 2003–4 season.

Nevertheless, I had never been more proud of a team's effort and improvement from one year to the next than at that point in my career. We didn't win many games, but we competed every night and made dramatic improvements. Nine of our 19 losses were by six points or less, which led me to begin writing a "plus sign" on my left hand with a Sharpie prior to games as a reminder to "stay positive." The close home losses also often led me to the Fox and Hound for a postgame beer to drown my oh-so-close tears. I always limited it to one beer so I could then go home and watch the game tape. But the bartenders definitely grew to know me well. As soon as I would sit down, one of them would always ask, "Did you lose another close one?" He would already have a Coors Light draft drawn for me.

The answer was often "yes." We lost to No. 24 Baylor at home by three points in a game we had led by 16 at the half; No. 3 Texas escaped Reed Arena with a 64–62 win; No. 7 Texas Tech beat us by one point at Reed Arena on Valentine's Day after we had a three-point lead with 20 seconds remaining; and No. 8 Kansas State outlasted us by three points four days later. After the close loss to Texas, Jody Conradt shook our hands and said, "I'd rather go to the dentist and get a root canal than play you guys." We took our compliments where we could, and we definitely were encouraged.

Even in some of the more lopsided losses, we made great strides. A&M had gone to Lubbock the year before and endured a 45-point loss, 83–38, in what was Tech's 22nd consecutive home win over the Aggies. But when we returned to Texas Tech in January 2004, we were down by one at that half and were shooting to cut the lead to three with a wide-open lay-up with three minutes to go. We eventually lost the game, 65–56, but we had earned the Red Raiders' respect, and people could clearly see the progress. I think we also put the Big 12 on notice that evening because we weren't going to be lifeless punching bags anymore. We were going to play hard, force the issue defensively, and compete every time we took the floor. Texas Tech realized that on January 28, 2004. And to my delight, our fans began to notice, too, as we began to draw interest from the Bryan–College Station community. A&M averaged 1,403 fans per home game in 2002–3, and that number increased to 2,403 in 2003–4. The Texas game attracted 4,336, while the Baylor game crowd of 5,565 set a Reed Arena record.

I'm sure some of those fans were kids who begged their parents to bring them because I was passing out candy in the stands before the games (an idea I stole from Van Chancellor when he was with the Houston Comets), but whatever the case, we significantly increased attendance from one year to another—despite being a last-place team. There were still issues to overcome, of course, like convincing fans and even athletic department staff members that a conference basketball game was more important than attending a football recruiting party. On the night of February 4, 2004, we were scheduled to play Oklahoma State at Reed Arena at 7 p.m., but some of the staff members within the athletic department and 12th Man Foundation asked me to move the game to 5 p.m. so that head football coach Dennis Franchione could have a bigger audience at his signing day social at

Kyle Field. In no uncertain terms, I said, "Hell no." Not only did I feel like I needed to stand my ground and not move my game time, but I really felt disrespected. After all, we were at least making great strides in our first season at A&M. In his first football season, Franchione's team was pummeled by Texas Tech (58–29), Nebraska (48–12), Oklahoma State (38–10), Missouri (45–22), and Texas (46–15). And in the worst defeat in Texas A&M football history, Oklahoma plastered the Aggies, 77–0. It could have been worse, as Oklahoma practically refused to score in the fourth quarter.

Incidentally, we beat Oklahoma State that night, 65–52, in our only conference home win of the year. We finished that season tied for last place, and Texas A&M's men's basketball team—in its final year under Melvin Watkins—finished dead last, despite having two future NBA Lottery Draft picks (Antoine Wright and Acie Law) on the roster. The A&M men went 0–16 in Big 12 play (0–17 including the opening-round loss in the conference tournament). The combined conference record of the Texas A&M women's and men's teams in 2003–4 was 2–30, which made us the worst basketball program in the country among Division I-A schools that year. But it's always darkest right before dawn, and I could sense things were about to change for the better.

First and foremost, the A&M fans weren't the only ones buying into our vision. Before that first season had even begun, we signed A&M's most impressive recruiting class in a decade by landing Morenike Atunrase (Shreveport/Southwood), Patrice Reado (Houston/Madison), LaToya Gulley (Fayetteville, AR/Fayetteville High School), and Ashley Bolden (Houston/Westfield). (Fellow class members A'Quonesia Franklin [Tyler/John Tyler] and Katy Pounds [Shallowater High School] signed their letters of intent after the early signing period.) It was a really good class—ranked in the top 25 nationally by the recruiting gurus—and it gave us a truly strong foundation. But we weren't exactly beating out the superpowers in women's basketball to sign them. Morenike, a 5-foot-10 forward from Shreveport, Louisiana's Southwood High School, was rated as the No. 111 best player nationally and was a *Street and Smith* honorable mention All-American. But when it came right down to it, neither LSU nor Louisiana Tech was recruiting Morenike in her home state. It came down to TCU, Tulane, and us, and she believed enough in our vision to come to Aggieland. It was similar with most of the other recruits. In almost every case, we were competing for these players with some of the major basketball powerhouses.

Adding that first recruiting class upgraded our overall talent level tremendously, and it signified brighter times ahead for Aggie women's basketball.

Another event my first year that had a significant impact on Texas A&M's basketball image, as well as the basketball facilities on campus, was men's head coach Melvin Watkins's resignation in early March. In six years at A&M, Watkins's teams went 60–111. A couple of weeks later, Bill Byrne announced the hiring of Texas–El Paso head coach Billy Gillispie, a Texas native who took UTEP from 6 wins and 24 losses in his first season at the school (2002–3) to 24 wins and only 8 losses the following year. The Miners won the WAC, advanced to the NCAA Tournament, and nearly upset Maryland in the first round. Gillispie was named the 2004 Texas Coach of the Year by the TABC and was a finalist for National Coach of the Year honors. At A&M, he inherited a roster with a couple of tremendously talented players (particularly future NBA players Antoine Wright and Acie Law) and a recruiting class that featured a major building block in center Joseph Jones.

Gillispie made an immediate impact at A&M, instilling a level of toughness, tenacity, and defensive intensity that didn't exist during Watkins's tenure. The overachieving Aggie men won 21 games—14 more than the previous season. They advanced to the quarterfinals of the NIT, marking the deepest postseason run for A&M since 1982. The men's team also attracted the four largest crowds ever to watch a basketball game in College Station, as A&M went 17–3 at home and 8–8 in Big 12 play (the best conference record for the men since the inception of the league).

Similarly, we also made major strides in 2004–5. Two true freshmen (forward Morenike Atunrase and point guard A'Quonesia Franklin) moved immediately into our starting lineup, joining the two junior college transfers (Charlette Castile and Erica Roy) we had signed upon arriving at A&M and Tamea Scales. Atunrase was the Big 12 Freshman of the Year and the only player in the conference to rank in the top four among the league's freshmen in scoring, rebounding, steals, and blocks. Franklin ranked second in the Big 12 in assist-to-turnover ratio, dishing out 155 assists with only 50 turnovers.

We lost our first game of the year to South Florida in a tournament in Miami, but then we rolled to nine consecutive wins over Bucknell, Tulane, Cleveland State, Texas–San Antonio, Texas State, McNeese State, Northwestern State, Arkansas–Little Rock, and North Texas (not exactly "murderer's row"). We were 9–1 heading into our conference opener against No. 3 Baylor and drew a good crowd of 4,383 on a Wednesday night. We gave the fans plenty to cheer about as the game was tied at 44–all with just eight minutes left. Unfortunately, Baylor, led by All-American Sophia Young, outscored us 20–6 to close the game and pulled away en route to a 64–50 victory. That Baylor team turned out to be pretty good, as the Lady Bears went 33–3 and finished the season with 20 straight victories to win the national championship. I was certainly happy for Kim Mulkey, who became the first woman to play for a national championship team and then coach one. Seeing Baylor win the national title—just five years after Mulkey took over a team that had gone 7–20 and was last in the Big 12—also provided an inspiring example for our players. If Baylor could complete that kind of turnaround, so could we.

Of course, we first had to learn how to finish games—unlike our conference opener against Baylor and most of our games the rest of the season. We closed out the year at 4–12 in conference play and 14–14 following our opening-round loss to Oklahoma in the Big 12 Tournament. While it wasn't a great season, it was good enough to earn a spot in the 2005 WNIT, as we joined the men's program in the postseason, marking just the second time in school history that both squads advanced to play past the regular season (the first time was in 1993–94 when Lynn Hickey took the women to the Sweet Sixteen of the NCAAs and Tony Barone took the men to the NIT).

The men won their first two games in the NIT, beating Clemson at home and winning at DePaul before losing in the quarterfinals, 58–51, to St. Joseph's before a sellout crowd of 13,151. While many schools barely draw a crowd at NIT or WNIT games, A&M fans were so hungry for basketball success that the school sold thousands of NIT T-shirts and exceeded the capacity of Reed Arena in the men's quarterfinals game. Like the men, we also advanced to the quarterfinals of the 2005 WNIT, beating Tulsa and Texas A&M–Corpus Christi at Reed Arena in the first two rounds. In the first round against Tulsa, we drew a spectacular crowd of 8,532. After winning the first two games, we also lost in the quarterfinals at Southwest Missouri State. We played an awful first half and fell behind 37–21 at the half, but we rallied to tie the game on an Erica Roy jumper with 2:10 left. The Lady Bears then hit two free throws to regain the lead, and we had a missed three-point attempt with just four seconds left that ended our season. Missouri State went on to win the WNIT, and we finished the season at 16–15. The men went 21–10, which led school officials to begin talking about building new practice facilities and locker rooms at Reed Arena.

Originally, the plan was to use existing space on the lower level to expand the facility underground, which would have cost approximately $3 million. But as plans and discussions progressed, the 2005–6 season approached. We added another strong recruiting class that included three more building blocks in 6-foot-3 post La Toya Micheaux (the daughter of former

University of Houston star Larry Micheaux, of "Phi Slamma Jamma" fame) from Missouri City Hightower, 5-foot-8 guard Takia Starks from Houston Westfield, and 5-foot-10 guard/forward Danielle Gant from Oklahoma City's Putnam City West.

Gillispie also added some integral recruiting pieces in 6-foot-10 junior college transfer Antanas Kavaliauskas and outside shooting specialist Josh Carter. The men started slowly in conference play and were only 3–6 following a loss at No. 7 Texas on February 4. But from that point forward, A&M won its final seven games and then won a game at the Big 12 Tournament for the first time. That was enough to earn the men a bid to the NCAA Tournament for the first time since 1987, where the Aggies sent shockwaves throughout the college basketball world by stunning Big East Tournament champion Syracuse in the opening round. The remarkable run came to an end seconds short of the Sweet Sixteen in a 58–57 loss to LSU at Jacksonville's Veterans Memorial Arena. But the success and the excitement generated by the men in 2006 played a huge role in dramatically changing the scope and grandeur of the proposed basketball facility additions at Reed Arena.

Instead of a $3 million facelift, it became a remarkable and magnificent makeover. After touring a couple other Big 12 basketball facilities with Bill Byrne and representatives from the 12th Man Foundation, longtime Texas A&M supporters and donors Jerry and Kay Cox pledged a lead gift of $4 million toward the project. I will never forget Jerry saying, "Let's build this thing right from the start!" Then Artie and Dorothy McFerrin followed suit with another $4 million pledge. The project grew to a $24 million, 68,000-square-foot facility that featured a foyer rotunda entrance, two practice gymnasiums, significantly larger locker room facilities than what the men's and women's teams previously used, players' lounges, coaches' offices, a weight room, team meeting rooms, a training/medical room, and video rooms. The Cox-McFerrin Center, as the facility became known, further elevated our basketball image and our ability to recruit premier players.

The men's success was the catalyst for the sensational new facilities, but the women also contributed to the overall momentum. We upgraded our nonconference schedule significantly in 2005–6, registering quality wins over Washington, UNLV, and Utah State. Once the conference race started, we were 5–3 when we kicked off an impressive stretch that began with a 65–48 win over Texas Tech, our first victory over the Lady Raiders since the championship game of the 1996 Southwest Conference Tournament (a stretch of

19 games). That made us 17–5 overall, and the following day we entered the Associated Press Top 25 for the first time since March 11, 1996.

We followed up that win with a more impressive victory, as we throttled Texas, 73–53, at the Erwin Center. It was the first win in Austin since 1995 and the largest margin of victory against the Longhorns on their home court. It also stopped Texas' 31-game home conference winning streak. We closed the regular season with three more wins, including a 79–67 home win over Texas. It marked the first time since 1995 that A&M had swept the regular season series with Texas.

We ended the regular season at 22–7, marking the first 20-win season for the A&M women since 1995–96. We also went 11–5 in the Big 12, which put us in a third-place tie and represented A&M's highest conference finish since 1994–95. We won our opening game at the Big 12 Tournament in Dallas, beating Nebraska, 73–64. We lost to Baylor for the third time in the season in the semifinals, but we made a statement in the loss. Sophia Young scored 29 points to lead the Bears to a 53–52 victory. The game featured 11 lead changes and 11 ties. "They play hard, they gamble, they make it tough on you, they contest shots," Baylor coach Kim Mulkey said of our team afterward. "I just thought they gave an effort that was just outstanding."

If we would have played that well in our next game—the first round of the NCAA Tournament—we would have been in great shape. Instead, we chose a bad time to play one of our worst games of the year. Our first NCAA Tournament appearance since 1996 was against TCU in Trenton, New Jersey. We were the sixth seed, while the Horned Frogs, who were just 2–27 against the Aggies when both were in the Southwest Conference, were 11th. The Horned Frogs were also playing without their leading scorer and rebounder, Natasha Lacy. But that didn't matter. We were just 1-for-12 on three-pointers in the first 20 minutes, which is a big reason we were down 11 at the half. We made it close late in the game, but lost, 69–65, for a disappointing finish to our breakthrough year. Nevertheless, we had taken a massive step in the right direction. Morenike Atunrase was selected to the All-Big 12 first team, while A'Quonesia Franklin was an honorable mention selection. Women's Basketball News Service also named Takia Starks to its national All-Freshman Team. The same organization honored me as the National Coach of the Year, which was really shared by my entire staff. Those honors are nice, but they are actually a reflection of the staff and the team.

Clearly, we had turned a corner, and with most of our roster returning for 2006-7, we set the bar even higher. We didn't just want to get back to the tournament in '07; we wanted to contend for the first conference title in school history. It was a lofty goal for a squad that was just 2–14 in the league three seasons earlier, but we all believed it was within our reach. We began the 2006–7 season with a 10-day team-bonding tour of Europe in August, where we played five games against foreign competition in France, Switzerland, and Monaco. We won all five games, but the trip also provided our players a great life experience in Europe. We became closer as a team and from a historical point of view.

Once we returned, we began receiving plenty of attention. We were ranked ninth nationally by *Sports Illustrated*'s website poll and in *Street and Smith's College Basketball Yearbook*, marking the highest preseason national ranking and overall national ranking in school history. In October, we were picked to finish second in the Big 12 in a vote of the league's coaches behind defending champion Oklahoma. Typically, I am guarded about preseason rankings and expectations, but I welcomed them at that point because they really helped boost our confidence.

We started the season well, going 10–2 in nonconference, but then we lost our opening Big 12 game at Kansas State. We bounced back to win a close game at Texas Tech (49–47) and then returned home to face Baylor for Dollar Day, which was presented by Campbell Custom Homes. Dollar Day specials included tickets and concession items while supplies lasted. We had done the same promotion the previous year and attracted a school record of 11,088 fans. But a couple of things went awry during the 2006 promotion. First, there weren't enough concession stands open or not enough workers to handle the near-sellout crowd. I was told over and over by many people who attended the game that they missed most of the first half waiting in the ridiculously long lines. We messed up big-time there.

We also messed up big-time on the court. Baylor went on a 25–8 run in the first half to take control of the game. We struggled from the field during part of the stretch, missing seven straight shots over six minutes. Baylor also took advantage of 11 turnovers by converting them into 14 points in the first half. Overall, Baylor scored 23 points off of 19 of our miscues and coasted to an 84–59 win. It was ugly—even though I didn't see all of it. With 8:57 left in the game, I was issued back-to-back technical fouls following a basket by Takia Starks and what I thought should have been called a charge taken by A'Quonesia Franklin. I was ejected because, according to referee Clarke Stevens, I came out onto the floor complaining about the block. I deserved that first technical, but then he gave me another one and ejected me because he said I continued walking onto the court. To this day, I don't believe I should have been ejected. The official said I didn't leave the court in a timely matter, even though I was already walking toward my bench! In any event, we all stunk it up that night before the huge crowd, which made the next year's home game against Baylor even more important to our players.

The crowd wasn't as big (8,886), probably because so many of the people who had shown up the previous year had left frustrated. But those who showed up saw a fantastic game that filled us with confidence. The Lady Bears opened the game with a 17–5 run as we missed 14 of our first 16 shots, many of them uncontested. We also coughed up four turnovers in the first eight minutes. After a timeout, however, I was able to settle our girls down and we went on a quick 7–0 run that shifted momentum back in our favor. Baylor never solved our tenacious, league-leading scoring defense, shooting 35 percent from the field. Takia Starks produced a double-double (12 points, 11 rebounds) to lead us to a 60–52 win that broke a 13-game losing streak to Baylor. More significantly, it was our first win over a top-10 ranked team since A&M defeated No. 5 Iowa State in January 2002 and made our girls truly believe that we could win the conference crown.

As the season progressed, we positioned ourselves to earn the championship by sweeping Baylor, Texas Tech, and Oklahoma during the same season for the first time since the school joined the Big 12. We then faced Texas on February 28, 2007, in the final regular season game of the year with a chance to win the championship. Earlier in the year, Texas had manhandled us, 64–45, in Austin to hand us our most lopsided loss of the year. In that first game against Texas, Tiffany Jackson scored 27 points and grabbed 14 rebounds for Texas, and the Longhorns forced 23 turnovers.

In the second game, we "limited" Jackson to 19 points, and A'Quonesia Franklin scored a career-high 27 points to lead us to a 67–60 win that earned us a share of the Big 12 Conference title. At 23–5 overall and 13–3 in the Big 12, we needed Baylor to beat Oklahoma to win the conference title outright. That didn't happen, so we shared the title with OU. That hardly mattered to the crowd of 7,478 fans (the fourth-largest crowd in school history), who began chanting, "Big 12 champs, Big 12 champs" in the final seconds as we won a regular-season conference title for the first time in school history and beat our arch rival in the process. After the game, our girls remained on the court, wearing their championship hats and T-shirts as we were presented with the Big 12 championship trophy. The crowd stood cheering as a banner proclaiming the title was unfurled. The win also marked our 18th straight win at home dating back to the previous year and gave us an unbeaten home record for the year (16–0) for the first time in school history.

We cut down the nets that day with the help of our key fans and faculty, who had stuck with us since the beginning.

By virtue of sweeping Oklahoma, we were the top seed in the Big 12 Tournament in Oklahoma City, where we opened with a 62–45 win over Colorado. We didn't play well in the next game, however, as we lost 57–51 to Iowa State, a setback that probably cost us in terms of our NCAA Tournament seeding. Still, we earned a four seed in making back-to-back NCAA Tournament appearances for the first time ever. We were placed in the Dallas Regional, but we first had to travel to Los Angeles for the opening two rounds.

We beat No. 13 seed Texas–Arlington on March 17 at the Galen Center in Los Angeles in front of a tiny crowd of maybe 400 people, which set us up to face Atlantic 10 Conference champion George Washington in the second round. A year ago that day, we had played poorly against TCU in the NCAA Tournament, and we did it again. We started well and built an early 16–8 lead. But the Colonials methodically gained the upper hand with a matchup zone defense, nicknamed "The Blizzard," that rattled us. After building the early lead, we were 0-for-8 shooting from the field with five turnovers in a 7-minute, 19-second span that allowed GW to turn an eight-point deficit into a 17–16 lead. We struggled offensively throughout much of the rest of the game against the Colonials, who gutted out a 59–47 victory. Fifth-seeded George Washington advanced to the Sweet Sixteen in Dallas, where it lost to top-seeded North Carolina.

The George Washington coach happened to be my best friend in the coaching business, Joe McKeown. I first met Joe back in the days when he was the assistant at Oklahoma (1983–86) before he became the head coach at New Mexico State (1987–89). He then spent the next 19 seasons at George Washington before going to Northwestern in 2008–9. When he knocked me out of the NCAA Tournament in Los Angeles, there were only about 300 people in attendance. It was an awful night for us, but I was happy for Joe.

In 19 seasons at George Washington, Joe was the winningest coach in Atlantic 10 Conference history. He has 15 NCAA tournament appearances, including three trips to the Sweet Sixteen. But McKeown left George Washington to take over Northwestern's long-struggling program because his high school–bound son, Joey, had been diagnosed with autism, and educational resources were lacking in Northern Virginia.

Joe went to the worst program in the Big 10, like I had gone to the worst program in the Big 12. We talked before he took the job, and he said he was just going to do this for his family and not complain about anything. But Joe gripes about everything.

When he beat us in Los Angeles, I was truly happy for him, but I agonized for our players and fans. The bottom line is that once again, our season ended in a disappointing fashion. In hindsight, winning the first-ever conference championship and finishing the highest final national ranking in school history with a No. 16 ranking in the final Associated Press Top 25 Poll signified that we were capable of reaching any goal and achieving even the loftiest milestones imaginable. In 2006–7, we were one of the top eight defenses in the country, holding opponents to 53.6 points per game. We played with tenacity and toughness, and with a spectacular new facility under construction at Reed Arena and a roster filling with talented veterans and excellent young players, we had a sense of purpose and a belief that bigger and better things were in our future. We believed we were headed straight to the top, and not just in our conference. We believed we could conquer the road to the Final Four in the very near future, which was saying something for a program that once lacked any sense of direction.

11 Maneuvering through March

On the night of October 14, 2003—exactly 95 years to the day that the 1908 Chicago Cubs wrapped up their second straight World Series title— Chicago led the Florida Marlins 3–0 in the top of the eighth inning at Wrigley Field. The Cubs also held a three-to-two lead in the best-of-seven National League Championship Series and were just five outs away from returning to the World Series for the first time since 1945. Wrigley was rocking with combustible energy and anticipation, as Cubs fans sensed the end of nine decades of disappointment and discontent.

Just as Cubs fans were sensing a sensational celebration, however, Florida infielder Luis Castillo lifted a foul pop fly down the left-field line just past the bullpen. Chicago outfielder Moises Alou hustled toward the stands, placed his bare hand on the padded wall, timed his jump perfectly, opened his glove wide, and made the—wait, no he didn't. Alou failed to catch what would have been the second out of the eighth inning because Cubs fan Steve Bartman reached up to catch the foul ball. Bartman, a 26-year-old youth baseball coach sitting in Section 4, Row 8, Seat 113, simply reacted like most fans would have with a foul ball drifting directly toward his seat. He stood, looked up, and lifted hands. The ball hit the heel of Bartman's hand and caromed farther back into the stands, preventing Alou from possibly making the catch and reducing the Cubs' magic number to just four more outs.

Inside the Marlins dugout—as Alou stomped his feet in frustration and fury—Florida pitcher Mark Redman turned to a teammate and said, "Let's make this kid famous." The Marlins did just that and won Game 7 the next night, adding to the Cubs' long list of postseason nightmares. Bartman was blamed, berated, and besieged by venomous Cubs fans who probably would've done the exact same thing.

The reality of the moment was that Bartman became the latest symbol—an easy, unassuming, naïve, defenseless target—of decades of postseason failures by a team that often referred to itself as "the loveable losers." If the Cubs hadn't blown multiple postseason opportunities since their last World Series title 95 years ago, Bartman probably wouldn't have been so tormented and cursed. But Cubs fans know—and can often recite—the franchise's sordid and sorrowful postseason past. They know the Cubs blew an 8–0 lead in Game 4 of the 1929 World Series because star outfielder Hack Wilson lost two fly balls in the sun and allowed the Philadelphia A's to score 10 runs in the eighth inning. They know that the Cubs lost Game 4 of the 1945 World Series after tavern owner Billy Sianis was denied admission to Wrigley because he refused to leave his smelly goat, Sonovia, outside. Sianis placed a "curse" on the team, saying they'd never play in a World Series again. Cubs fans also know about Game 5 of the 1984 NLCS when Leon Durham allowed a routine ground ball to go through his legs, which enabled the Padres to rally from a 3–2 deficit in the game. All those failures—and others—contributed to all the animosity that was dumped on Bartman. Although, as I write this in the fall of 2016, the Cubbies are having a pretty good year. Maybe the curse will be broken.

The bottom line is that sports fans ultimately judge a team's success or failure by its postseason history. Anybody who watched Dan Marino play throughout his brilliant professional career would likely rate him as one of the greatest quarterbacks in NFL history. Yet the fact that he never won a Super Bowl is like a scarlet letter that causes many sports fans and radio talk show hosts to regularly question the validity of his accomplishments and his status as one of the NFL's all-time best quarterbacks. Ditto with Fran Tarkenton, Dan Fouts, Jim Kelly, and Warren Moon. Conversely, it would be preposterous to argue that Brad Johnson, Trent Dilfer, or Jeff Hostetler belong in any discussion about the greatest quarterbacks in NFL history, but they tend to receive more credit and are given more respect because they were signal callers on Super Bowl championship teams.

The same goes for other sports and coaches as well. Jerry Sloan won 1,221 games in 26 seasons as an NBA coach, but he is often overlooked as one of the great all-time coaches because he never won an NBA title. Same with Gene Mauch or Jimmy Dykes in Major League Baseball. As the MLB television promo regularly reminds us each year during the baseball playoffs, "Legends are made in October." In college basketball, legends are made during the Madness of March.

Rick Majerus, Norm Stewart, Gene Keady, Lefty Driesell, Lou Carnesecca, John Chaney, Ray Meyer, Guy Lewis, and Eddie Sutton were all great men's college basketball coaches. Andy Landers, Vivian Stringer, Joe Ciampi, Jim Foster, Sue Gunter, and Kay Yow were all great women's basketball coaches. They never won a national title, however, which has undoubtedly negatively affected their reputation and overall legacy. What you do in college basketball in March determines your perceived value and worth as a coach. Period. That's also the case on the women's side. Geno Auriemma and Pat Summitt will always be considered among the greatest collegiate basketball coaches ever because of the multiple national championships they won at UConn (11) and Tennessee (8). They are in a legendary postseason class of their own on the women's side, one that could only be shared by the likes of John Wooden (10 national titles), Mike Krzyzewski (five through 2016), and Adolph Rupp (four national championships)—all of whom are in the College Basketball Hall of Fame—on the men's side. Winning one national title doesn't place you in the same elite class as those legends of the game, but it at least gets you into the same school.

Image, perception, and legacy are certainly not the reasons I became a coach, nor are they for most other coaches. Nevertheless, if you are any sort of competitor, you are certainly driven to be recognized as among the best in your field, whether that's an entrepreneurial endeavor, a corporate environment, professional athletics, or the coaching profession. Making a deep run in March Madness is what separates good college basketball teams from great ones, solid players from sensational ones, and respected coaches from revered ones. March is what matters most in our game. Always has, always will.

That's the focus we held entering the 2007–8 season. We were excited about making consecutive trips to the NCAA Tournament for the first time in school history and hanging the 2006–7 Big 12 championship banner from the rafters of Reed Arena, especially considering how far we had come in a span of four years. On the other hand, we had not done particularly well in March. In my first four seasons at A&M, we were 2–4 in the Big 12 Tournament, winning one game in '06 and one in '07 before being eliminated. Losing to Iowa State in the semifinals of the '07 Big 12 Tournament was particularly disappointing because we were the No. 1 seed after winning the regular-season conference crown. And in two trips to the NCAA Tournament, we were just 1–2 after being eliminated by lower seeds in both years. To ever be considered one of the great teams in America—even in our conference, for that matter—we needed to be better in March, and the 2007–8 season was a great time to start our ascension. After all, that roster was made for making a run in March.

We possessed great senior leadership with the players from our original recruiting class (Morenike Atunrase, Patrice Reado, LaToya Gulley, A'Quonesia Franklin, and Katy Pounds) still on the roster. We featured some stars in the junior class (Danielle Gant, Takia Starks, and La Toya Micheaux), and our younger players had dramatically improved our overall talent level. Our freshmen class in 2008, for example, included Maryann Baker from the Dallas area, who had been rated the No. 25 best shooting guard in the country; Houston's Sydney Colson, the No. 8 point guard in the country; and Kansas City shooting guard Tyra White, a McDonald's High School All-American, who had originally signed with LSU during the early period but was granted a full release in June, which made her eligible for the 2007–8 season. She was rated as one of the top 20 overall players in the country and was the Missouri Gatorade Player of the Year. Quite frankly, we were lucky to land White. We were at the right place at the right time with a scholarship available. Associate head coach Kelly Bond and assistant coach Johnnie Harris did an outstanding job in developing a relationship with White and staying with it through the middle of our current recruiting season. And our players also did a great job convincing her to come to A&M.

We began the season ranked in the top 10 nationally in many preseason polls, and we kicked off the year in mid-October with a modified "Midnight Madness" on our first day of practice, Friday, October 12. One thing you learn right away at Texas A&M is that you don't allow anything to conflict with Midnight Yell Practice at Kyle Field in the fall. The first time ESPN College GameDay—the football version—was held at Texas A&M was in November 2000, prior to an A&M–Oklahoma game. Of all the things they witnessed on campus, the GameDay personalities were most mesmerized by Yell Practice. "On Friday night, the school holds yell practice at midnight, where 25,000 people practice their yells in a pep rally," cohost Kirk Herbstreit wrote on ESPN.com after his 2000 trip to Aggieland. "It is amazing to see that many people that fired up. They're all doing the same thing, with no megaphone or speaker system to aide them. They have five yell leaders, who use hand signals to communicate each cheer. It's an incredible scene that carried over into Saturday's game." Cohost Chris Fowler added: "Aggie fans are accustomed to it, but packing 25,000 to 30,000 fans inside the stadium the night *before* the game is one of the great traditions and spectacles in college football. I've always been impressed by how the tradition has been passed on from one generation to the next. Not many schools could pull something like midnight yell practice off on a continuing basis. Once, maybe. But week after week and year after year, no way. A&M is unique." By the way, these days, the crowd count is more like 50,000 fans, especially for big games like UCLA, Alabama, or LSU.

A&M has also evolved over the years, especially in its basketball atmosphere, which includes an all-female dance team and a pep band that plays much different music than the marching band. A&M is now a massive, diverse university with more than 60,000 students on campus, but opposing schools' coaches sometimes try to convince recruits that Texas A&M is still a country cow college located in the sticks where service in the military is a requirement. That hasn't been the case since the early 1960s, but it's sometimes necessary and beneficial to combat those negative stereotypes with edgy, trendy, and new-school marketing concepts or personalities. Case in point: We tipped off the 2007–8 season with a Maroon Madness celebration that began at 10 p.m. at Reed Arena, included the introduction of both teams—it was Mark Turgeon's first season at A&M following Billy Gillispie's departure to Kentucky—and the headliner of the evening was rapper DeAndre Cortez Way, better known as "Soulja Boy," whose smash hit "Crank Dat" had reached No. 1 on the US Billboard Hot 100 a month earlier.

I have to admit that I probably can't understand more than about a handful of words in "Crank Dat" or most other songs that reach the top of the Billboard Hot 100 chart these days. Listening to American Top 40 reruns with the late Casey Kasem or even *American Bandstand* from the Dick Clark days would be more my speed. But when you are the head basketball coach at a major university that is attempting to recruit inner-city kids from across the country—many of them African American student-athletes—you better embrace the music of Soulja Boy, Jay Z, Eminem, Lil Wayne, Drake, or whoever the latest rap star is. I didn't know the difference between Soulja Boy and Soul Train, and I sure didn't know the lyrics he was singing, but I was damned happy to help promote him at Texas A&M.

Of course, that event didn't need much of my marketing. Reed Arena was sold out and rocking to Soulja Boy, and we followed his lead once the season began, "cranking" out a 12–2 record in nonconference play with wins over numerous good teams, including SMU, TCU, Indiana, Michigan, Florida State, and Auburn. We were the preseason favorites to win the Big 12, and we looked the part through much of the nonconference season. We then opened the conference portion of our schedule at home against Kansas State, the same team that had beaten us the year before to open Big 12 play. This time, however, we were playing at home, where we were riding a 26-game winning streak.

We had plenty of incentives to play well. Instead, we fell flat on our faces. We lost that game (67–54), lost the next game at Baylor (59–56), and wound up losing four of our first five conference games. When we lost at Nebraska, 73–60, we fell to 1–4 in league play. The worst part of the loss in Lincoln was the way we turned the ball over. We had a season-high 30 turnovers against Nebraska, marking the first time since Peggie Gillom was the head coach that the Aggies had that many turnovers. The problem wasn't just turnovers, though. After winning the conference the year before and starting so strongly in 2007–8, we were the team that our opponents were most geared up to play. We weren't prepared for the targets on our backs, especially in a league as strong as the Big 12. After that loss to Nebraska—a game in which we lost senior LaToya Gulley to a career-ending ACL tear—I told our team and the media, "This isn't going to be our last loss because of how tough the league is on a nightly basis."

Perhaps I should have spoken those words much earlier in the season, because my players almost proved me wrong. In one of the defining moments of that season—or my tenure at Texas A&M, for that matter—we traveled to Lawrence, Kansas, to face to face a KU team that was also 1–4 in league play and had been picked to finish 10th in the Big 12 preseason coaches' poll. Kansas wasn't a particularly good team, but the Jayhawks were playing at home in historic Allen Fieldhouse, and they could sense our blood in the water like a frenzy of sharks. We were struggling to find our rhythm and our confidence, and we suffered through a dismal first-half shooting performance, hitting only 10 of 33 shots (30.3 percent). Meanwhile, Kansas shot 50 percent from the field in the first half and took a 30–29 lead at the intermission.

We had not won a game in 10 days, and it was not out of the question that our season could spiral to rather severe depths if we didn't figure out a way to beat Kansas. Fortunately, we stepped it up on the defensive end. Like the legendary men's coach Bob Knight said, "Good basketball always starts with good defense!" That's so true, because there will always be games where the shots just won't fall with any consistency; but while you can't always shoot well, you can always give great effort on the defensive end. As another legendary men's coach Mike Krzyzewski said, "Effort is fully replenishable. There is no need to save any of it. Leave every bit you have on the court."

As I've mentioned, Vic Schaefer is a tremendous defensive technician and strategist, and we decided at the half to go with a smaller, quicker lineup so that we could hopefully force Kansas into turnovers with a full-court press. We had a plan of action going into the game, but basketball is a sport of adjustments—from one half to the next and even one possession to the next. Our adjustments worked tremendously well, as Kansas committed 15 turnovers in the second half. During one nine-minute stretch, the Jayhawks managed only four shots, while turning it over seven times. But the key was that we forced those mistakes and then capitalized on them. Danielle Gant recorded her ninth career double-double with 14 points and 12 rebounds, while Takia Starks produced a team-high 17 points and six rebounds to lead us to a 58–51 victory. I loved the pressure we put on Kansas, and I loved the fact that we only turned the ball over nine times, the fewest in almost two years and 21 less than we had in the previous game against Nebraska.

That game didn't register a blip on the national or regional radars, but it was monumental for us. We needed to find a way to win. Period. While it wasn't particularly pretty, it allowed us to breathe easily again as we traveled home to face another team, Missouri, that was inferior to us from a talent prospective. We rolled past Mizzou and then beat Texas Tech and Texas to improve to above .500 (5–4) in the Big 12 Conference standings for the first time all year. We had weathered some difficult storms, and we were beginning to play with much more confidence and swagger. One of the great misnomers in coaching is that you don't just recruit new players each year and throw them into a locker room with the returning players and instantly produce team chemistry. You build that team chemistry as you play through tough games and stretches, and the players discover that they need each other, as well as the coaches. Nobody looks forward to difficult times, but you often look back on those times as the biggest periods of personal growth. That goes for individuals and teams.

After winning four straight games, we had a momentary stumble, losing at Oklahoma, 68–56, before a school-record crowd of 12,168 at the Lloyd Noble Center. Patrice Reado played through severe migraine headaches to score 19 points, and we had a 32–26 lead at the half. But behind All-American Courtney Paris, the Sooners outscored us, 42–24, in the second half. We dropped the game, but we didn't allow the loss to deter us. We bounced back from the OU loss with four consecutive victories over Texas Tech, Iowa State, Texas, and Oklahoma State, and as the calendar flipped to

March, we had won eight of our last nine games. We were truly hitting our stride at just the right time, and the final two regular-season games of the year offered our fans a preview of our March Madness potential.

Morenike Atunrase had suffered a foot injury the previous December, which had sidelined her for much of that season and continued to affect her into the 2007–8 season. She was tentative and worried that she would injure her foot again if she went too hard. But as we moved into March of her senior season, Morenike kicked into high gear, finally putting the injury out of her mind. On March 1, 2008, Morenike came off the bench and scored a season-high 24 points in our surprisingly easy and thoroughly dominating 72–53 win over eighth-ranked Baylor before a Dollar Day crowd of 5,686 at Reed Arena. Assistant coach Kelly Bond challenged Morenike to attack the basket against Baylor's Melissa Jones, and she took full advantage of that mismatch by scoring 18 points in the first half alone.

While Morenike was the lead story of the day, our defense was just as important. For the fourth-straight contest, we held a Big 12 opponent to either their fewest or second-fewest points scored this season. Baylor, one of the top teams in the league in scoring offense averaging at 73.6 points per game, scored just 53 points, its second fewest of the year. Baylor had won the first game on a last-minute three-pointer, but we dominated every aspect of the contest on March 1. The Bears had a chance to clinch at least a share of the regular season Big 12 title against us but instead suffered their worst loss since a 24-point defeat by then-No. 5 Stanford in December. The win over Baylor was a huge confidence boost and set up our regular-season finale at Reed Arena against No. 11 Oklahoma in a nationally televised game on Fox Sports Net.

Against the Sooners, Oklahoma native Danielle Gant celebrated her 21st birthday by scoring 21 points and grabbing 12 rebounds to lead us to another big win of 73–59. It was our third win in a row against a top-25 team, as we started that streak with a victory at No. 17 Oklahoma State. It was also our 10th win in our last 11 games, giving us great momentum heading into the Big 12 Tournament in Kansas City. Once again, our defense was tremendous, as Oklahoma didn't even score during a seven-and-a-half-minute stretch in the second half. At one point, we led 62–36 with about five minutes left. I moved Morenike into the starting lineup, and she responded with another double-digit scoring effort. Our fans literally stormed the court for the first time ever, led by the "gray hairs, the blue hairs, and the no-hairs" among our faithful fans and also by the parents of our players, because there were so few students in attendance.

I really felt like we were firing on all cylinders as we went to Kansas City, and I challenged our girls to play with great energy and passion. I really believed we had a chance to win the tournament if we just continued playing the way we had been since that dreadful loss to Nebraska. Looking at the bracket as we traveled to Kansas City, I figured one of our biggest challenges would be trying to beat Oklahoma for the second time in a week. As one of the top four seeds, we had a first-round bye, while Oklahoma (the fifth seed) played last-place Missouri in the first round. We were preparing for Oklahoma, but it's a good thing I'm not a gambler because Mizzou pulled off the stunning upset on the opening day of the tournament to become the first 12 seed to ever win a game at the Big 12 Tournament. So instead of a difficult rematch with the Sooners on March 6, we faced the Tigers. Takia Starks led the way with a game-high 18 points and La Toya Micheaux scored seven of our first 11 points in our 65–39 win. We only led 29–22 at halftime, but our defense really turned it up a notch, causing the Tigers to turn over the ball 20 times. We also held Missouri without a basket for the first three and a half minutes of the second half, taking complete control.

Looking at the bracket before the tournament started, I would have bet that we would face top-seeded Kansas State in the semifinals. But once again, an upset altered our route to the championship. Eighth-seeded Iowa State knocked off regular-season champion Kansas State in the quarterfinals, meaning that we would face ISU in the semis for the second consecutive year. The Cyclones had beaten us the year before in Oklahoma City, which meant I had no trouble getting our girls' full attention on the job at hand. Our goal was to take control right away with a full-court press from the opening tip. The result was just what we wanted, as a technical foul was called on Iowa State head coach Bill Fennelly at the 17:20 minute mark after our quick 5–0 start to the game. And after A'Quonesia Franklin drained her second three-pointer of the game, we led 10–2. Franklin played great at the point, and we did not commit a single turnover in the first half. Fellow senior Morenike Atunrase was also great, coming off the bench and immediately draining a three-pointer with 14:05 remaining in the half to push the lead out to 17–4. She scored a game-high 19 points on 7-of-11 shooting from the floor.

That win advanced us into the championship game of the Big 12 Tournament for the first time ever, and before a rowdy crowd of 4,420 inside Municipal Auditorium, a national television audience, and a significant contingent of media members throughout the Big 12 region, Takia Starks scored 10 points and was named the Most Outstanding Player in the tournament as we held off a furious rally from third-seeded Oklahoma State to claim the conference tournament crown with a 64–59 win. Shortly after the victory, multicolored confetti and streamers exploded from the rafters of the old building, while our school officials, including Director of Athletics Bill Byrne, passed out championship T-shirts and hats. Big 12 Conference representatives then rolled out the platforms for an awards ceremony and a ladder for the players to cut down the nets, and we soaked up every minute of the spotlight.

We had also cut down nets the previous year at Reed Arena following the Big 12 regular-season title. But winning the postseason title was the most significant and rewarding moment of my five-year coaching career at A&M at that point because everyone who cared about women's college basketball would have been watching the national television broadcast. We were one of the last women's games in the country on March 15, so it was really sweet knowing that all eyes were on us. And those who tuned in saw a team with plenty of resolve and senior leadership.

Our first two wins in the Big 12 Tournament had been easy, but OSU pushed us to the limit, which I thought was a great test heading into the NCAA Tournament. We led throughout most of the game, but it was an all-out war in the second half. When OSU's Andrea Riley, who scored a game-high 28 points, hit a high-arching, jaw-dropping three-pointer with 25.4 seconds left in regulation, the Cowgirls drew to within one point of us, at 60–59. Municipal Auditorium, filled predominantly with orange-clad OSU fans, was rocking and rejoicing over Riley's phenomenal outside shooting. But even with the pressure mounting, our seniors—like Morenike Atunrase, A'Quonesia Franklin, and Patrice Reado—and our juniors, Takia Starks and Danielle Gant, never flinched. We calmly finished the job—as Franklin hit four free throws in the final 22 seconds—and then celebrated yet another milestone achievement for a program that was mired in the cellar of the Big 12 as recently as five years ago.

Two days later, the NCAA Selection Committee honored us by naming Texas A&M a program-best No. 2 seed in the 2008 NCAA Tournament. That's quite an accomplishment for any team, but considering that we had tied for third place in the regular-season standings, the two seed was a tremendous honor. We earned it by playing the seventh-toughest schedule in the nation and winning 13 of 14 down the stretch. As a No. 2 seed in the Oklahoma City Regional, we traveled to Baton Rouge to face No. 15 seed Texas–San Antonio at LSU's Pete Maravich Assembly Center.

Louisiana native Morenike Atunrase, playing in the Pelican State for the first time in her collegiate career, came off the bench and knocked down a game-high 19 points to lead us to an easy 91–52 rout of UTSA. The outmatched Roadrunners seemed stunned by our pressure defense throughout the first half, committing 23 of their 30 turnovers in the first half alone. UTSA, making its first-ever NCAA Tournament appearance, attempted only 15 shots in the first half as we scored 28 of our 49 first-half points off of turnovers.

The next game was closer, but we were once again in complete control as we coasted to a 24-point blowout of 10th-seeded Hartford, 63–39, to earn a trip to the Sweet Sixteen for just the second time in school history. Danielle Gant scored a game-high 21 points to lead us back to her hometown of Oklahoma City. Our defense forced Hartford to commit 12 first-half turnovers, which resulted in 19 of our 34 points in the first half. The win was our 11th straight and set up as showdown with third-seeded and tournament-tested Duke (25–9) on Sunday, March 30, at the Ford Center. Duke, making its 14th consecutive NCAA Tournament appearance, was an outstanding basketball team, but we were not in awe of or intimidated by any opponent. We believed we could beat any team in the country, and we went to Oklahoma City with a mission in mind.

We accomplished the first part of that mission by pounding Duke, 77–63, to reach the Elite Eight for the first time in A&M's history. Patrice Reado led a group of four Aggies to reach double-figure points with 17 and also pulled down a team-high eight rebounds. Takia Starks added 15 points, while A'Quonesia Franklin and senior Morenike Atunrase added 13 apiece. But once again our defense made the difference. We forced 14 Duke turnovers while committing only six in the first half of play. The only negative was that we had to play the second half without defensive leader Danielle Gant. After playing every minute of the first half and posting eight points and five rebounds, Gant suffered from dehydration and had to be administered nearly four bags of IV fluid during the halftime break.

The win over Duke earned us the opportunity to face top-seeded Tennessee (33–2) in the regional finals on April 1 on ESPN. The defending national champion Lady Vols downed fifth-seeded Notre Dame, 74–64, in the second regional semifinal game of the Oklahoma City Regional. The Lady Vols had reached their 27th consecutive Sweet Sixteen appearance (25 more times than us at that point) by beating Purdue on March 25, making Hall of Fame coach Pat Summitt the first coach to ever win 100 NCAA Tournament games. The Lady Vols, one of only three teams in the country with fewer than two losses, were led by two-time All-American Candace Parker, who was averaging a team-leading 21.5 points and 8.4 rebounds per game and was best known for being the first woman to dunk in an NCAA Tournament game and the first woman to dunk twice in a college game.

It was going to be a huge challenge to beat Tennessee, but our team was filled with warriors, and by that point in the season, we believed we could win the national title. And for much of the game against Tennessee, we looked like a team that could win it all. We took our biggest lead at 42–37 with 6:19 left in regulation, but the Lady Vols answered with an 8–0 run to take a 45–42 lead with 2:10 to go. Tennessee led by only two points, 45–43, with 1:18 remaining when Alexis Hornbuckle drained a three-pointer with 50 seconds remaining to put Tennessee ahead, 48–43. Morenike Atunrase answered with a jump shot to cut the lead to three again, but the Lady Vols hit five of six free throws to down the stretch to win the game.

Parker was sensational for Tennessee, even though she was struggling to keep her arm in its socket at one point. Parker dislocated her left shoulder but still scored 26 points to lead the Lady Vols' comeback. She twice left the game in the first half with the injury and didn't return until about halfway through the second half. She scored six of the Lady Vols' points in the game-deciding 8–0 run. We pushed them harder and farther than any other opponent, but Parker was too much for us to handle, and the Lady Vols went on to win their eighth national championship and second straight.

But still, just think: We were up five with 6.19 seconds left against the best team in the nation. We didn't finish it, but we played Tennessee better than any team in the NCAA tournament, as the Lady Vols learned while cruising to an easy victory in Tampa. This would be Tennessee's last national championship under Summitt and the last time since that they have been to the Final Four. All that being said, the Texas A&M women nearly derailed this historic run by Tennessee. In all honesty, in retrospect, I have to wonder how many more chances Pat Summitt would have had, given the way her health would soon begin declining.

But meanwhile, the best season in Texas A&M history concluded in disappointing fashion and one game short of the Final Four. We finished the season at 29–8 overall, marking a school record for wins after having won 16 of our final 18 games. And while it is always difficult to say good-bye to your seniors, it was particularly tough to bid farewell to a class that had meant so much to our program, A'Quonesia Franklin, Morenike Atunrase, and Patrice Reado played a huge role in our special season, while teammates La Toya Gulley and Katy Pounds continued to sit on the bench and cheer us on after suffering career-ending injuries. They believed in us right from the start, buying into our vision of what Texas A&M women's basketball could be when we first arrived in Aggieland. To this day, I love and appreciate those seniors so much. They were great players and left quite a legacy.

That senior class led us to 93 victories over a four-year span in comparison to just 44 victories for Texas A&M in the four-year span prior to their arrival on campus. No other senior class comes remotely close. The Class of '96 was the previous best with 79 victories. The five-member senior class led A&M to back-to-back-to-back NCAA Tournament appearances and back-to-back conference titles. More than all those things, however, that class taught Texas A&M fans, future Texas A&M teams, and recruits across the nation that anything was possible for the Aggies because we had learned to win in March. In 2008, we were within six minutes of making it to the Final Four and beating the team that won the national championship. We had also won a regular season and postseason championship in a conference that included three previous national champions—Texas, Texas Tech, and Baylor. In other words, we were really close to achieving the ultimate goal in women's college basketball. Those seniors had put Texas A&M on an elite map and had proven that the Aggies were capable of winning it all.

12 Perspective Is Everything

In 1985, Chicago Bulls rookie Michael Jordan began his relationship with Nike, signing the largest basketball endorsement at that time: $2.5 million plus royalties over five years. Nike then fused the company's new technology with the player's high-flying reputation, resulting in Air Jordan. The investment proved to be a wise one, as the Air Jordan line of athletic shoes and apparel surpassed $130 million in revenues within its first year, stabilizing Nike's bottom line and turning the company around to take back the lead from Reebok in the sports shoes market by 1990.

An air-bound silhouette of Jordan became Nike's dominant image, as Jordan was featured prominently in the company's marketing materials and its commercials. Of all the Nike commercials that spotlighted Jordan throughout his career, though, he was most proud of the 1997 spot that captured his humanity. The commercial, filmed at Soldier Field in Chicago, showed a well-dressed Jordan exiting his limousine and strolling past banks of fans, humbly acknowledging the custodians and security workers along the way. Amid these outward signs of success, Jordan's voice-over revealed his inner thoughts: "I've missed more than 9,000 shots in my career. I've lost almost 300 games. Twenty-six times I've been trusted to take the game-winning shot—and missed. I've failed over and over and over again in my life."

Such self-doubt from perhaps the greatest basketball player ever caught viewers' attention. Then the camera showed Jordan heading into the locker room and the voice-over added one last thought: "And that is why I succeed."

Jordan admired the "9,000 shots" spot because it delivered the message that his fallibility was an inherent component of his success. Not everyone could "be like Mike" in terms of Jordan's tremendous athletic abilities, but the ad delivered a message similar to the one American inventor Thomas Edison shared decades earlier: "I have not failed. I've just found 10,000 ways that won't work."

Indeed, perspective really is everything in life. I remember reading the book *Roy Story*, an inspirational account of Aggie legend Roy Bucek, who thrived on the athletic fields, survived World War II battlefields, and became a millionaire businessman. Bucek, a member of Texas A&M's 1939 national championship football team, lost his left eye while serving in World War II at the Battle of the Bulge. A sharp-edged, rusted piece of German metal ricocheted off a tree, sliced his left eye in two, continued to travel behind his nose, and lodged permanently in his right cheek. "To add insult to injury, I later developed spinal meningitis from the rusted shrapnel and nearly died," he wrote. "Those damned Germans did everything in their power to make sure that we—the Allied soldiers—died in the most agonizing and gruesome manner. Every January since 1945, I have awoken on the 19th day of the month, pausing for reflection, recalling the loss of my eye, recalculating my steps that day and thanking God in heaven for allowing me to experience the single *greatest day of my life!*"

Bucek explained that, according to various reports, roughly 600,000 Americans were involved in the Battle of the Bulge, and 81,000 of them never made it home alive. The surgeons who worked on Bucek told him that he came ever-so-close to being one of the members of the "Bulge bodybag club." "But God spared me," he wrote. "And He provided me with something that has been so extremely valuable to my successes in this life: Perspective. It's a little thing that makes all the difference between success and failure in practically anything. I lost my ability to see out of one eye on January 19, 1945, but God actually expanded my vision in the aftermath of that battle wound. I realized I didn't need both eyes to be a visionary."

Wise words from a wise man. The bottom line is that there are some losses—regardless of whether it is the loss of a body part in battle that sends a soldier home alive, the loss of a job that opens up another door, or the loss of a game that drives a team to future greatness—that are more meaningful and valuable than victories. The key is to remember the words from the late American author F. Scott Fitzgerald, who reminded us to "never confuse a single defeat with a final defeat."

After making our triumphant run to the Elite Eight in April of 2008, there was a natural assumption that we would continue to take the next step the following year just as we had been doing every other year since we arrived at A&M. We went from a losing season in 2004 to the WNIT in 2005, and from making it to the NCAA Tournament in 2006 to winning the Big 12 regular-season championship in 2007. We won the postseason Big 12 title in 2008 and made it to the Elite Eight for the first time in school history.

Things were going so well for us following that Elite Eight that we signed highly recruited junior college All-American guard/forward Tanisha Smith in late April of 2008 from the University of Arkansas at Fort Smith. Originally from Kansas City, Smith spent one season at the University of Arkansas prior to transferring to UA–Fort Smith. She previously starred at Kansas City's Lincoln College Prep Academy, and she had played youth basketball alongside Tyra White, who was then a redshirt freshman on our team. Assistant coach Johnnie Harris, who had joined our staff prior to the 2007–8 season after Amy Tennison accepted a new position as women's athletics coordinator and head girls basketball coach at Mansfield Legacy High School, first signed Tanisha while she was an assistant at Arkansas. Harris did a great job of resigning her for Texas A&M. Our players also did an excellent job of making her feel comfortable. The addition of Tanisha gave us a tremendously versatile class for the 2008–9 season. We had already signed Sydney Carter, a combination guard from DeSoto High School; Skylar Collins, a shooting guard out of Cedar Hill High School; and Adaora Elonu, a small forward out of Alief Elsik High School. That Texas trio was joined by Floridian Kelsey Assarian, a post player out of Barron Collier High in Naples, Florida, and Tanisha Smith.

We were recruiting well regionally and nationally, and even my golf game was earning some headlines. In June of 2008, I hit my first and only hole-in-one (at least to this point) on the par-3 sixth hole of the Tom Fazio–designed No. 4 course at the Pinehurst Resort in Pinehurst, North Carolina, which played host to the US Open Golf Championships in 1999 and 2005. I was on a trip with the Traveling Aggies, coordinated by the Association of Former Students at Texas A&M, and I definitely felt like our basketball program was going places. In August 2008, the Texas A&M University System Board of Regents approved a salary increase and contract extension for me, bumping my pay to $800,000 annually through May 31, 2012. We started the 2008–9 season ranked in top 10 nationally, and we signed another fantastic recruiting class in November 2008 that included combination guard/forward Cierra Windham from Corona, California; post player Diamond

Ashmore from Midwest City, Oklahoma; wing player Kristi Bellock from River Ridge, Louisiana; and point guard Adrienne Pratcher from Memphis, Tennessee.

Once the season started, we took all the momentum we had generated from the run to the Elite Eight the previous year along with our impressive recruiting accomplishments and compiled the greatest nonconference start in the history of Texas A&M women's basketball. When we beat George Washington, 78–59, on January 3, 2009, at Reed Arena, we avenged two previous losses to the Colonials and improved to 12–0 before a season-high crowd of 6,892 at Reed Arena. In that game, senior All-America candidate Takia Starks scored 22 points, senior All-America candidate Danielle Gant contributed the 14th double-double of her career, and preseason Big 12 Newcomer of the Year Tanisha Smith added a career-high 16 points as we won for the 28th time in a 30-game stretch dating back to a 58–51 win at Kansas in Big 12 Conference play on January 26, 2008.

We were ranked No. 3 nationally at the time (another school record), and our 12 consecutive victories to start the year included wins over Pittsburgh, Michigan, Arizona, Penn State, TCU, and New Mexico. In a win that was especially meaningful to me personally, we were also on the celebratory side of a 41-point rout at Stephen F. Austin, 77–36, in Nacogdoches on the night I was inducted into SFA's Hall of Fame at halftime. University President Dr. Baker Pattillo and several of my former SFA players were in attendance. It was somewhat awkward because the game was so lopsided, but it was actually only the second win ever for A&M at SFA and only the Aggies' fourth win in the 17-game series between the two schools, which speaks volumes about how good SFA had been in previous decades—and how down A&M had once been in women's basketball. I was most pleased that night with my assistants at A&M, who did a great job of preparing for that game, which I had not been thrilled about coaching because of all the emotions it stirred up.

Nevertheless, it turned out to be a memorable night during a practically unforgettable nonconference run. Only a loss at Florida State on January 5, 2009, prevented us from a perfect nonconference season. In that game, we had a 17-point lead with 13:27 to go, but FSU closed the contest with a 20–3 surge to seal the upset. That was a disappointing way to finish the nonconference portion of the schedule, but what was really frustrating about that season was that we couldn't figure out how to beat Baylor. We lost at home to the Lady Bears, 64–61, in late January when Baylor's Danielle Wilson converted a crucial three-point play with 4.8 seconds left. Then we lost to Baylor, 64–60, before a sellout crowd of 10,118 at the Ferrell Center on the final day of the regular season after trailing by 10 at the half. Tanisha Smith and Danielle Gant led a great rally that tied the game at 44–44 with 11:23 remaining in regulation, but we were unable to close out the game.

As a result, we finished the regular season with a 23–6 overall record and an 11–5 mark in Big 12 Conference play, tying Iowa State for third place in the final league standings. We then went to the Big 12 Women's Basketball Championship in Oklahoma City as the No. 4 seed, where we beat No. 21–ranked Kansas State in a 65–63 thriller and upset top-seeded and No. 3–ranked Oklahoma for the second time in a month, 74–62, behind 22 points from Oklahoma native Danielle Gant and 15 points from sophomore point guard Sydney Colson. That set up yet another rematch with Baylor in the championship game of the tournament.

Unfortunately, the third time was not the charm. We were whistled for 21 fouls, which resulted in a major advantage for the Lady Bears at the free-throw line in Baylor's 72–63 victory. Despite that loss, the NCAA Tournament Selection Committee again rewarded us with a No. 2 seed for the second consecutive year. At 25–7 overall, we were paired with 15th-seeded Evansville in the first round of the Trenton, New Jersey, Regional. We easily coasted past Evansville, 80–45, and then routed Minnesota, 73–42, in South Bend, Indiana, to reach the Sweet Sixteen for the second consecutive year and the third time in program history. We played really well against Minnesota, as four players (Danielle Gant, Takia Starks, Tanisha Smith, and Sydney Colson) scored in double figures. Our reward for reaching the Sweet Sixteen was a return trip to Sovereign Bank Arena in Trenton, the same location where we had not played well against TCU during my first trip to the NCAA Tournament as the head coach of the Aggies in March 2006.

It wasn't any better the second time around in New Jersey. Arizona State shot an opponent season-high 62.0 percent from the floor and scored an opponent season-high 84 points en route to a 15-point victory. It was uncanny how many times they hit a shot with two or three seconds to go on the shot clock. Their kids stepped up and made plays, and that was the story of the game. We ended the season with the second-most wins (27) and tied for the second-fewest losses (eight) in 35 seasons of Aggie basketball. Meanwhile, our senior class of Takia Starks, Danielle Gant, and La Toya Micheaux ended their four-year careers as the winningest seniors in program history, with an impressive 104–32 (.765) record since their freshman season in 2005–6. For all that we accomplished, however, it felt like we had not truly taken the next step for the first time since we had been at A&M. We didn't win a conference championship in the regular season or the postseason, and we didn't advance as far in the NCAA Tournament as we had done the previous year. In no way, shape, or form was the 2008–9 season a failure, but we were also missing that satisfactory feeling of moving closer toward the ultimate prize.

We lost to Arizona State on March 29, but the loss on April 1 was almost just as demoralizing. We had been recruiting Houston's Kelsey Bone for five full years—literally since she was in seventh or eighth grade—and my staff had done a tremendous job in building a relationship with her and her mother, Kim Williams. By the time she was a senior at Sugar Land's Dulles High School in 2008–9, Kelsey was an imposing 6-foot-5 center who averaged 20.2 points, 9.1 rebounds, and 2.3 blocks per game during her senior year. She had opted not to sign during the early period in November, saying she couldn't decide between the Aggies and Longhorns. As time progressed, Illinois and South Carolina also entered into the recruiting equation, but we felt really good about our chances. I had even traveled to Argentina to watch Kelsey play as part of Team USA.

For many reasons, we believed Kelsey was a real difference-maker and someone we needed to keep pace with Baylor, at the very least. Bone was a McDonald's All-American and the No. 2–ranked player in the state behind 6-foot-8 Brittney Griner of Aldine Nimitz, the No. 1 high school player in the country according to Rivals.com, who had already signed with Baylor in November 2008. In a head-to-head meeting in November 2008, Bone led Dulles past Nimitiz and Griner, 64–63, where the two post players were compared to the high school versions of Wilt Chamberlain and Bill Russell.

Bone, the nation's No. 2 recruit in 2009 according to ESPN HoopGurlz, decided to make her collegiate destination announcement on national television during a courtside interview with ESPN at the McDonald's All-American game at the University of Miami's BankUnited Center.

Ultimately, Bone decided that South Carolina was the place for her, although her mother had been pushing for Texas A&M. We were heartbroken to lose her. But we did something important in the aftermath of that telecast—we wished Kelsey and her family the best, and we certainly didn't burn any bridges. We simply moved on immediately in an effort to sign another impact player who could possibly help us in the paint. Fortunately, we had developed quite the pipeline to Kansas City thanks to Tanisha Smith and Tyra White.

That connection, along with the hard work of Vic Schaefer and Johnnie Harris, opened the door for us to recruit the National Junior College

Player of the Year, 6-foot-1 power forward Danielle Adams. We had not taken Danielle into serious consideration until December of 2008 because we strongly believed we would sign Kelsey Bone. Now that the one scholarship was once again available, we turned our full attention to Danielle, who averaged 22.1 points and 2.8 blocked shots as a sophomore and led Jefferson (Missouri) College to a 34–1 record and the NJCAA championship game. She wasn't a true post player at 6-foot-1, but she occupied plenty of space in the paint and was physical enough to play against much taller opponents. She also had the ability to hit shots from the outside, which could potentially open up the paint as defenders were forced to guard her on the perimeter.

In the prep ranks, Adams had earned first-team All-State honors as a senior at Summitt High School in Kansas City after averaging 21.4 points per game. Johnnie Harris, who was then at Arkansas, had recruited her out of high school and developed a great relationship with her. Meanwhile, Vic handled our junior college recruiting, and he had developed a solid relationship with her coach, Kevin Emerick, who guaranteed us that she would make an impact the first time she stepped on the floor. "She can shoot the three or she can take it to the hole," Emerick said. "Danielle is not only a great player, but she's a great kid. She has no ego at all. She is as well liked as any kid on campus. She's just a big teddy bear."

Danielle was also being recruited by NCAA runner-up Louisville, as well as Mississippi State and Oklahoma State. She was naturally big-boned and burly, and there was concern about her weight and her ability to play a full-court type of game. In fact, her junior college coach liked us, but he was strongly encouraging her to pick Louisville because the Cardinals ran more of a half-court system, and he told her that she would probably struggle keeping up with our fast-paced tempo and pressure-oriented defensive philosophy. But she visited us and loved our facilities and our players. She also loved the fact that the Big 12 Championship Tournament would be held in Kansas City the next two years, so she would have a chance to win a title or two back in her hometown. And ultimately, she told us that she was tired of hearing people tell her what she couldn't accomplish.

Looking back on it, signing Danielle reminds me of the Rolling Stones lyrics, *"You can't always get what you want, but if you try sometimes, you just might find you get what you need."* We didn't land Kelsey Bone right away, but Danielle Adams would eventually prove to be exactly what we needed.

We entered the 2009–10 season with extremely high expectations despite the fact that we were only picked fourth in the Big 12 in the preseason coaches' poll. Coming off back-to-back NCAA Sweet Sixteen and Big 12 postseason championship game appearances, we returned 10 letter winners from the 2008–9 team that had gone 27–8. Not only did we return the 2009 Big 12 Newcomer of the Year in senior Tanisha Smith, but we also featured strong guards in Sydney Colson, Tyra White, Maryann Baker, and Sydney Carter, along with solid frontcourt players like Adaora Elonu, Damitria Buchanan, and Kelsey Assarian. And we welcomed in one of the top 10 recruiting classes in the nation, which included the preseason Big 12 Newcomer of the Year, Danielle Adams.

For the second consecutive year, we also opened in extremely impressive fashion, beginning with a near-perfect 95–77 win over No. 6 Duke in which Danielle Adams scored 24 points in her Texas A&M debut. Tanisha Smith added 19 and Sydney Colson scored 17 in front of the largest-ever home crowd for a women's basketball season opener, with 6,866 fans in attendance at Reed Arena. In the process of going 12–1 in the nonconference schedule for the second year in a row, we also beat a really good Gonzaga team in the Las Vegas Holiday Hoops Classic. In that same tournament, we gained a measure of revenge by beating Arizona State—the team that eliminated us from the NCAA Tournament the previous year—by 10 points as both Tyra White and Tanisha Smith scored 18 points.

Once the Big 12 race started, however, we lost five times in a seven-game stretch from January 17 to February 10. Most of those losses came against outstanding teams like No. 13 Oklahoma, No. 14 Baylor, No. 15 Oklahoma State, and No. 4 Nebraska. But the bottom line was that we were just 4–5 in league play after losing at Texas Tech on February 10, 2010. We managed to right the ship by beating Kansas State, Oklahoma State, and Texas to sweep the season series against the No. 12–ranked Longhorns for our seventh straight win over Texas. But while we seemed to have Texas' number, Baylor was the major thorn in our side. On February 22, 2010, for example, Brittney Griner scored 22 points and grabbed a whopping 21 rebounds as No. 17 Baylor knocked us off once again in College Station, 65–63. It was Baylor's fifth win in a row against Texas A&M.

We ultimately finished the 2009–10 regular season at 10–6 in the Big 12 and 22–7 overall, tying Texas for fourth place in the final regular-season standings. But since we beat the Horns twice, we won the tiebreaker for the fourth seed at the league tournament, while Nebraska (29–0, 16–0) earned the No. 1 seed with a perfect season, followed by Iowa State and Oklahoma. Entering the league tournament, Nebraska was clearly the favorite, but in all honesty, I was probably more concerned about the prospect of facing Baylor again than meeting Nebraska at some point, although the Huskers, who had beaten us 71–60 in Lincoln, were clearly the better team.

In hindsight, winning the 2010 Big 12 Tournament championship in Kansas City was probably an even more impressive accomplishment than winning our first Big 12 postseason title in '08. After all, we faced only one ranked opponent (Oklahoma State in the championship game) as we won it all in 2008. In comparison, our road to the title in 2010 was far more difficult, beginning with our third matchup of the year against the then-No. 15 Longhorns in the quarterfinals. We needed a huge effort to beat Texas for the eighth straight time, and that's what we received from our Kansas City trio of Tanisha Smith, Danielle Adams, and Tyra White, who combined for 57 points in our 77–64 win over Texas. Smith, Whitem, and Adams sparked a 20–2 run to build a double-digit lead midway through the second half that put us in complete control.

The win over Texas advanced us into the semifinals against unbeaten Nebraska, and while the Huskers were loaded, perhaps our girls saw a golden opportunity when Oklahoma eliminated Baylor in the quarterfinals. From a psychological standpoint, it was Baylor—not regular-season champion Nebraska—that seemed to be in our players' heads, and once the Lady Bears were eliminated, we were ready to make a statement on March 13. We did just that in perhaps our most impressive effort of the season.

Danielle Adams scored 22 points, and we forced Kelsey Griffin to the bench with early foul trouble to spoil No. 3 Nebraska's unbeaten season with an 80–70 victory before a stunned crowd at Municipal Auditorium. Nebraska was bidding to become just the 12th team to make it to the NCAA Tournament unbeaten, but Griffin, the Big 12 Player of the Year, was saddled with three fouls at halftime and was called for her fourth early in the second half. With the 6-foot-2 senior sitting on the bench, the Huskers had no answers for Danielle. At one point, we led 65–47 when Adaora Elonu stole a pass and Adams converted it into a layup.

With that victory, we advanced to the tournament championship game for the third year in a row and faced No. 12 Oklahoma—our third consecutive ranked opponent—in the championship game. Once in the title game, the Kansas City girls stepped forward once again, as Tyra White scored all 16 of her points in the first half and Danielle Adams scored 17 of her 19 points in the second half to lead us to a 74–67 win. The victory was our 11th win over a ranked opponent in 16 games against ranked foes throughout the course of the season. It was also an emotional, uplifting moment for Danielle Adams, who had never previously won a championship. To do it in her hometown and to be named the Most Outstanding Player of the Big 12 Tournament was extremely gratifying.

After the win over Oklahoma, I began lobbying for our placement in the NCAA Tournament. I know many coaches who hate postgame press conferences and maintain an adversarial relationship with all members of the media. That's certainly not the case with me. Perhaps it's because I once dreamed of a career in sports media or just a case of my gift for gab. Whatever the reason, I've learned that media can be your friends if you treat them with respect and use them to deliver a message, whether it's to your own team, school officials, or the powers that be in the NCAA, as I happened to do during the postgame press conference: "We've earned the right not to be in Geno Auriemma's region," I said, referring to the undefeated UConn women's team. "We've earned that right. I think both of us—A&M and Oklahoma—deserve not to be the last No. 2 seed, which I have been the last two years. And it better not happen to us again, committee."

Maybe the Selection Committee listened to me or perhaps it just worked out to our benefit. Regardless, we were placed as the No. 2 seed in the Sacramento Regional behind No. 1–seeded Stanford. The Big 12 tied the Big East for the most schools in the 2010 tournament with seven each. Nebraska was a one seed in the Kansas City Regional, where Oklahoma was a No. 3 seed. Meanwhile, the UConn machine rolled through the Dayton Regional and into the Final Four by beating Southern, Temple, Iowa State, and Florida State. The closest game UConn played while advancing to the Final Four was a 38-point win over the Cyclones. That's not a misprint. The 38-point win was the smallest margin of victory for the Huskies. That's why I really wanted to avoid UConn, led then by Maya Moore, until the Final Four in San Antonio. My hope was that we could make it to the Final Four before running into the Huskies, where we would play them in front of tens of thousands of Aggies.

It was a great plan, but our execution fell far short of the Final Four. After beating Portland State by 31 in Seattle during the opening round of the NCAA Tournament, we faced seventh-seeded Gonzaga, a team we had beaten earlier in the year in Las Vegas. In that first game, we dominated the smaller, less athletic Bulldogs in the first half and built a 20-point lead. But Gonzaga turned its season around the second half and played much better before losing to us by four points. They didn't lose again for the rest of the year.

I figured we would have our hands full in the Bulldogs' home state, and sure enough, Gonzaga bolted to an 11-point halftime lead in the second round of the NCAA Tournament, forcing us into uncharacteristic mistakes and closing the first half on a 12–2 run to take a 42–31 lead. That lead increased to 44–31 in the first moments of the second half after I was called for a technical foul for disputing a no-call and walking onto the court during play. I was hoping to ignite my team, and we outscored Gonzaga 21–6 over the next eight minutes, taking our first lead on Tanisha Smith's three-pointer with 11:49 left. Kayla Standish answered for the Bulldogs and started a back-and-forth final 11 minutes where neither team ever led by more than three points.

With 1:21 remaining and the Zags up 70–67, Gonzaga point guard Courtney Vandersloot committed her fifth foul trying to defend Sydney Colson. Colson made two free throws and Smith drained a jumper to give us a 71–70 lead with only 39 seconds remaining. At that point, I thought we were on the verge of surviving and advancing—the theme of the NCAA Tournament. But Vivian Frieson took advantage of a mismatch with a smaller defender to sink a 12-footer with 18 seconds on the clock. And on the other end, Frieson forced Danielle Adams into a contested 18-footer that came up short.

Our season ended, while the Bulldogs were on their way to the regional semifinals for the first time in school history, setting off a wild celebration for Gonzaga. That was a really tough loss to take because I believed we could make it to San Antonio—just as Baylor and Oklahoma eventually did—for the Final Four, and I believed we could ride the wave of passionate A&M fans to force UConn into a battle, just as Stanford did. In the national championship game, the Cardinal led the Huskies by eight at the half, before Maya Moore scored 18 of her 23 points in the second half, as Connecticut defeated Stanford, 53–47, for its 78th straight victory and its second straight unbeaten season. UConn was going to be extremely difficult to beat, but Stanford gave the Huskies a run for their money, and I believed we could have done so too.

It was not meant to be, though, and we said good-bye to a senior class that included Tanisha Smith, Damitria Buchanan, and Katrina Limbaha. The loss to Gonzaga was particularly tough to swallow because I believed we were the better team and that we had missed an opportunity to do something remarkable. We still had a great group of returning players in Danielle Adams, Sydney Colson, Sydney Carter, Tyra White, Adaora Elonu, and so forth, but replacing the contributions made by Tanisha Smith would be difficult, even though we once again had compiled a great recruiting class headlined by 6-foot-4 center Karla Gilbert from College Station's A&M Consolidated High and 5-foot-9 guard Kristen Grant from Arlington's Lamar High School. Gilbert was rated the No. 9 overall prospect in the country in the Class of 2010 and the No. 1 post player in the country by ESPN HoopGurlz. We also received great news from a long-term standpoint when Kelsey Bone requested a transfer from South Carolina to Texas A&M. She was the highest-ranked recruit we ever signed.

Bone, the Associated Press's Newcomer of the Year in the SEC in 2009–10, led the SEC with 9.2 rebounds a game and ranked among the top 10 in scoring with 14 points per game as a true freshman. But USC was simply not the right place for her, and she requested the opportunity to come to Aggieland.

Unfortunately, because of the NCAA's transfer rules, Bone was not eligible for the 2010–11 season. But her transfer at least temporarily eased the pain of that loss to Gonzaga, which seemed to linger a little longer than any of our other eliminating losses the previous four years, partly because I felt like I had lost control in the first half and let my players and assistant coaches down. Quite frankly, I may have thought so much about what I could have done differently that I allowed myself to dwell on the negative—something I rarely did and something I preached to my players to guard against. Even into the summer of 2010, I was thinking about how unfortunate we had been—as opposed to how blessed we had been in turning the A&M program around in the course of five years.

As a coach of young people, sometimes you teach perspective to your players. Other times, life teaches you about perspective. That's what happened in the summer of 2010 when our team, our coaching staff, and our entire community was brought to their collective knees following a freak accident that nearly took the life of Logan Schaefer, the son of our associate head coach and my dear friend, Vic Schaefer. In the early morning hours of July 12, 2010, Logan Schaefer was involved in a serious wakeboarding accident at Frontier Camp, a Christian-based adventure retreat in East Texas, that nearly took his life.

To make a long story short, Logan ended up at Tyler's East Texas Medical Center ICU. Surgeons diagnosed the injury—a subdural hematoma—and concluded that it was a result of severe whiplash. A craniotomy had been performed, removing a side of the skull to alleviate the intense pressure from the swelling and allow the blood to drain. Of all the ordeals and complications Logan endured in his 11 days at the East Texas Medical Center, including pneumonia and a bad IV that caused his right arm to balloon, perhaps the worst were the uncontrollable and violent shakes that kept him from sleeping for more than an hour or two at a time. For 10 straight days, he shook so much that he sweated profusely. Some people with that kind of head trauma have the shakes and sweats for months as a result of the brain firing and missing and trying to figure out what has happened.

Logan's condition was so dire at times and so uncertain at others that Vic and Holly were purposely vague in sending out updates to the masses of well-wishers. And while the Schaefers certainly appreciated the prayers, cards, flowers, and other forms of support, they wanted to keep visitors and distractions to a minimum. Following 11 days in intensive care at East Texas Medical Center, Logan then spent the next 28 days at the Institute for Rehabilitation and Research at Memorial Hermann Hospital in Houston.

Logan's ordeal, his remarkable recovery, and his family's faith truly inspired us all and gave us something absolutely invaluable heading into what turned out to be the greatest season in Texas A&M history: perspective. We didn't spend another second anguishing about what could have been last season. Instead, we followed Logan's lead by keeping our eyes on the prize rather than focusing on long odds or obstacles.

13 Mission Accomplished

From a theatrical standpoint, Hollywood would have approved of the grand finale at the conclusion of the 2010 American League Championship Series and the Cinderella-like tale of how the Texas Rangers finally won their first-ever AL pennant on Friday, October 22, 2010. One out away from reaching the organization's first World Series and ending 39 years of frustration in Arlington—50 years overall, including the franchise's origins as the Washington Senators—the Rangers' rookie closer Neftali Feliz was on the mound before a towel-waving, combustible crowd of 51,404 inside Rangers Ballpark in Arlington. Feliz, the composed righty who won 2010 Rookie of the Year honors, was one of the key acquisitions from the 2007 trade that sent Mark Teixeira to Atlanta and invigorated Texas' farm system. Stepping into the batter's box for the Yankees—the team that had eliminated Texas in all three of its previous playoff forays in the mid- to late-1990s—was Alex Rodriguez, the symbol of everything that went wrong for the franchise under former owner Tom Hicks. If you were looking to pinpoint one reason above all others that Hicks was broke—the Rangers had been in bankruptcy throughout much of the 2010 season and Texas entered the year with 27th-lowest payroll in the MLB—it started with A-Rod.

New school versus old guard. Flamethrower versus former franchise flame. What irony for the Arlington crowd, how intriguing for the national television audience, and what a story for the media covering the game. Feliz's first pitch, a ball up high, was a four-seam fastball clocked at 100 miles per hour. He then threw back-to-back 99-mph fastballs, one for a called strike, the next fouled back to the screen. With the crowd on its feet and growing more feverish on every pitch, Rodriguez dug in, wiggled his bat, and obviously guessed fastball.

Wrong.

Feliz threw a wicked curve. A-Rod froze. Home-plate umpire Brian Gorman called, "Strike three," and pandemonium inside the ballpark ensued. Red fireworks immediately burst high into the air as Pat Green's "I Like Texas" blared across the public address system and a dog pile of celebratory Rangers' players formed in the infield. As a Rangers fan ever since the franchise had moved to Arlington in 1972, the images of that night are moments frozen in time that will remain with me with the permanence of a tattoo. For so long, the Rangers were the laughing stock of all of baseball. The first team in Arlington went 54–100 in the strike-shortened 1972 season (a .351 winning percentage). The second edition produced an almost identical winning percentage (.352) with a 57–105 record. And over the next 35 years—until 2010—the Rangers had won exactly zero playoff series.

I often wondered if I would ever see my Rangers actually win a playoff series, let alone reach the World Series. It seemed like a farfetched dream for so long. As a lifelong sports fan, though, I've seen the improbable (the 1969 Mets), the implausible (the 1980 US Hockey Team), and the unbelievable (the 2004 Red Sox) become reality time and time again. But seeing the Rangers reach the 106th Fall Classic in October of 2010 really hit close to home and reminded me again of the jubilation, the pride, and the sheer joy that team sports can bring to fans of all ages. I certainly never played for the Rangers, was never employed by the organization, and had never been in a position to own season tickets. But as a fan, I took ownership in that AL pennant and beamed with pride as I looked back on how far the franchise had come, from laughing stock to last team standing in the American League.

Obviously, there was a correlation in my mind as we prepared for the opening of 2010–11 women's basketball season. If the Rangers could make it to the World Series, anything was possible for us—including making it to the Final Four. Our team could also draw inspiration from the fact that two schools from our division in the Big 12 South—Baylor and Oklahoma—had reached the Final Four the previous season. We had beaten Oklahoma twice in 2010, and we should have beaten Baylor at home before falling, 65–63. After reaching the NCAA Tournament for five consecutive years, we also possessed a roster full of veterans with major expectations, including a senior class comprising three young women—Sydney Colson, Maryann Baker, and

Danielle Adams—who were determined to leave a memorable legacy during their final season in Aggieland.

Quite frankly, I wasn't necessarily thinking about winning a national championship when we started the 2010–11 season, but I did sense something special on the horizon, especially when we received great news out of Indianapolis in late October. After some successful lobbying on my part, the NCAA announced that the first and second rounds of the 2012 NCAA Tournament would be hosted at Reed Arena. Our athletic director, Bill Byrne, had been extremely influential getting Texas A&M to host for the first time since 1994, when the Aggies still played at G. Rollie White Coliseum. I felt like a politician who'd just won the race. We had been sent all over the country the previous five years, and I was delighted that our athletic department was providing financial support and truly backing us. Playing those first two games at home doesn't guarantee you'll advance to the Sweet Sixteen, but it certainly increases your odds. Beginning in March 2012, we were able to host the first and second rounds of the NCAA Tournament in College Station for four of the next five seasons. Being selected as one of the host sites obviously didn't help us right away, but it was a clear indication that we were being recognized as one of the premier programs in the country. The NCAA had recognized our consistency and was confident that we were a program that would be in the Big Dance year after year. Furthermore, we would be a host site that could be depended on to put butts in seats.

We began the 2010–11 season as the No. 8–ranked team in the country in both major polls, another positive indication, and we were picked second in the Big 12 by the league's coaches behind Baylor. Meanwhile, Danielle Adams, who was chosen as the Big 12 Newcomer of the Year in her first season at A&M, was a first-team preseason selection to the All-Big 12 team. We were generating some serious respect, although we were definitely playing second fiddle in our own state in terms of the national spotlight. All eyes that were interested in women's basketball in the state of Texas were fixed firmly on Baylor, where sophomore-to-be Brittney Griner was projected as the Big 12's preseason Player of the Year, Brooklyn Pope was the preseason Newcomer of the Year, and Odyssey Sims was projected as the preseason Freshman of the Year. The Lady Bears were picked second nationally behind Connecticut, the two-time defending national champion that entered the 2010–11 season riding a record 78-game winning streak.

Obviously, Baylor was recruiting exceptionally well, but we were also doing great things to attract the top players in the country. Even before the 2010–11 season had begun, we signed the highest-rated recruiting class in

A&M history (No. 3 nationally according to the *Collegiate Girls Basketball Report*). The class included 6-foot-7 center Rachel Mitchell out of Atascocita High School in Houston; 5-foot-10 guard Tori Scott from John Ehret High in Marrero, Louisiana; and 5-foot-8 guard Alexia Standish out of Colleyville Heritage High in the Dallas–Fort Worth area.

Deservedly, Vic Schaefer received plenty of credit for his work as a defensive coach while he was at A&M, but Kelly Bond-White has always done a remarkable job of coaching and recruiting. Her recruiting ties across the country have been key for Texas A&M. She is a tremendous evaluator of talent, and year after year after year, she has displayed a tremendous ability to build genuine relationships with the players and the parents we are recruiting. For that matter, Johnnie Harris was also a really good recruiter when she was here, but Kelly is one of a kind and deserves so much credit for all that we have accomplished at Texas A&M. She is so much more than just an assistant coach to me; she feels like family.

Likewise, one of the things I loved about that 2010–11 season was the togetherness of that squad. The chemistry of that team was positively unique and led by two of the most charismatic, personable, quotable, and photographable players we've ever had at A&M, senior Sydney Colson and junior Sydney Carter. In addition to being tremendous players and individuals, Colson and Carter could have easily been spokeswomen for Disney, television news anchors, or models. We loved bringing them out to the media because they were so articulate, and it certainly didn't hurt our image to have them serve as the faces of the program. They are beautiful young ladies and great ambassadors for Texas A&M.

Seniors Danielle Adams and Maryann Baker were both great team-first players as well. Danielle was not a vocal leader; that's just not her personality. But she possessed a warrior's mentality and definitely led by her example. Maryann was a brilliant young woman who had graduated in the top 20 percent of her prestigious private high school (Dallas Bishop Lynch Catholic School) and earned back-to-back Academic All-Big 12 First Team honors at A&M. She displayed tremendous resolve in fighting through numerous injuries throughout her career.

The rest of the roster was filled with talented, tough, and team-oriented young women who were not afraid to work hard. And we worked extremely hard, beginning with 6 a.m. workouts in August and September and conditioning in the afternoons, pushing the girls to their physical limits and testing their mental toughness in pools of sweat. We weren't the biggest team in the country or even within a 100-mile radius of College Station. Our two biggest players were 6-foot-5 true freshman Karla Gilbert and 6-foot-4 sophomore Kelsey Bone. But Bone wasn't eligible, and Gilbert was still more of a role player at that point in her career. We also were not going to be able to simply out-talent most teams in our conference. We were good, and we had good balance, as nine of our players would eventually come pretty close to averaging at least 10 minutes of action per game.

To win at a championship level and advance further than any other team in school history, however, we needed to make the games ugly. We needed to be even more physical and aggressive in our defensive intensity than we had previously been—and that was already our calling card. To play at a fast pace and focus on playing great defense for 40 minutes was going to require sheer toughness, tremendous physical conditioning, and a total commitment to be sold out to each other and our singular vision. It can be difficult getting every player on the same page and having everyone in the program in complete synch. As a coach, that's what you're always striving to achieve, but it doesn't happen often. And when it does, it doesn't always stay harmonious throughout an entire season. It's not enough to merely have everyone in the same boat; you also have to make sure everyone is paddling at the same time and in the same direction. Otherwise you will never reach your full potential. And obviously, you are not going to win the Triple Crown with a mule; you need thoroughbreds to compete with the horsepower of schools like UConn, Notre Dame, Tennessee, Stanford, and Duke. It's sometimes difficult to push, break, and train those thoroughbreds who have been told all their lives that they are already championship-caliber.

Throughout my collegiate coaching career, we've typically been blessed with really good people. We have not had many jerks or troublemakers at Louisiana Tech, Stephen F. Austin, Arkansas, or A&M. For the most part, we've recruited the right kids with the right work ethic. Nevertheless, it's rare to compile a team with the right mix of high quality, high character, and high commitment. But going into that 2010–11 season, I believed that team had a chance to form a special bond and accomplish some historic achievements.

We started strongly once again, beating our first six opponents—Arkansas–Little Rock, Rice, Liberty, Arizona, Michigan, and California—by an average of 27 points. We then went on the road for a big test at No. 5 Duke in Durham, North Carolina, playing in the ninth women's Jimmy V. Classic (an annual game, named for Jim Valvano, the great North Carolina State men's coach). Adaora Elonu scored 15 points and Sydney Carter added 13, but we only shot 34 percent and couldn't convert on three chances in the final minute. Ultimately, we lost that game, 61–58. We were disappointed with the outcome, but hardly dejected. We returned home and beat Purdue by 45 points, 100–55, as Danielle Adams scored 27 points and we hit 10 three-pointers. That was the start of a 12-game winning streak in which we scored at least 80 points nine times. And with the way we played defense, we were not going to lose when we scored 80 points. During the 12-game winning streak, we also ran our nonconference home game winning streak to 43 consecutive games, the Texas A&M University System Board of Regents extended my contract, and only two of those 12 opponents—ranked foes Iowa State and Oklahoma on the road—stayed within double figures of us.

Those two road wins were especially meaningful. We had never won in five previous trips to Ames, Iowa, where the Cyclones were riding a 19-game winning streak. The Cyclones built a five-point lead in the first half, but Danielle Adams scored 25 points and we beat No. 20 Iowa State 60–51. That set up another big road test, as we traveled to Norman, Oklahoma, where we had not won since 2007 and where the Aggies were only 3–16 all-time.

Once again, Danielle Adams was sensational, scoring 31 points, including the decisive free throws with 7.6 seconds left to lead us past 12th-ranked Oklahoma, 80–78. Danielle Robinson led Oklahoma with 33 points and almost single-handedly fueled a comeback from a 15-point first-half deficit. But Robinson, an 87 percent free-throw shooter, missed the front end of a one-and-one opportunity with 30.6 seconds left, as well as two driving layups in the final minute. After Robinson missed the free throw, Sydney Colson missed on a driving layup attempt, but Adams rebounded and was fouled by Lyndsey Cloman, setting up the winning free throws. The victory extended our program-best overall start to 18–1, improved our best-ever Big 12 start to 6–0, and helped us tie the longest winning streak we'd set two years earlier to open the 2008–9 season.

Those two road wins against ranked teams prepared us for the biggest test of the season, a matchup against No. 1 Baylor before a sold-out crowd of 13,162 at Reed Arena. It was the largest crowd in school history for a women's game. Those fans were treated to quite a show, as Baylor sprinted out to a 10-point halftime lead and we came storming back to take a 48–46 lead with about nine minutes left. Baylor battled back to take a seven-point lead, but we answered with a 10–3 run and tied it at 60-all on a three-pointer by Colson with 49 seconds remaining. Unfortunately for us, Odyssey Sims scored 25 points and hit a short jumper with 26 seconds left to lead the Bears to a 63–60 win. We used several different players to slow down Brittney Griner, and we held her to 17 points and 12 rebounds. Danielle Adams spent the most time defending her, even though she's 7 inches shorter than the 6-foot-8 Griner. Adams's aggressiveness ultimately resulted in her fouling out. It was our first loss since falling at Duke in early December, and while it was disappointing, it proved to everyone—our players included—that we could play with the Lady Bears and beat them on any given night.

After beating Texas Tech, Oklahoma, and Kansas in our next three games, we had another chance at the Lady Bears on Valentine's Day in Waco. The second meeting wasn't quite as close (Baylor won 67–58), but we actually led most of the game thanks in large part to holding Griner to just three points in the first half. But Griner scored 23 in the second half and the Lady Bears took the lead for good at 57–56 with three minutes left in the game. Again, we were disappointed but certainly not disheartened.

The Lady Bears were 24–1 overall and had won 21 consecutive games. Only two of their victories at that point in the season were by less than 11 points, and both of those games were in a span of 16 days against us. One thing Baylor did really well once again was to defend Danielle. In our previous game against Kansas, Danielle scored an A&M-record 40 points, but she was held to a season-low nine points on 5-of-16 shooting against the Lady Bears. She came into the second Baylor game averaging 23.7 points, slightly more than Griner's 22.4 average. The key statistic of the game was our season-low 31 percent shooting. The bottom line was that in order to beat Baylor—and we figured we would receive at least one more shot at the Lady Bears—we had to shoot better and play a more complete game. Good wasn't going to be enough. Playing well in one aspect of the game wasn't going to cut it either.

We followed up the loss in Waco with wins over Oklahoma State, Texas Tech, and a gritty 68–65 win over Texas in Austin—our 10th consecutive win over the Longhorns—before losing at Kansas State, 71–67, in the next-to-last regular-season game of the year. The loss at K-State was a wake-up call of sorts. In our other three losses—at No. 5 Duke and twice against No. 1 Baylor—we could walk away from those games feeling good about ourselves. For the first time that season, we had lost to a team that wasn't as talented as us. But Kansas State wanted that game really badly, and the Wildcats played with a greater sense of energy. They built a 15-point lead in the first half, weathered our comeback runs, and shot 50 percent from the field for the game. They also had one player, Brittany Chambers, who had an unforgettable night, scoring 35 points and drilling seven three-pointers. I'm not sure if I would ever go so far as to say a loss is a good thing, but that one may have served a purpose. We spoke often to the players about not taking anything for granted or overlooking any opponent the rest of the way. We lost to K-State on the second day of March—the make-or-break month of the season in college basketball.

We bounced right back on Senior Night and whipped Nebraska, 84–59, to close the regular season at 25–4 overall and 13–3 in the Big 12. It was a great Senior Night effort, as Danielle Adams scored 23 points and fellow senior Sydney Colson produced 15 assists, the most ever against a Nebraska team. She was like a magician out there, making passes and running our offense to near-perfection.

We then traveled to Kansas City as the No. 2 seed behind Baylor in search of our second consecutive Big 12 postseason championship. We started off in great fashion, playing a tremendous defensive game and forcing Texas into 31 turnovers. Heading into that game, I was uneasy about facing the Longhorns in the quarterfinals. We had already beaten them twice that season and 10 times in a row. Fortunately, our players were more than up to the challenge, holding Texas to its lowest point total of the season in our 77–50 win that improved our winning streak against our rivals to 11 games in a row. After the game, Texas guard Yvonne Anderson said, "I think we just let them get in our heads tonight." Indeed, we certainly controlled things from start to finish.

We essentially did the same thing in our next game against Oklahoma as we cruised to an 81–68 victory that advanced us into the finals of the Big 12 Tournament for the fourth consecutive year (we became the first women's team in the conference to ever do that). What I was most pleased about in the Oklahoma game was that we didn't wait around for Danielle to score 40 points. To reach the Final Four, we needed other players to step up. In that particular game, Oklahoma held Danielle to 16 points, but Sydney Carter scored 19 points—all in the second half—and Tyra White added 18 as we beat the Sooners for the fifth straight time to set up another rematch with Baylor. In the postgame press conference, one of the reporters asked me how I felt about facing Baylor for the third time this year. I told the media: "We want to play Baylor four times. If we do, we'll be in the Final Four. That's how good Baylor is."

On March 12, before a crowd of 4,250 at the old Municipal Auditorium in Kansas City, we embraced the challenge of facing Baylor once again and started in near-perfect fashion. In the previous two games against Baylor, we had tried a number of defensive strategies against Griner, and we tossed a new wrinkle at her in that championship game. Each time Baylor fed the ball to Griner in the paint, either Sydney Colson or Sydney Carter collapsed in the post as soon as Griner placed the ball on the floor. The two Sydneys combined for six steals in the first half, and we frustrated Baylor from the opening tip, building a 12–0 lead during the first four minutes and 50 seconds.

Like two heavyweight contenders in a championship fight, however, the Lady Bears countered with big blows of their own. After finally scoring, Baylor went on a 23–6 run and eventually took a 30–28 lead at the half. Griner started slowly but finished the half with 16 points after a 1-for-5 start. Once the Lady Bears kicked things into gear, it was an absolute classic game in which the lead changed seven times and was tied 12 times. During one stretch, Griner scored 20 consecutive points for Baylor. Still, we had a great look at the end. Trailing 61–58 in the closing minute, Danielle Adams missed a three-pointer with four seconds left that would have tied the game. It looked like it was good when she released it, but it didn't happen and we lost to Baylor for the third time that year. Afterward, Kim Mulkey and I shook hands and she said she'd see me at the Final Four in Indianapolis.

The funny thing about that loss is that the media really believed—or assumed—that after three straight setbacks during the 2010–11 season and eight straight losses to Baylor overall, we would be utterly demoralized. We weren't even discouraged. We knew we were closing in on probably the best team in the country and that every time we played them, our odds of beating them increased. They were a great team in every aspect, but for each of our losses that season, we were within a play or two of winning. After the game, Sydney Colson summarized our entire team's thoughts when she said, "We know we're on their level." All we wanted was one more opportunity to prove it. We all assumed that if we met Baylor again, it would likely be at the 2011 Final Four, because we didn't figure the NCAA Selection Committee would put us both in the same region.

Wrong.

On March 14, the Selection Committee announced we had earned our fourth consecutive No. 2 seed, becoming the first team in NCAA Tournament history to be selected a No. 2 seed four straight years. The surprise was that we were placed in the Dallas Regional, where Baylor was the top seed. We expected to be sent to the Dayton, Ohio, or Spokane, Washington, Regional. A month earlier, ESPN women's basketball writer Charlie Creme wrote that putting Baylor and us together would violate a major principle used by the committee that no more than one team from a conference may be seeded in the top four of the same region unless a conference has five or more teams seeded fourth or higher. The committee went against that in 2008 by placing top-ranked Connecticut and No. 2 seed Rutgers together.

The Big East rivals met in the regional final with UConn winning, and Creme noted that the committee took flak for that.

During the Selection Show, when we were announced as the No. 2 seed in Dallas, the cameras flashed to Waco and the Baylor watching party. There seemed to be a sense of disbelief. From Baylor's standpoint, it was a show of disrespect to put us in that regional. Afterward, Kim Mulkey said, "I can't ever use the word 'shocked' with the NCAA anymore. You want to see new faces, you want to see new teams. I don't think anybody wants to see the same teams that you see from your conference."

From our perspective, we loved being in the Dallas Regional. We knew we were likely to face Baylor, so we'd rather do it in Dallas than in Indianapolis. Of course, first things first. We opened our NCAA Tournament in Shreveport, Louisiana, against Southland Conference regular season and tournament champ McNeese State. The winner of that game would meet seventh-seeded Rutgers or 10th-seeded Louisiana Tech. Considering our previous early-round travels to faraway places like Trenton, New Jersey, and Spokane, Washington, Shreveport was practically in our backyard.

In hindsight, it was quite the pleasant business trip, as we coasted to a 40-point win (87–47) over McNeese State and followed up that with comfortable 70–48 win over Rutgers. Those two victories earned us the right to travel to Dallas for a Sweet Sixteen matchup against Georgia. Looming beyond that, of course, was the potential showdown against Baylor in the Elite Eight. Practically anyone and everyone who was remotely interested in women's basketball was salivating at the possibility of a fourth head-to-head confrontation between the Bears and the Aggies, which worried the hell out of me. While the media could look past our matchup with Georgia, we couldn't.

The sixth-seeded Bulldogs traveled to Dallas with a 23–10 overall record and were making their 12th overall appearance in the Sweet Sixteen. This was a tournament-tested program that was appearing in its 17th consecutive NCAA Tournament and was coached by Hall of Famer Andy Landers. Earlier in the year, Landers became just the fifth major college women's hoops coach to secure 850 career victories. Georgia even brought in its most famous athletic alum—Herschel Walker—to deliver the pregame speech to the team. Georgia absolutely deserved our full attention from the opening tip, and I preached that to my team all week leading up to the March 27 game against the Bulldogs inside the American Airlines Center.

Fortunately, I had nothing to worry about because my team arrived in Dallas with a laser-like focus. Georgia was focused on stopping Danielle

Adams, and they did a decent job of limiting her early in the game, holding the All-American to just a 3-of-11 shooting performance from the floor midway through the first half. But the complete focus on Danielle left gaping holes in the zones, and we had a field day from the three-point range. Sydney Colson hit three of her first four attempts from three-point range as we bolted out to a 27–2 lead. As a team, we shot nearly 60 percent from the three-point arch in the first half. Even our desperation shots found the bottom of the net. For example, a heave by sophomore guard Adrienne Pratcher with 2:52 left in the half beat the shot clock to push the lead above 30. Overall, we connected on eight of 14 attempts from three-point range in the first 20 minutes, building a 48–17 halftime lead.

Our hot outside shooting forced Landers to abandon the zone, and Georgia just didn't have anyone strong enough to guard Adams one-on-one. Adams produced a game-high 23 points even though she started slowly. And I may have been most proud of her defense. All-SEC forward Porsha Phillips, who became the first Lady Bulldog to average a double-double for the season in more than two decades, was limited to six points and seven rebounds in 31 minutes. Most people never credited Danielle for her defense because of how many points she averaged. She was, however, a tremendously underrated defensive player and embraced our defensive philosophy, which was responsible for Georgia starting the game by making just one of its first 14 shot attempts.

Our large lead in the second half allowed me to freely use my bench. Freshman Karla Gilbert had nine points and five rebounds in nine minutes, and our reserves scored 22 points as we coasted to a 79–38 victory. The 41-point victory was our 30th win of the year for the first time in school history and was the most lopsided NCAA Tournament win in school history. Meanwhile Georgia's 38 points were the second-fewest in regional history. I wasn't at all surprised that we won, but I was stunned by how dominant we were. Honestly, I kept looking up at the scoreboard in disbelief. I was even telling the officials that I had never been part of an NCAA Tournament game like that against a quality team of Georgia's stature. In the other game that day, Brittney Griner scored 40 points, as Baylor was forced to exert more effort than us in an 86–76 victory over Wisconsin–Green Bay. That, of course, set up the matchup that everyone wanted to see: Baylor versus Texas A&M for a trip to the Final Four. It was a battle of heavyweights, like Muhammad Ali versus Joe Frazier, Larry Holmes versus Ken Norton, Jack Dempsey versus Gene Tunney, Evander Holyfield versus Mike

Tyson, or even the Ultimate Fighting Championship matchup between Conor McGregor and José Aldo.

Immediately after beating Georgia, our school officials began organizing round-trip buses from College Station to Dallas for the Elite Eight game. Baylor fans had long been bitten by the women's basketball bug, because for quite some time it was the school's marquee team sport. Besides, Baylor fans knew the Lady Bears would be the top seed in Dallas and were able to purchase tickets for the regional weeks and months in advance.

Texas A&M, on the other hand, had long been considered a football school and a basketball wasteland. With the help of men's coaches like Billy Gillispie, Mark Turgeon, and Billy Kennedy, we vastly improved our basketball reputation through the years. Still, I was concerned about the arena being filled predominantly with green and gold as we battled for the right to represent the state of Texas in the Final Four. I was thrilled to have buses coming in, but the night before the game, I made it a point at the press conference to challenge A&M fans in the Dallas–Fort Worth area not to be outnumbered in the arena. I built up the game, saying it would be the best women's basketball game ever played in Dallas. I also played to my roots, reminding people that it was my hometown. Likewise, I reminded fans it was the hometown area of Sydney Carter, Maryann Baker, Kristen Grant, and Skylar Collins. I really challenged Aggies to show up because they would be treated to something really special. I stopped short of going "Joe Namath" at the press conference and guaranteeing a victory, but I liked our chances.

I loved the way we were playing, and perhaps history was on our side as well. Gabe Bock of TexAgs.com pointed out on the day of the game that since 1996–97, only one women's NCAA basketball team had managed to beat the same opponent four times in the same season, according to Stats.com. Oral Roberts had four wins over Missouri–Kansas City in 2004–5. One of the final things I told the media at that press conference was that I hoped for a really close game, even a tie game with about three minutes left to play. I figured it would be like that, I anticipated a nip-and-tuck nail-biter, I believed we were due for a good shooting game against the Bears, and deep down, I believed that Danielle Adams was due for a big game against Baylor after struggling in the first three contests. Baylor had been Danielle's kryptonite of sorts. In the first three games against Baylor, Danielle had averaged just 11.3 points per contest, while shooting 24 percent from the field. For the season, however, she was just about twice as good in both categories. It seemed like it was her time to shine.

In retrospect, I was wrong in just about all my assumptions except for my hunches that we would, indeed, win and that the atmosphere inside the American Airlines Center would be energized. As I had done with my Arkansas team that reached the Final Four in 1998, I told our girls not to step off the bus unless they truly believed we were going to win. It was our time, and I wanted to make sure all our players were in a positive mind-set before we entered the facility. Fortunately, there was no hesitation on anyone's part. We practically burst off the bus and into an arena that was combustible. Fans of both teams showed up in masses—a total of 11,508 filled the venue—creating a supercharged atmosphere.

We did not shoot particularly well (just 34.4 percent from the field and just 11.8 percent from three-point range), though. Likewise, Danielle did not have a great offensive game, especially not in terms of her statistical standards. She made just three of 12 shots from the field, missed all five of her three-point attempts, didn't shoot a free throw, didn't score in the first half, grabbed only four rebounds, and finished with six points. If you had told me in advance that her statistical line, as well as our team shooting numbers, were going to be so ordinary, I would have been quite worried. And if you had told me about those numbers and the fact that one team would be comfortably ahead in the last three minutes—as opposed to my prediction the day before during the press conference—I would have been especially concerned that we would be the team on the negative end of the scoreboard.

As it turned out, though, our defense made the difference. Dallas/DeSoto native Sydney Carter stole the show, and Sydney Colson made the steal of the game to lead us to a 58–46 victory. While Danielle didn't have a great offensive day, she played well on the defensive end against Brittney Griner, despite picking up two early fouls and sitting out all but eight minutes of the first half. Freshman Karla Gilbert then took her turn against Griner and picked up three quick fouls. Despite our early foul trouble in the post, our guards did a great job defensively, and our 1-3-1 zone helped keep Baylor off guard. Griner was 1-for-8 from the field when Danielle Adams was in the game. When Kelsey Assarian and Karla Gilbert were in there, she was 5-for-10. That just shows how underrated Danielle was as a defender.

Baylor, which averaged 51.9 shooting from the field in its first three tournament games, shot 31.3 percent against us. Griner finished with 20 points, but she labored in doing so, hitting just six of 18 shots and going scoreless for almost six and a half minutes to open the game. Griner also missed a one-handed dunk attempt—to the delight of our fans.

Primarily because of the early foul trouble, Adams was held scoreless in the first half, but Carter was sensational. Carter set a tone from the start, hitting a three-pointer, dishing out an assist, and canning a jumper in the game's first two minutes for a 7–0 lead. Overall, Carter scored 15 of her 22 points in the first 20 minutes as we took a 32–21 lead into halftime. We felt good at the intermission, but we were certainly not taking anything for granted. After all, we'd lost a nine-point second-half lead against Baylor on Valentine's Day, and we squandered a 12–0 start in the Big 12 title game almost three weeks earlier in Kansas City. We knew Baylor would make its run, but we wanted to be in full attack mode to start the second half. We did just that and extended our advantage to 15 (41–26) with just over 14 minutes left on a layup by Carter.

To the surprise of no one, Baylor made its run. With a little over four minutes remaining, Griner made two free throws to bring the Lady Bears to within seven, at 48–41. That's when we put the clamps down and made our triumphant run to the Final Four. With Baylor fans sensing a now-or-never moment, Colson blew past Griner and missed, but she was fouled and made both free throws to extend our lead to 50–41. Right after that, the Bears attempted to put the ball in the hands of Odyssey Sims, but Colson stripped it at center court and took it all the way for a layup and was fouled again. With our bench going wild, and the stunned Baylor players sitting in bewildered shock, Colson pumped her fist and shrieked in joy. She then finished the three-point play to make it 53–41 with 2:41 remaining. At that point, our fans began making travel plans to Indianapolis while Baylor fans began streaming out of the arena.

Once the final seconds ticked away, maroon mayhem ensued at center court as our players and coaches stormed the floor and celebrated Texas A&M's first-ever trip to the Final Four. It was such a great moment to savor in front of so many of our fans and former players. So many great images come to mind when I recall that moment. We held an impromptu press briefing before the actual press conference as—this will probably come as no surprise—I took the microphone from the scorer's table on media row and began addressing the crowd over the arena's PA system. I told the thousands of fans who stuck around long after the game ended that they had watched something very special with these young ladies, and as we all took turns cutting down the nets, the crowd began chanting, "Final Four! Final Four! Final Four!" I held up four fingers during the chant and walked off the floor while being escorted by former players such as A'Quonesia Franklin and Danielle Gant. Before I left the floor, however, I had invited practically everyone in maroon to celebrate with us at Dick's Last Resort in the West End of Downtown Dallas after the press conference. I also invited the media covering the game to the party and promised I would buy the first round.

Sure enough, we finished the press conference at about 11:30 and went to Dick's Last Resort, where we celebrated until about 1 a.m. It was so special because our fans were able to share that incredible moment and the sheer jubilation of the accomplishment with our players and coaches. The place was rocking and rolling, and I ended up on top of a table, toasting the Aggies. We didn't get back to the hotel until about 1:15 in the morning, where my wife was sound asleep because she had to wake up at 4:30 to drive back to Arkansas. It was a whirlwind time, and I knew that everybody associated with our program could have ridden cloud nine back to College Station the following day. But once the sun rose, it was my job—along with Vic Schaefer's, Kelly Bond's, and Johnnie Harris's—to keep us grounded and focused on the mission ahead.

We'd just beaten the best team in America, but we needed to stop basking and start tasking on the two games ahead. In 1998, I had taken an Arkansas team to Kansas City for the Final Four, and we were just happy to be there. We were the heavy underdogs, and we were going to the Big Dance as Cinderella. In 2011, though, we were going to Indianapolis as Rosa Parks, meaning that we were not going to take a backseat to anyone.

Of course UConn (36–1), making its 12th Final Four appearance and a run for its third consecutive national title, was the favorite heading into the Final Four. But they weren't invincible and we knew it. The Huskies were damned good, and on December 28, 2010, Geno Auriemma's winning streak reached 90 straight wins following a victory over Pacific. That win also made UConn 12–0 for the season, including an 80-point win over Holy Cross, 31-point wins over Ohio State and Florida State, and a one-point home win over Baylor. But on December 30, the streak came to an end when Stanford shocked the Huskies, 71–59, in Palo Alto. From that point forward, the Huskies did not lose another game en route to the Final Four. But several opponents had proven that UConn was vulnerable. For example, Notre Dame had lost by only three during the regular season and by only nine in the championship game of the Big East Tournament.

The other two teams heading to Indianapolis were No. 1 seed Stanford (33–2) and No. 2 seed Notre Dame (30–7). Obviously, Stanford had proven that it was capable of beating anyone by knocking off UConn and going unbeaten in the Pac-10. But the Cardinal has also proven vulnerable, losing by double digits at DePaul and at Tennessee. Meanwhile, Notre Dame—like us—had pulled off a big upset to reach the Final Four, knocking off top-seeded Tennessee, 73–59, in the Dayton Regional. Notre Dame, making its first trip to the Final Four since 2001 when Muffet McGraw's team won it all, also was similar to us in that one team from its own conference had been a huge thorn in its side. The Irish came to Indianapolis, only 140 miles north of their campus in South Bend, having gone 0–3 against their Big East antagonist, UConn.

In the National Semifinals on April 3, we faced Stanford in the first game, and Notre Dame would have its fourth shot at UConn in the night-cap. Most of the experts predicted a championship game between Stanford, which was making its fourth consecutive trip to the Final Four, and UConn. But I truly believed we could win it all because we'd already beaten what I thought was the best team in the country thanks to our defense. In winning our first four games in the NCAA Tournament, none of our opponents had even managed to score 50 points in a game. We could frustrate any opponent, we could handle any obstacle thrown at us, we'd been tested under fire, and we could beat any team in the country. We were going to Indy with a tool box in tow instead of a tour guide because we had a job to do. That was my message on March 30, the morning after we beat Baylor and boarded a bus back to College Station, that was the "sermon" I preached back on campus, and that was the theme of our discussions once we arrived in Indianapolis. I was so focused on that that I almost forgot my wife's birthday on April 1. Since I was usually at the Final Four on April 1, I was always getting last-minute gifts. Nan went with me in 1998 when we were at Arkansas, and she teased every year afterward, saying that if I was any damned good, my team would be at the Final Four more so she could go too. So in 2011, I flew her to Indianapolis for the Final Four.

Family and friends are things you don't really think about when you are watching a big sporting event like the Super Bowl, the World Series, or the Final Four. But when you are a participant in one of those events, you want your friends, family, and the people who have helped you along the way to be a part of it. But arranging for tickets and travel accommodations really cuts into your preparation time. You have to be careful with your time and focus on the most important thing. If you're just satisfied and happy to get to the Final Four, you'll be coming home on Monday morning instead of Wednesday morning.

One of the hardest things is putting up the cell phones. The cell phones were blowing up after we beat Baylor, and it's really hard for the teenagers and young adults now who grew up with cell phones and social media to put their phones down. I had 132 messages the morning after we beat Baylor that I just did not have time to answer before we left for Indianapolis. I told the girls on the team that their friends were their friends before the Final Four and they will be your friends after it. The most important thing is being able to focus. When we arrived at the Final Four, we took up those kids' cell phones, which made them mad, but they appreciated it in the end.

We also kept our focus on practice day before the game. Instead of merely conducting a laid-back shootaround on April 2 when all four teams were given practice time on the floor of Conseco Fieldhouse, we turned up the intensity and had a real practice. At the end of practice, I summoned my inner Gene Hackman/Norman Dale and climbed up a ladder, busted out the tape measure, and gave a speech similar to the one that Hackman gave in *Hoosiers*, which was loosely based on the Milan High School team that won the 1954 Indiana state championship. In the movie, the small-town team, Hickory, shocks the state by reaching the championship game in Indianapolis. In a large arena and before a crowd bigger than any they've seen, the Hickory players face long odds to defeat the defending state champions from South Bend, whose players are taller and more athletic. When the Hickory team first arrives at the arena, head coach Norman Dale, played by Hackman, measures the height of the basket and the distance from the free-throw line to the basket and informs his players, "I think you'll find it's the exact same measurements as our gym back in Hickory." The point is that despite the big stage, the game is the same. I couldn't help but make the same comparison, and our team took the message to heart. We then went over to Marion College for another workout, and I could see in our players' eyes that they believed we were going to beat Stanford on April 3.

Heading into the game, our big challenge was to slow the versatile attack of Stanford, a team that was averaging 79.8 points per game. I told the media before the game that we were not going to play "hope you miss" defense. Instead, we were going to play "make you miss." To do that, we were going to have to be physical, and we needed a big game not just from Danielle Adams but also from Tyra White, Adaora Elonu, and the rest of our help-side defense. In contrast to Baylor and its one big threat in 6-foot-8 center Griner, Stanford had plenty of size and skill: six-two Nneka Ogwumike, six-three Chiney Ogwumike, and six-four Kayla Pedersen were starters, and six-three Joslyn Tinkle, six-five Sarah Boothe, and six-three Mikaela Ruef were available to come off the bench. With so much size at their disposal, rebounding was a huge concern—probably our biggest—heading into the game. We tried to recruit the Ogwumikes out of Cypress–Fairbanks

High in the Houston area really hard, and we knew how good they were, but we were determined to throw all our energy and defensive effort at them to make it a crazy, frantic pace.

Unfortunately, we didn't exactly set Conseco Fieldhouse on fire to start the game. In fact, we only made 2 of our first 11 shots—a three-pointer by Adams and a three by White in the first six and a half minutes. But we were able to keep it close with our defensive intensity, and when Sydney Carter canned a jumper with 10:43 left in the first half, we took a 12–11 lead. We soon increased that lead to 17–11 following a layup by Maryann Baker and another three by Carter. At that point, Stanford made a concerted effort to pound the ball into the post, beginning by putting the ball into the hands of Ogwumike. As the intensity in the paint began to increase, Danielle Adams suffered a minor injury on her right hand after falling hard to the floor. Moments later, she took an unintentional blow to her nose that sent her to the floor for several minutes. She managed to remain in the game and quickly drew a charge on the defensive end, hitting her face in the process. At that point, she was forced to take a seat for the final seven minutes of the half while she received treatment for her nose.

With Danielle on the bench for an extended period, the Cardinal took advantage in a big way, ripping off a 15–4 run to close the half. In doing so, Stanford was able to turn a seven-point deficit into a four-point half-time lead, 27–23. We only shot 30.3 percent from the field, and we did not get to the free-throw line at all in the opening 20 minutes. Stanford also outmuscled us on the glass in the first half—our biggest worry entering the game—grabbing 23 rebounds compared to our 15.

Things certainly did not turn in our favor once play resumed in the second half, although we did cut the lead to 29–28 when Sydney Carter drained a three-pointer a little over two minutes into the second half. From that point, however, the Cardinal answered with a 9–0 run to take a 38–28 lead with 15:08 left. During part of that stretch, we were without Colson, who had taken an Ogwumike elbow to the face on a hard screen. Colson didn't see it coming and was woozy for a short time. The physical nature of the game was taking its toll on us, and even though we cut the lead to one point again, Stanford answered with another run to go back up by 10 once again, 54–44, with only 6:01 left in the game. That was about the same time when associate head coach Kelly Bond came up to me and said that Sydney Carter was out of gas. But I couldn't take her out because we were essentially in dire straits. We needed her in the game, so we had to quit calling as many plays for Carter. Instead, we started calling plays for Tyra White, and she delivered.

We talked about digging deep and putting every ounce of energy into the final six minutes, and we then began an amazing comeback by scoring eight straight points in 96 seconds. But the key to the comeback was our relentless effort on the defensive end. We held Stanford scoreless for two and a half critical minutes, which allowed us to cut the lead to 54–52. The teams traded a few baskets over the next couple of minutes, including a big three-pointer by Carter, and we finally pushed ahead on a pair of Sydney Colson free throws with 53 seconds left on the clock. Eighteen seconds later, Adams was called for a questionable foul on Ogwumike. Upset by the call, Danielle picked herself up and started running toward our bench, with one of the referees telling her to calm down. Ogwumike made both shots to give Stanford a 60–59 lead with 35 second left.

Those 35 seconds were practically an eternity in this game. White was magnificent down the stretch, scoring nine of our final 17 points over the last 4:31. She finished with a team-high 18 points, and she gave us back a one-point lead with 19 seconds left on a layup. After Stanford called a timeout, Ogwumike answered with a tough layup of her own with only nine seconds left, giving the Cardinal a 62–61 lead. We didn't have another timeout at that point.

Fortunately, we didn't need one because we had a heady senior point guard who knew exactly what needed to be done and who needed the basketball in her hands. Sydney Colson took the inbounds pass and raced up the floor, her ponytail bobbing up and down as she sped toward the other end. As Colson reached the paint on the Stanford end of the floor, she found White and delivered a perfectly executed bounce pass. White connected—despite two defenders crashing toward her—with the biggest layup of her career, putting it through the net with 3.3 seconds remaining to give us a 63–62 advantage.

All we needed at that point was one more stop, and Sydney Colson, despite running on empty for the last couple minutes of the game, intercepted the Cardinal's desperation pass to seal the victory, sending Stanford home from the Final Four and sending our players jumping for joy. In the process of overcoming a 10-point deficit in the final six minutes, we orchestrated a comeback that was the 10th largest deficit in Final Four history. And our girls were absolutely so clutch. After not attempting a free throw in the first half, we finished 10-for-10 from the free-throw line, becoming the 15th team to finish perfect from the stripe in a national semifinal game.

Despite a slow start, Adams finished with 16 points and Carter added 14 points, including four three-pointers. We had just enough offense, and we once again were stellar on the defensive end. We held Stanford's potent offensive attack 18 points under its average, and we forced the Cardinal into a season-high 22 turnovers. Even being the first tourney team to top 50 points against us in a game wasn't enough for Stanford, because we outscored the Cardinal 19–8 during the final six minutes. As a result, we advanced to the national title game for the first time in Texas A&M history and the first time in my career as a head coach. It was a sweet win, and it absolutely stunned the world of women's college basketball. On the other hand, it wasn't even the biggest upset of the night. Hours after our victory, Notre Dame pulled an even bigger shocker by sending Maya Moore and top-seeded Connecticut home, 72–63.

That set up a championship game that no one anticipated: the Aggies versus the Irish. The traditional powers and top seeds in 2011—Tennessee, Connecticut, Stanford, and Baylor—were gone, marking the first time since 1994 that a women's title game would take place without a No. 1 seed. Quite frankly, it was good for women's college basketball to feature some fresh faces on the biggest stage, and it just so happened that we resembled each other. Both teams relied on stingy defense, both beat No. 1 seeds in Indy, and both had to take down foes that had beaten them three other times this season. "In some ways, we're mirror images of each other because we've got great guard play and an outstanding defense throughout the tournament," Notre Dame coach Muffet McGraw said the day before the title game. "I thought throughout the tournament, as I watched them, they would be a very, very tough team to play. Be careful of what you wish for because now we've got them."

Deep down, we also knew that we had a national championship firmly within our reach. Going into the Final Four, we truly believed Stanford was the toughest of our three possible opponents, followed by UConn and Notre Dame. That certainly didn't mean we could take the Irish lightly in the championship game, but the reality is that we believed we were better than Notre Dame. We also knew that we had already beaten the two best teams in the entire 2011 NCAA Tournament field in Baylor and Stanford. Now it was just time to finish the journey. It wasn't going to be easy, but every one of our players, coaches, trainers, and so forth knew we would be national champions on April 3. We weren't just thinking positive thoughts; we knew we were going to get the job done and that we were going to win a national championship on national television for Texas A&M.

Prior to April 5, 2011, Texas A&M had won a national championship three times in women's softball ('82, '83, and '87), once in men's golf in 2009, and twice in the men's and women's outdoor track-and-field in 2009 and 2010 (thanks to the guidance of legendary coach Pat Henry, who went on to win two more national titles a couple months later in the summer of 2011). But that was the extent of A&M's national championships since 1939, when the football team went undefeated and beat Tulane in the 1940 Sugar Bowl. But times were much different back then, and the national championship didn't deliver the kind of publicity that it generates today. "We didn't know there was such a thing as playing for No. 1," said Tommie Vaughn, the center of the '39 team, prior to his death. "When you look back at what we did, it's very impressive. But it wasn't even a big deal back then." Obviously, it's a monstrous deal nowadays, and not just in football.

Athletics are often called the "front porch of a university" because they offer a brief glimpse of the entire university to visitors who come to games from other campuses or watch televised sporting events. Universities spend millions upon millions each year to build great athletics programs because successful sports teams that appear on national television can educate spectators from South Florida to Seattle and from New York City to New Mexico about a university's distinguishing traditions, its commitment to excellence, its overall uniqueness, and so forth.

Of all the places I have ever coached or even visited, I have never experienced a student body and former student population with more passion, pride, and pure love for their school than Texas A&M. That passion is often best displayed at Kyle Field, the renowned home of the Aggie football team, and its famed fan base, known throughout the college athletics universe as "the 12th Man." When it comes to its one-of-a-kind game-day atmosphere, Texas A&M can stand toe-to-toe with any program in the country, as Kyle Field may be the best of the best. In banner years and bleak decades, A&M continually achieves national recognition for the unmatched, ear-splitting, goose bump–inducing environment generated at its home football games and other athletic venues.

In those venues, many of Texas A&M's storied and unique traditions are on display to the masses of people who attend games or watch them on television. Visitors from other schools are often awestruck by a visit to Aggieland, where camaraderie is coveted, sportsmanship is stressed, booing is discouraged, respect is revered, friendliness to visitors is emphasized, and supporting the team through thick and thin is practically mandated. But the reality is that because A&M has not won a football championship since 1939 and had never even been to the Final Four in men's or women's basketball prior to 2011, much of the county's average sports fans were not particularly familiar with A&M's traditions, enrollment numbers, and so forth.

In comparison, the school we were playing in the 2011 national championship game was well known across the country largely because its football program had won 13 national championships, the 1979 men's basketball team had made it to the Final Four, and the women's basketball team had made a Final Four appearance in 1997 and won the national title in 2001.

After we beat Baylor, and especially after we beat Stanford, I began to sense just how important a national title would be to our students and former students of all ages. Before and after the Notre Dame game, I received countless messages from Aggies who had attended Texas A&M in the '40s, '50s, and '60s, when the school was still a small all-male institution that hadn't changed much since the school first opened its doors on October 4, 1876, as the land-grant college near the banks of the Brazos River. In 1891, a former two-term governor of Texas named Lawrence Sullivan Ross arrived as the school's president and declared that in order to survive, A&M's central mission would be military training. Classes soon took somewhat of a backseat to military training, and A&M began to establish its legacy as the all-male, all-military outpost that welcomed brave, common young men of meager means without reservation. It wasn't until the 1960s, under the leadership of President James Earl Rudder, that women began to be welcomed as students on a full scale.

Since then, the university has grown and prospered in many ways. Texas A&M now possesses a stellar academic reputation and an enrollment of roughly 55,000 students. It's a spectacular university that has been continually sited by numerous organizations as one of the top academic institutions in the country. The former students and current students are remarkably proud of what A&M has become, and they have desperately wanted their athletic teams to receive the kind of positive exposure that a nationally televised national championship can deliver. It wasn't so much about a love for women's basketball; the maroon-tinted, flag-waving, 12th Man towel–wielding bandwagon that followed us on our journey to Indianapolis was all about the love they have for Texas A&M. We just were in the great position to play on ESPN for the ultimate prize and to showcase to the nation our oak-lined, tradition-rich campus of passionate and proud students who—in good times or in bad—may be more spirited toward their university than any other student body in the country.

As we prepared for Notre Dame, we all felt the power, the purpose, and the support of the huge Aggie network behind us. I was totally relaxed on the day of the national championship game for a couple of reasons. First and foremost, I just knew we would find a way to win. I knew Notre Dame would make it a battle, but I knew we would win. I also wanted to make sure that my team could see that I was completely confident. I knew that after knocking off UConn, Notre Dame was going to be completely confident that this was their championship to win, but I absolutely wanted to exude confidence in our team. Before we departed the bus to enter the arena, I stood up and told the entire team that this was their game and their national championship. "You've got to feel it right now," I said. "Second is last. We're going for first."

Prior to the opening tip-off, Vic Schaefer—as he always did—addressed the team before I did. He said the game was not about who was the more talented team, pointing out that we were both great teams, and that the game would be decided by the team that displayed more resilience and toughness. In the midst of his speech, Sydney Carter lit up like a Christmas tree. She said, "If the game is about toughness then we have this in the bag. There is not another team in the country as tough as us."

My speech after that was almost anticlimactic. We just needed to take care of business. Period. Play our game. Make history. Bring a major title back to Texas A&M for the first time since 1939. Once the game actually began, it went better than I could have possibly imagined. In front of an amazing crowd of 17,473, we jumped out to an early 12–4 lead in the opening half, and we led by 13 points, 29–16, with 8:32 left in the first half. Notre Dame certainly didn't back down, however, after a difficult start. And we were hamstrung by the fact that our playmaker, point guard Sydney Colson, picked up her second foul with 12:41 left in the first half. Notre Dame heated up on the offensive end and switched to a full-court, man-to-man pressure defense. Without Colson on the floor, the Irish went on an 11–2 run to pull to within four points, 31–27. At that point, I gambled and inserted Colson back into the lineup. She calmed the team down and hit a pair of key free throws, but she also picked up a third foul on a reach-in that she should have never attempted. The Irish ended the half on an 8–0 run and scored 17 of the final 21 points, holding us without a point over the final 5:50. Notre Dame shot 59.1 percent from the field in the half and took a 35–33 lead into the locker room at the half.

I remember going into the locker room absolutely livid that we were losing. We had controlled so much of the first half, yet we were losing. I had to remind myself that we were only trailing by two, and I think I looked down toward the Sharpied plus sign on my hand—something I had done since first taking the job at A&M to remind myself to stay positive—to keep my focus on staying upbeat. As soon as we entered the locker room, Vic and I were discussing strategies, then came the ESPN cameras. They were setting up to hear the halftime speech I was going to give. They wanted to provide viewers with the adjustments that we were going to make, but I needed a few minutes to be bluntly honest with my team. I told the ESPN camera crew, "Give me four minutes. I don't want you in here until four minutes from now."

I then went into the dressing room and kept it really simple. Notre Dame had been undefeated throughout the course of the season, but I didn't care about that crap. I peppered my speech with a few "damns" and "hells," but then I hammered home a couple of points. First, I told Danielle Adams that she was not allowed to settle for outside shots anymore. I wanted our offense to go through her in the paint, not the perimeter. Next, I told Colson to quit going for the steal and to get the ball inside to Danielle. I wanted to set up Sydney Carter, Tyra White, and Adaora Elonu for open jumpers. Second— and this is what I didn't want the ESPN cameras to broadcast—I reminded our girls that we had already beaten a couple of teams that were better than Notre Dame. "Don't let Notre Dame steal this from us," I said. Then I let ESPN come in and I made a few motivational comments. But the takeaway of my halftime message was this: get the ball inside to Danielle and don't let an inferior team beat us when we had already taken down two Goliaths.

My speech was certainly not Knute Rockne–like, but our team took the message to heart. Danielle Adams—the first first-team All-American in Texas A&M women's basketball history—saved her absolute best for the last half she would ever play in an A&M uniform. She was nothing short of brilliant. Adams scored 22 of her 30 points in a dominating second half and answered the Fighting Irish basket for basket. She was absolutely sensational. With us trailing 48–43 early in the second half, Adams simply took over. She scored 10 of our next 13 points to give us a 56–53 lead midway through the second half. We then extended the advantage to 64–57 behind the two Sydneys. Not surprisingly, Notre Dame didn't back down, battling back behind Diggins and Devereaux Peters. The Irish scored nine of the next 11 points to tie the game at 66 on Skylar Diggins's jumper with 3:56 left.

Without hesitation, we went right back to Adams on the next two possessions and she delivered, hitting back-to-back layups. Remarkably and inspirationally, Adams hit nine of her first 10 shots in the second half. After

Peters's put-back cut our lead to 70–68, we called timeout with two seconds on the shot clock and the ball under our basket. The play was "31 fist," a back-screen lob play to Danielle Adams, with Tyra at the top of the key. I told Tyra to run the arc, just in case Danielle was double-teamed, which she was. Sydney Colson realized that and hit the second option for the play, feeding the ball to Tyra. White launched the shot over Notre Dame's Skylar Diggins, and it went in. White, who scored 18 points, drained the clutch three-pointer as the shot clock buzzer sounded to put us up 73–68 with 1:07 left. It was very reminiscent of Acie Law's historic buzzer-beating shot that clinched an A&M men's victory over Texas in 2006.

"I really didn't know the ball was coming to me," White said after the game. "The play was designed for Danielle. But when I came off a screen, I saw that they were triple-teaming her, and I knew Sydney Colson was going to pass me the ball, so I just wanted to hit it. The defender kind of hit my elbow, too, so I didn't really think it was going to go in. But it did, and I'm glad it went in."

So was everybody else who bleeds maroon. White was often referred to as "the silent assassin" by her teammates and friends, but her comments during her postgame interview with ESPN's Holly Rowe showed her great confidence and personality. "Not silent anymore, baby," she said with a huge grin on her face. Conversely, Notre Dame knew that the end of their run had arrived when White thrilled A&M fans and drilled the trey. "That was the knife in my heart. That was the game," Muffet McGraw said afterward, bowing her head when the question was asked. "I thought that was just an amazing play on White's part, and that play was the game."

Despite White's dagger, Diggins made two free throws with 40.7 seconds left, and the Irish had one last chance after our turnover with 29 seconds remaining. McGraw then called her final timeout, but Diggins—under duress from our outstanding defense—turned it over. White then hit two free throws to seal the win. We shot an astounding 68.2 percent from the field in the final 20 minutes and had nearly everything rolling down the stretch offensively. And of course, we knew that when the game was on the line, we would play with enough defensive intensity to win it all.

It's still difficult to describe the scene after the final buzzer sounded because the moment was just so damned surreal. We had come so amazingly far since first arriving at Texas A&M eight years earlier. After the game, so many things happened that I will never forget. I remember kissing my wife on the floor of Conseco Fieldhouse and thanking her for all the travels and trials we had been through over the course of decades. I remember looking toward the stands, where my grandson, Logan Burch, was holding up a sign that said, "I may be little, but I'm a HUGE Gary Blair fan! (a.k.a. Papaw Gary)." (He also had one that read "When we win . . . Coach Blair is taking me to Disney World.") I remember looking toward the stands, where my beautiful daughter and wonderful son were absolutely euphoric for me, and I recall thanking God that they had allowed me to pursue my dreams, which interfered with so much of the time that I would have otherwise spent with them during their childhood.

I also recall the blue, green, and gold Notre Dame–colored confetti falling and flashbulbs popping inside Canseco Fieldhouse as the Aggie Band played triumphantly and our players and coaches wildly celebrated the biggest win in women's basketball history at Texas A&M. I remember glancing toward one group of fans on the front row as they sobbed uncontrollably. Their tears of joy were evident in front of hundreds of euphoric Aggie supporters who held their arms aloft and celebrated the school's first women's basketball national title. The tears were literally streaming down the faces of former players A'Quonesia Franklin, Damitria Buchanan, and Jamila Ganter—three blue-collar building blocks of our program from previous years. I still have an image of Tyra White holding her hands up in celebration, tears streaming down her face, hugging teammates and former players like Katy Pounds-Lee, and then climbing into the stands to embrace family members. I looked over toward them, and Danielle Adams rushed over to embrace her family just moments after the final buzzer. Danielle played the game of her life on the biggest stage, and I just remember thinking about how happy I was for our seniors—Sydney Colson, Danielle Adams, and Maryann Baker—as well as our upperclassmen like Tyra White, Adaora Elonu, and Sydney Carter.

I was so delighted for my staff. Vic, Kelly, and Johnnie had worked so hard and had done such a great job in building and shaping our team. And I was also incredibly happy for the rest of my staff: director of basketball operations, Erich Birch (a Texas A&M graduate); video coordinator, Char-lee Miller; strength and conditioning coach, Jennifer Jones; trainer Mike "Radar" Ricke (also an A&M graduate); my administrative assistant, Claudia Walker; the women's basketball sports information director (SID), Deanna Werner; our assistant athletic director, Steve Miller (an A&M graduate), who was once the women's basketball SID and had been part of our radio broadcast for many years; and our radio play-by-play host, Mike Wright. And there are so many others from our athletic department who were at the title game, soaking up the moment. I was so happy for Texas A&M director of athletics, Bill Byrne, the man responsible for me coming to Texas A&M in the first place.

At some point during the craziness, I was dancing with Sydney Carter and Sydney Colson, attempting an old white man's version of "the Dougie." As luck would have it, the moment was captured on camera, and it became the opening sequence for an ESPN broadcast for the whole next year.

In the midst of the celebration, I remember thinking that I wished I could somehow stop time. I didn't want to just appreciate the moment; I wanted to savor and document every second, and I wanted time to go in slow motion. But time marches on, and that night was such a whirlwind— from appearing live on the ESPN set right after the game with Trey Wingo, Carol Lawson, and Carolyn Peck to the postgame press conference, and from the trophy presentation with our entire team and staff to hamming it up for photographs as we cut down the nets. I remember wanting to thank every- one who had contributed to this moment as we were on the stage inside the arena. Holly Rowe asked me how I felt, and I just started thanking groups of people from my past: the people at South Oak Cliff, Louisiana Tech, Stephen F. Austin, Arkansas, and, of course, Texas A&M.

I don't really recall what I said to my team in the locker room after the game, but I do remember the postgame press conference and demanding that Vic Schaefer accompany me to the interview room. I wanted him to share in that moment, and I knew that he would have a head coaching opportunity in the very near future. Walking toward the interview room, so many thoughts came rushing to my mind. I was so happy for A&M fans and former students from across the globe. Before the game, I had received letters and e-mails from Aggies stationed in Afghanistan, Iraq, and other locations around the world wishing us luck and letting me know that they were going to wake up at four in the morning to watch the game and to see their school make history.

Before anyone could even ask me a question in the press conference, I went into rambling mode—typical for me—and thanked the NCAA; the WBCA; the people of Indianapolis; Notre Dame head coach Muf- fet McGraw; and the Notre Dame players, especially Skylar Diggins and Devereaux Peters. Finally, I thanked my staff and my players, especially the seniors. It was so great to sit on a stage in front of the media and just listen to my players speak so proudly. Sydney Colson, Tyra White, and Danielle Adams were sensational in the press conference, and so was Vic. We prob- ably set some kind of record for the longest press conference in history, as I was rambling on and on until I introduced Vic. I told the media that Texas

A&M gave the country the secretary of defense in Bob Gates but that now I am presenting the secretary of defense for women's basketball, Vic Schaefer. I even asked him a question to start off, to which he replied, "That's got to be a first, a coach asking a coach the question."

On the stage right after the game, on the ESPN set, and at the press conference, I just wanted to be gracious. Throughout my career, I have always attempted to show class and give credit not only following losses but also following victories, all while remaining humble. When the blue, green, and gold confetti came down, I was oblivious to it all, but our fans were not. We were told that those colors had been planned three months ago, but that was bull crap. I thought about bringing it up at the press conference like some other coaches might have done, but I decided to let it go. At the moment, it could have been Baylor green and gold and I still wouldn't have given a damn. As long as it wasn't burnt orange, I could live with it. I had waited all my life to prove that nice guys could finish first. I wanted to shower people with praises and stay away from any agendas.

When we finally finished with the press conference, we loaded up the bus and headed for the hotel, where another trophy presentation would be held to award us the crystal ball trophy. I'll never forget walking through the crowd of A&M yell leaders, band members, fans, administrators, athletic department employees, friends, and family members who lined the lobby of the hotel after midnight to cheer for us, shake our hands, and pose for pictures. We were celebrating with all those friends in one of the ballrooms of the hotel until four in the morning. Usually, my wife is in bed by 10, but she was still going strong with the entire crew into the wee hours of the morning. I was supposed to be joining ESPN Radio's Mike and Mike Show the following morning at seven, so I finally took my grandson, Logan, up to the hotel room with me a little after four and began watching the game again on a DVD as Logan drifted off to sleep.

I fell asleep watching the game and then woke up in time to do the national radio interview with Mike Greenberg and Mike Golic, who is a former Notre Dame football player. Greenberg, who was from Northwestern University in Chicago, was giving Golic a really hard time, and I really loved that interview. We had so much fun on that interview that Golic was practically apologetic for predicting the day before that Notre Dame would win. As I had done the night before on ESPN's television set, I also sold Texas A&M, women's basketball, and the beauty of college athletics. I also continued to lobby for a free trip to Disney World (Disney owns ESPN), as I had done the night before. "I'm 65 years old, so maybe this is part of an

AARP plan," I told Mike and Mike. "I plan to continue coaching. If UConn men's coach Jim Calhoun can keep going, so can I. I forgot to mention on air last night that I want to take my grandkids to Disney World. I think Calhoun and I would be great taking the grandkids to Disney, as opposed to the normal way where the star athlete takes his kids."

Greenberg said he might have a little pull in that area, and he finished the interview by saying that he hoped to see me on Space Mountain soon. I certainly felt like we had scaled the mountaintop as we boarded the plane later that day in Indianapolis and headed back to College Station, where we were treated to another rousing celebration at Reed Arena. We received a police escort back to campus as people were lined along the streets waving at us. As we pulled into the loading docks of the arena and walked in the building, we were nearly floored by the fact that 7,500 people had shown up in the middle of the work day because they wanted to share in the exhilaration of our national championship. Our other coaches at A&M at that time, including track-and-field coach Pat Henry and men's golf coach J. T. Higgins, who had also led their teams to national championships, were so gracious to me and my staff. Head football coach Mike Sherman, men's basketball coach Mark Turgeon, baseball coach Rob Childress, volleyball coach Laurie Corbelli, softball coach Jo Evans, soccer coach G. Guerrieri, women's tennis coach Bobby Kleinecke, men's tennis coach Steve Denton, swimming and diving coaches Steve Bultman and Jay Holmes—along with all their assistants—were all so supportive, as were our university administrators, beginning with university president Bowen Loftin, who shared a dance with me on stage at Reed Arena, which proved that neither one of us possess an ounce of rhythm. But I did out-dance President Loftin.

I also received so much support and so many congratulatory messages from friends and former coaches around the country. I had just learned how to text two weeks before the national title game, and when my administrative assistant helped me retrieve the congratulatory texts upon our return, I had 657! I think I may still be trying to answer those messages.

For many years, I had dreamed about what it would be like to win a national championship as a head coach at a major university like Texas A&M. Quite frankly, my dreams paled in comparison to reality. It was better than I could have ever imagined. And it was even better than watching my Texas Rangers in the World Series—which they lost.

14 Success Is a Journey, Not a Destination

In 1939, at age 20, Edmund Hillary completed his first major climb, scaling Mount Ollivier in the Canterbury Region of New Zealand's Southern Alps. Twelve years later, Hillary was part of the 1951 British expedition to Mount Everest, the highest mountain in the world with a summit at 29,035 feet. Although it was unsuccessful—the eighth expedition that failed to reach the summit—the ninth British expedition to Everest in 1953, led by John Hunt, did succeed. At 6:30 a.m. on May 29, 1953, Hillary, then in his mid-30s, and Tenzing Norgay left camp for the final leg of their historic climb to the summit of Mount Everest.

Hillary and Norgay, the Sherpa mountain guide, had begun their climb up the world's tallest mountain seven weeks earlier, and Hillary had spent much of his life dreaming about completing this climb. At 11:30 a.m., Hillary and Norgay reached the summit of Mount Everest, becoming the first men to ever successfully reach the top. After risking their lives daily for nearly two full months, the two men spent only 15 minutes at the top of the world, because the scanty air supply made it difficult to breathe. After taking photos and enjoying the amazing view, the two men began their descent.

Interestingly to me, Hillary, who died in 2008, didn't stop climbing or taking on new challenges because he had reached his ultimate goal. After achieving international fame on Mount Everest, Hillary took up exploration.

He reached the South Pole by tractor on January 4, 1958, and he was among the first to scale Mount Herschel in the Antarctic expedition of 1967. In 1968, Hillary traversed the wild rivers of Nepal on a jet boat. He did the same up the Ganges, from its mouth to its source in the Himalayas, in 1977. In 1985, Hillary (then in his mid-60s) and astronaut Neil Armstrong flew a twin-engine plane to the North Pole, making Hillary the first person to stand at both poles *and* the summit of Everest, also known as the "third pole."

Beyond his explorations, the humble Hillary was devoted to helping the Sherpa people. He founded the Himalayan Trust, which built schools, hospitals, and transportation hubs in Nepal. He served as New Zealand's high commissioner to Nepal, as well as India and Bangladesh, from 1985 to 1988, and he was made an honorary citizen of Nepal in 2003, on the 50th anniversary of reaching the summit. *Time* magazine also listed him as one of the 100 most influential people of the 20th century.

Many inspiring quotes have been attributed to Hillary:

- "It is not the mountain we conquer, but ourselves."
- "People do not decide to become extraordinary. They decide to accomplish extraordinary things."
- "I have enjoyed great satisfaction from my climb of Everest and my trips to the poles. But there's no doubt that my most worthwhile things have been the building of schools and medical clinics."

I find all those comments quite intriguing and fascinating. First and foremost, Hillary saw Mount Everest as a mere obstacle that could help make him a better man. After his first failed expedition, he said, "Mount Everest, you beat me the first time, but I'll beat you the next time because you've grown all you are going to grow . . . but I'm still growing!" Second, his take on "extraordinary" is exceptional. You don't simply become a great climber, a great writer, a great entrepreneur, or a great coach by writing it down as a goal; you become extraordinary in your field—any field—by tackling great challenges. Finally, reaching the tops of mountains was how Hillary became an international name, but it was his impact on people that meant the most to him.

Quite frankly, I can relate to every single one of those comments, as well as many others Hillary made. Winning the national championship in 2011 was something I had dreamed about since first becoming a head coach at the collegiate ranks. Because I achieved that goal in April 2011, roughly four months shy of my 66th birthday in August, I am sure that some people naturally assumed it would be a great time for me to hang up the whistle and leave on top. I understand that line of thinking, but it never really crossed my mind. Like Edmund Hillary, I still had many more adventures I wanted to explore and conquer. I was not satisfied with merely climbing to the top of the mountain in women's college basketball; my competitive drive was still in high gear after reaching the summit in 2011.

Winning the national championship was wonderful on many different levels, but that's not what I want on my tombstone. It's not what defines me as a person or coach either. When I do finally ride into the retirement sunset, I want to be known primarily for how I influenced young people since first entering the coaching profession in 1973.

Don't get me wrong; I am really proud of the state championships, the conference crowns, and the national title. I am also genuinely appreciative that I have been fortunate enough to have been inducted into six hall of fames (Texas High School, Stephen F. Austin Athletics, Southland Conference, Texas Sports, Women's Basketball, and Arkansas Sports). But what really delights me is to see how God has allowed me to positively influence others. I am very proud, for example, of my longtime affiliation with the Special Olympics by raising funds and creating opportunities for children and adults with intellectual disabilities through sports activities. That has been one of my passions for many years through my foundation, Gary Blair Charities. And, of course, it thrills me to see so many of the young women I've coached through the decades use their basketball experiences as a stepping stone toward great careers and also their abilities to bless others as role models, mothers, and leaders in their communities.

I am absolutely overjoyed whenever I look at the media guide page titled "Gary Blair Coaching Tree." To see how many of my former players and assistant coaches have continued to impact young people by entering—or staying in—the coaching field is deeply gratifying. Entering the 2016–17 basketball season, 30 of my former players (Tennille Adams, Trenia Tillis, Maryann Baker, Damitria Buchanan, Skylar Collins, Sydney Colson, A'Quonesia Franklin, Jamila Ganter, Kristen Grant, Shae Henderson, Sytia Messer, Kristin Moore, Deneen Parker, Carol Price-Tortok, Taqueta Roberson, Amber Shirey, Christy Smith, Amy Wright, Stephanie Bloomer-Shieldknight, Sarah Pfeifer, Ashlaa Horton, Kimberly Jenkins [Wilson], Shaka Massey-Hare, La Toya Micheaux, Carrie Satterfield-Redman, Adrienne Pratcher, Rochelle Vaughn, Brandi-Whitehead-McEnturff, and Wendi Willits) were in either the high school or college coaching ranks or had been at one time. That roll call delights me because I know those women are shaping generations of young people—and will continue to do so long after I have left the profession.

I've also been so blessed to work with some incredibly talented assistant coaches through the years. Men and women like Kelly Bond-White, Bob Starkey, Vic Schaefer, Amy Wright, Johnnie Harris, Amy Tennison, Mike Neighbors, Tom Collen, Nell Fortner, Candi Harvey, Sue Donohoe, Lee Ann Riley, Julie Thomas-Stapp, and Kit Kyle-Martin have helped shape me as a coach and have contributed so much to everything we've been able to accomplish at Stephen F. Austin, Arkansas, and Texas A&M. I've said many times that one of the keys to success in any walk of life is to surround your-self with great people. I've been surrounded by wonderful men and women throughout my career, and for that I am truly grateful. They have allowed me to go to places I could have never imagined, and they have taken me on adventures I will never forget.

In that regard, I can also relate to Edmund Hillary. When it comes right down to it, I am an adventure/adrenaline junkie, and reaching the summit in 2011 just whet my appetite for more journeys, voyages, and basketball-focused escapades. In fact, winning the national championship was just the beginning of the adventures in 2011. Shortly after coming home to College Station and being greeted by the magnificent crowd at Reed Arena, we took the entire team to the state capitol in Austin, where we were honored by Senator Steve Ogden and several other senators on the Senate floor. We then proceeded to the Governor's Reception Room, where Governor Rick Perry (a former Texas A&M yell leader) posed for pictures and congratulated the team. We also toured to the House floor, where several Aggie representatives, including Representative Fred Brown, and even non-Aggie representatives were eager to meet and congratulate the team.

In May, I joined UConn men's coach Jim Calhoun at a gala event in midtown Manhattan's New York Athletic Club, where we were presented with the Winged Foot Award, given annually to the winning coaches of the men's and women's NCAA Division I Basketball Tournaments. In June, I was invited to throw out the first pitch prior to the Atlanta Braves–Houston Astros game on Aggie Night at Minute Maid Park, and in July, the Brazos Valley Bombers of the Texas Collegiate League allowed me to lead off the game against the Acadiana Cane Cutters as the designated hitter. I worked the count full, fouling off one pitch before striking out. Nevertheless, we won the game and I signed autographs for fans for over an hour after my appearance at the plate.

In June, Nan and I escorted Adaora Elonu, Sydney Carter, and Maryann Baker to the ESPYs at the Nokia Theater in downtown Los Angeles. The ESPYs, short for Excellence in Sports Performance Yearly, commemorate the previous year in athletics by recognizing major sports achievements, reliving unforgettable moments, and saluting the leading performers and performances. We were nominated for the award of Best Team, and although we didn't win (at least we lost to my favorite NBA team, the Dallas Mavericks), we were able to rub shoulders with the who's who of the sports world on the red carpet with the likes of Serena Williams, Dirk Nowitzki, Blake Griffin, and Aaron Rodgers.

In the summer of 2011, we also unveiled the most difficult schedule in the history of the program, as 18 of our 20 opponents had advanced to postseason the previous year. The highlight of the nonconference schedule was a showdown against seven-time national champion and 2011 Final Four participant Connecticut in the Jimmy V. Women's Basketball Classic.

In the midst of our whirlwind travels during the spring and summer of 2011, something else happened that forever changed the direction of Texas A&M athletics. Rumors had first swirled in 2010 that the University of Texas was leading a mega realignment movement that proposed Texas, Texas A&M, Oklahoma, Oklahoma State, Colorado, and Texas Tech moving to the Pac-16. But leaders at Texas A&M then began exploring alternative options, such as joining the SEC. Ultimately, only Nebraska and Colorado decided to leave the Big 12 in 2010, a move they completed in 2011.

In the summer of 2011, the rumor mill again heated up after Dave Brown, the vice president for programming and acquisitions of the new "Longhorn Network," announced in an interview on ESPN Austin affiliate KZNX 104.9 FM that the Longhorn Network planned to air as many as 18 high school football games.

"We're going to follow the great [high school] players in the state," Brown said in the interview:

> Obviously a kid like [then-unsigned UT-Austin verbal commit and Aledo High School senior-to-be] Johnathan Gray—I know people are going to want to see [him]. . . . So we're going to do our best to accommodate them [on LHN] and follow the kids who are being recruited by a lot of the Division I schools, certainly some of the kids Texas has recruited . . . and everyone else the Big 12 is recruiting. . . . I know there's a kid [unsigned Texas verbal commit] Connor Brewer from Chaparral High School in [Scottsdale] Arizona. We may try to

get on one or two of their games, as well, so [LHN viewers] can see an incoming quarterback that'll be part of the scene in Austin.

Such comments raised a major red flag at other Big 12 institutions, especially at Texas A&M, because of the recruiting advantages that broadcasting high school games would give to Texas. To make a lengthy story short, the Texas A&M System Board of Regents on August 15, 2011, unanimously authorized then-A&M president Bowen Loftin to act on conference realignment, after which he first described the possible move to the SEC by A&M as a "100-year decision." After numerous legal hurdles were cleared, then-SEC Commissioner Mike Slive called Loftin on September 25 and officially invited Texas A&M to join the SEC beginning in the 2012–13 school year. Two days later, inside the Zone Club at Kyle Field, Slive, Florida president Bernie Machen, and other SEC staffers joined A&M officials to celebrate the beginning of a new era.

Quite frankly, those decisions were made way above my head and were really all about conference television networks and football revenues. Nevertheless, that decision affected all the coaches at Texas A&M and drew the ire of other Big 12 coaches and representatives. In October at the Big 12 Basketball Media Day in Kansas City, for example, Kim Mulkey was asked if she would schedule A&M in the nonconference. Mulkey cited that Bowen Loftin had likened the action to a divorce and stated, "My feeling is this: If a man wants to divorce me and says our relationship has no value to him, and then he asks me if he can sleep with me, the answer is, 'No!'"

Obviously, the media asked me to respond to her comments, and I tried to be as politically correct as possible. I simply said that it was all about recruiting and that I'd play anyone at any time. But I also pointed out that scheduling is a two-person effort. I stayed away from a battle of words with Kim, but I understood that we had gone from being the darling that won it all and represented the Big 12 as national champions to being the villain, even though the decision had nothing to do with women's basketball. It didn't matter, though. We had a bull's-eye on our backs entering the 2011–12 season for numerous reasons. We understood that, and we embraced the challenges.

Before the season began, though, we were able to take one more reward trip. In October 2011, we finally were able to go to the White House. The UConn men's team had their visit back in May 17, 2011, but because of scheduling conflicts, we couldn't go until October. It was a great trip, and I was so happy that all my players, as well as many A&M officials and my family members, were able to attend. We waited in line to enter the Oval Office and Kelly Bond-White was right beside me, followed by Vic Schaefer and Johnnie Harris. I shook hands with President Barack Obama, and he was wonderfully courteous and engaging, congratulating us and recognizing our efforts in giving back to the community. He even thanked our players for being role models to young girls, including his two daughters, Sasha and Malia. As we are standing there making small talk, I told him that Kelly went to the same Chicago high school, Whitney M. Young Magnet School, as his wife, Michelle Obama.

President Obama then shook hands with everyone else until it was just the president, Bill Byrne, and myself in the Oval Office as the others went into the Rose Garden. Bill was fascinated by the president's desk and began asking him about it while his people were trying to rush us along, but President Obama said it was OK and took time to give him a little background about the desk. Then it was just the president and me, and since the reelection was coming up soon, I mentioned to him that we both needed to win again to be more than one-hit wonders. He really liked that analogy, and I only wish that I had been able to record that moment.

We continued to the Rose Garden, for a presentation and photo opportunities. President Obama welcomed us with a loud "Howdy." He was quite prepared, referring to A&M's all-male school history in the 1960s as extra reason to praise the team's accomplishments. Noting that I often threw candy to the crowd before games, Obama joked that he was going to try that with Congress. He also acknowledged Danielle Adams for scoring 30 points against Notre Dame in the title game; Sydney Colson for her aggressive offense; Sydney Carter for her tenacious defense; and Tyra White, referring to her as the "Silent Assassin," for her clutch shooting.

During the ceremony, we gave the president a white A&M jersey with No. 12 and "Obama" on the back. We presented a second jersey for the First Lady with a No. 1 on it, and he enjoyed a great laugh about his wife being No. 1 and him being 12. I told him that I knew how much he liked to play basketball, and I mentioned that Danielle Adams and Sydney Colson would love to play him and Joe Biden in a game of two-on-two on his court. It was a great visit, and my grandson, Logan, even had a memorable trip. As the president was shaking Logan's hand, I mentioned that he had to miss three days of school to come to the White House and his teacher said he might need a note to get back into class. President Obama didn't miss a beat. He said, "We can take care of that." He asked his aide for a piece of White House Stationery and wrote Logan a note for an excused absence. That note is framed at Logan's home. During our visit to Washington, DC, College Station Rep. Bill Flores, Sen. John Cornyn, and Sen. Kay Bailey Hutchison also led the team on a tour of the Capitol. Our team members also took time to give pointers to local youths in a basketball clinic at the White House, and we attended a dinner honoring the team. It was an incredibly special time that none of us will ever forget.

Once we returned home, the whirlwind continued. We started the year with our highest-ever preseason ranking in both polls at No. 6, even though we were replacing some outstanding players in Danielle Adams, Sydney Colson, and Maryann Baker. Nevertheless, we returned three starters and 10 letter winners from the national championship team, and we opened the year with six straight victories, including a 76–58 win over ninth-ranked Louisville on the day our team members received their national championship rings and unveiled a banner commemorating our title in a pregame ceremony. Kelsey Bone scored 15 points, Sydney Carter added 14, and Tyra White scored 13 as we continued to build on the previous year's momentum.

Speaking of which, we also signed one of the most impressive recruiting classes in program history, a class ranked as high as No. 2 in the country by ESPN HoopGurlz, the *Collegiate Girls Basketball Report*, *Premier Basketball Report*, and *All-Star Girls Report*. We signed some big-time building blocks for the future in point guard Jordan Jones from DeSoto; wing Courtney Walker from Edmond, Oklahoma; and forward/guard Courtney Williams from Houston. Wing Chelsea Jennings from Fort Worth, combo guard Curtyce Knox from Humble, and wing Peyton Little from Abilene were also part of that great class.

On the court, we cruised through November, but we ran into some road blocks in December. On December 4, we lost at No. 13 Purdue, 60–51, in the Big 12/Big 10 Challenge, breaking a 12-game winning streak dating back to the previous season. Two days later, we received a hefty dose of reality when second-ranked Connecticut beat us by 30 points, 81–51, in the Jimmy V. Classic. The victory was UConn's 91st straight at home, extending its NCAA record. We were not ready for that type of competition. We didn't attack, but it was a learning process for us.

We bounced back and played pretty well the rest of December and through January. We were 17–5 overall, 8–3 in the Big 12, and ranked 14th nationally following a really impressive 67–36 win over Kansas State when we traveled to Baylor on February 11, 2012, for a matchup against the No. 1–ranked Lady Bears. It was our first time playing Baylor since the Elite Eight the previous spring, and Baylor wasted no time proving why it was No. 1. They jumped out to a 17–2 lead and never looked back as Brittney Griner scored 21 points and Baylor coasted to a 71–48 win to improve to 25–0 overall and 12–0 in the Big 12. In front of a record-tying sellout crowd of 10,627 at the Ferrell Center, it was a dominating performance, especially on the defensive end.

We represented ourselves much better a couple weeks later when Baylor came to Reed Arena on February 27. Our plan was to attack and show no fear against Griner. Too many teams had lived and died with jump shots against Baylor. We alternated six-four Kelsey Bone and six-five Karla Gilbert to try slowing Griner, and they both were in foul trouble early in the second half. Gilbert fouled out with about 12 minutes remaining and Bone picked up her fourth just seconds later, sending her to the bench. But we also managed to slow Griner down, and she was saddled with foul trouble as well. Ultimately, the game was decided at the free-throw line. Baylor made 23 of its 28 attempts, while we hit just 9 of 19. That was the big difference in Baylor's 69–62 win, which improved Baylor's overall record to 30–0 and 17–0 in the Big 12.

As fate would have it, we received one more shot at Baylor as fellow members of the Big 12. We finished the regular season at 20–9 overall and were 11–7 in league play after also being swept by Texas for the first time since the 2004–5 season. We went to Kansas City as the No. 3 seed in the Big 12 Tournament and promptly took care of Kansas and Oklahoma with no issues, becoming the first Big 12 team ever to reach the championship game of the postseason tournament five straight years. Awaiting us in the title game was Baylor. Unfortunately for us, the top-ranked Lady Bears used a season-high 26 points from Odyssey Sims to roll to a 73–50 victory. We held Griner to a season-low 11 points, but I had to rest our leading scorer Tyra White because of a foot injury, and we just didn't have enough offense to keep up with Baylor.

Still, it had been a great run to the title game, and we returned home quite optimistic about hosting the first and second rounds of the NCAA Tournament in College Station for the first time in my tenure at A&M. On March 12, we earned a No. 3 seed in the NCAA Tournament, becoming one of only four teams to be selected as a No. 4 seed or higher for six straight years. We faced No. 14 seed Albany (23–9) in the first round of the Raleigh Regional, and interestingly, the NCAA also sent my former school, Arkansas, to Reed Arena to play Dayton.

We coasted past Albany and then held on for dear life to beat Arkansas. Tyra White, who was still ailing, took just two shots, and Kelsey Bone was just 3 of 12 from the field, but fortunately Adaora Elonu was up for the challenge, tying a career high with 23 points as we survived, 61–59, to advance to the Sweet Sixteen. With the game on the line and 23 seconds remaining, our best free-throw shooter, Sydney Carter, hit the go-ahead foul shots. It's a good thing we were playing at home. Otherwise, Arkansas and my former assistant Tom Collen would have likely moved forward.

The defense of our national title came to an end in the Sweet Sixteen when we fell to No. 2 seed Maryland in Raleigh, North Carolina. We started great, jumping to a 12–2 lead and pushing that margin to 18 points twice in the first half. But Maryland closed the half on a 21–6 run to cut our halftime lead to 44–41. We also led 72–65 on Kelsey Bone's layup with 7:49 left, but we managed just one field goal the rest of the game as Maryland rallied for an 81–74 win. That game also marked the end of my longtime coaching partnership with Vic Schaefer, who accepted the head coaching position at Mississippi State. Schaefer had spent 15 seasons with me at Arkansas and A&M. He helped me become a better coach by always telling me what I needed to hear, not what I wanted to hear. I was happy for him and his family. Seeing your assistants go on to be head coaches is almost like watching your son or daughter graduate from college and start their career. Vic also took Johnnie Harris with him to Mississippi State as associate head coach and hired two of our former A&M players: assistant coach Aqua Franklin and director of operations, Maryann Baker.

I was pleased for them all, but I was also delighted that Kelly Bond-White stayed in Aggieland and that I was able to hire two great assistants in Bob Starkey and one of my former Arkansas players, Amy Wright, to complete my staff. Starkey came to A&M after a season as an assistant coach at the University of Central Florida and following 22 seasons at LSU. As we entered the SEC, I thought it was especially important to hire an assistant who was already familiar with the conference. Starkey had been on my short list of coaches for a long, long time, but I thought he was always untouchable, having been at LSU for so many years. He's an excellent defensive coach, a great teacher for post players, a great tactician of the game, and helped take LSU to the Final Four five times.

Meanwhile, Amy came back to Aggieland after one season as an assistant coach at Arizona State and following a three-year stint at Cleveland State. She was also a four-year letter winner for me at Arkansas, and she had previously spent time at A&M as an academic assistant and a radio color analyst for road games. As one of the rising young stars in the coaching community, we were excited to have her back with us at A&M. Amy is full of energy, and she definitely helped us prepare for that first season in the SEC.

As we prepared for our inaugural journey through the SEC, we first went on a summer adventure, taking a 10-day European Tour in August as we traveled through Rome, Florence, Pisa, Venice, and Milan on a four-game schedule. I always love it when we can do something like that because for many of our players, it's a once-in-a-lifetime opportunity. We visited some of Italy's most scenic and famous landmarks, including the Colosseum, Vatican City, the Leaning Tower of Pisa, and Lake Como. It was a great trip, and it helped us prepare for arguably the toughest three-game opening-season stretch I could have ever put together. We began the 2012–13 season by facing three top-10 foes: at Louisville, Penn State at home, and UConn at home. We lost all three games, but some of our youngsters, particularly freshman Courtney Walker, grew up in a hurry by facing such tough competition.

As we began to grow and Kelsey Bone began to truly assert herself, we won 12 of our next 13 games, with the only loss coming in a rematch of the 2011 national championship game. A few days before Christmas in Las Vegas, we dropped an 83–74 decision to No. 5 Notre Dame in the championship game of the World Vision Classic at Cox Pavilion. Kelsey Bone led all players with 28 points and also had a team-high 10 rebounds, but Notre Dame had four players in double-digit points, including tournament MVP Skylar Diggins, who had 24 points.

As SEC play began, we were shaping into a strong team by mid-February. In fact, on Valentine's Day, Bone collected her 12th double-double to lead us to a 78–71 victory over Florida at Reed Arena. Bone scored 31 points and grabbed 10 rebounds, while seniors Kristi Bellock and Adrienne Pratcher added 13 points and 12 points, respectively. The win, our eighth straight, moved us into a first-place tie with Tennessee at 10–1 in the SEC. The 10–1 start also set the record for best conference start by the Aggies in program history, and it marked our 20th victory of the season for the eighth straight season.

From that point forward, however, we lost four of our last five regular-season games to absolutely stumble into the postseason. We lost a close game (70–66) at home against No. 8 Kentucky, beat Ole Miss (82–53), lost at Vanderbilt (61–51), and lost to No. 8 Tennessee on the road (82–72). After each of those losses, I was disappointed, but I was disgusted when we lost the last game of the regular season before a really good crowd on Senior Day to LSU, 67–52. Although we were the more talented team, I told LSU head coach Nikki Caldwell as we were leaving the floor that she had a much better team at that point because they were playing with a purpose. They were only playing with eight people because of injuries, but at least they were all doing their job.

I told that story to the media after the game, and I also told the media that Nikki Caldwell was doing a better job coaching than I was. I even questioned whether my team had hit the wall. I was not happy about falling to the fourth seed at the SEC Tournament in Duluth, Georgia, and I was really frustrated by how we had just played against LSU. At that point, I was challenging my team through the media. You can't do that too often or it will fall upon deaf ears, but we needed a wake-up call, and we needed to go to the SEC Tournament with a renewed focus and a resolute mission in mind.

Fortunately, that's how we played right from the start. Against 14th-ranked South Carolina—Kelsey Bone's former team—Bone was limited to just seven points and three field goals because of foul trouble. But Kristi Bellock scored 17 points and Karla Gilbert added 13 off the bench to lead us to a 61–52 win in the quarterfinals of the SEC Tournament. Rachel Mitchell also gave us some big-time minutes, as did Jordan Jones. We hit the key shots, our defense stayed steady, and we hit our free throws down the stretch. The win allowed us to shed the monkey on our back and allowed us to face top-seeded and ninth-ranked Tennessee.

In front of a stunned crowd that was filled primarily with Tennessee supporters, freshman Courtney Williams drilled a jumper with 33 seconds remaining to give us the lead and propel us to a 66–62 win, ending the Lady Vols' bid for a fourth straight championship. Fellow freshman Courtney Walker scored 18 points to lead four scorers in double figures for us. Adrienne Pratcher (15 points) stepped up in the first half, while Kelsey Bone (also 15 points) was really solid in the second half. At that point, I think she was the best post player in the nation and we had regained our swagger, which carried into the championship game against Kentucky—a team that had swept us during the regular season.

With a championship at stake in the third meeting, Bone produced 18 points and 15 rebounds, with most of her numbers coming in the second half. After stumbling down the stretch of the regular season, we beat Kentucky, 75–67, to win the Southeastern Conference tournament championship in our first year in the league. It was extremely gratifying on so many different levels.

Kentucky led 36–34 at halftime, but Bone, after a foul-plagued first half, led us to a title in the second half and was named the tournament MVP.

I had challenged Kelsey before the game, telling her, "Give me 15 boards, give me 10 defensive ones, five offensive ones, give me five assists, and play great defense." When it was all said and done, she grabbed 10 defensive rebounds and five offensive rebounds. She owed me an assist, but that was OK. We won the game and brought home the first SEC trophy to College Station. In an act of genuine friendship and total unselfishness, Kelsey Bone accepted the MVP Award of the SEC Tournament and presented it to Karla Gilbert, who had been in her shadow throughout the year but had played exceptionally well in the SEC tourney.

Unfortunately, we were not able to keep the good times rolling much longer. After earning a three seed yet again in the NCAA Tournament, we beat Wichita State, 71–45, in the opening round of the Big Dance in College Station but then fell to former Big 12 rival Nebraska, 74–63, in the second round. Nebraska used a 12–0 run in the first half to take a 25–16 advantage, and the Huskers never lost the lead the rest of the way. A little more than a week later, Kelsey Bone announced that she would forgo her senior season to enter the WNBA Draft. She had an exceptional junior season, scoring the fourth most points in a single season in program history with 582, while ranking third in the SEC at 16.6 points per game. Bone was eventually selected by the New York Liberty with the fifth pick in the first round of the WNBA draft, and she's been a great ambassador for Texas A&M.

We certainly missed her the next year, although our 2013–14 team went 23–7 during the regular season and 13–3 in league play for only the third time in program history, matching the 2006–7 Big 12 championship season and the 2010–11 national championship teams. We once again earned a three seed in the NCAA Tournament, marking the seventh straight year we had done so. We opened the Big Dance in College Station, beating North Dakota and James Madison to advance to the Sweet Sixteen for the sixth time in school history. In Lincoln, Nebraska, Courtney Walker scored 25 points, and we rolled past DePaul, 84–65, to advance to the Elite Eight for the third time since 2008 and the first since winning the national title in 2011. That was as far as we could go, however. Defending national champion UConn beat us 69–54 to improve to 38–0 for the season, as the Huskies won their 44th straight game. UConn went on to win the national championship, while our seniors, Karla Gilbert and Kristen Gant, finished their careers with a 12–3 record in NCAA Tournament games. Under different circumstances—like if Kelsey Bone had decided to return for her senior season—we may have wound up back in the Final Four once again.

Honestly, I am not sure if we could have beaten that UConn team with or without Bone. And quite frankly, UConn and head coach Geno Auriemma have accomplished some amazing things in recent years. On April 6, 2016, for example, the Huskies defeated Syracuse, 82–51, to win their fourth consecutive national title. John Wooden's UCLA men (seven straight titles from 1967 to 1973) are the only other team in Division I basketball history to win at least four straight titles. The 2016 championship was Auriemma's 11th overall at UConn, moving him past Wooden for the most collegiate championships. The 2015–16 Huskies finished the season at 38–0, their sixth unbeaten season in program history, and they extended their winning streak to 75 games. UConn has achieved a level of "sustained greatness" that is virtually unmatched in the history of women's collegiate basketball.

Obviously, we're not quite at UConn's level, but I am extremely proud of the fact that we have reached a level of "sustained excellence" that is unmatched in the history of Texas A&M basketball. In 2014–15, we went 23–10 overall and 10–6 in the SEC and made our 10th consecutive NCAA Tournament appearance. One year later, we went 22–10 overall and 11–5 in the SEC, finishing in a tie for second in the conference. We lost to Florida State in the second round of the 2016 NCAA Tournament (our 11th straight trip to the Big Dance), but we've joined an elite group of schools that have become known as the premier programs in women's college basketball. In 2016, we joined Baylor, Connecticut, DePaul, Notre Dame, Oklahoma, Stanford, and Tennessee as one of only eight schools to have qualified for at least 11 consecutive NCAA Tournaments.

Our 2016 senior class (Chelsea Jennings, Jordan Jones, Rachel Mitchell, Courtney Walker, and Courtney Williams) finished their careers with a 97–39 record and a 56–12 record at home. Walker became Texas A&M's all-time leading scorer (1,989 points), passing Takia Starks's (2005–9) previous record of 1,977. Jones finished her career third on A&M's all-time assist list with 708 career assists, while Mitchell finished fifth all time with 116 career blocks. And on April 14, 2016, Walker was selected with the 16th pick of the WNBA Draft by the Atlanta Dream, while Jones was taken with the 34th overall pick by the Chicago Sky. Walker, a three-time All-American, and Jones, an All-American in 2014–15, became the 12th and 13th WNBA Draft selections from Texas A&M, 11 of which have come since 2008. The list since '08 features Morenike Atunrase, A'Quonesia Franklin, Danielle Gant, Tanisha Smith, Sydney Colson, Danielle Adams, Tyra White, Sydney Carter, Kelsey Bone, Walker, and Jones.

Texas A&M has become a destination for elite players, where the expectation every year begins with contending for a conference championship and playing in the NCAA Tournament. Considering where we were when I first started at A&M in 2003–4, that's not a bad place to "start," and there's no reason to see that ending anytime soon.

Nowadays, people always ask me when I plan on retiring. I suppose the answer to that is, "When I don't enjoy it anymore." Right now, I can't foresee that in the immediate future. I love representing Texas A&M, working with my staff of professionals, training and teaching young people from all different backgrounds, recruiting the next batch of potential superstars, marketing the program to a community that continues to grow and prosper, competing in the SEC against some of the country's premiere programs, and taking on new challenges. I've even learned a thing or two about social media in recent years, which has really made me step outside my comfort zone.

Of course, I've always been rather comfortable with discomfort, which is probably one of the reasons I have been able to stay in the game much longer than some of my counterparts. I was playing golf one day with legendary former Texas A&M head football coach R. C. Slocum, who mentioned something to me that really stuck. As we were playing and talking about what makes coaches great, R. C., the winningest coach in the history of A&M football, said, "Growth and comfort do not coexist." I nodded in agreement at the time, but that thought really stuck with me.

I suppose "comfort zone" means different things to different people. But to me, it's a behavioral pattern that minimizes stress and risk. The problem is that when you minimize risk taking for the sake of comfort, you also eliminate the possibility of new growth, new adventures, and accomplishing great new things. I am not done growing, although I wouldn't mind it if my waistline stopped expanding. Right now, the rocking chair of retirement just doesn't seem that tempting. I am sure it will be one day, but not yet.

The bottom line is that I love coaching women's basketball and thoroughly enjoy the adventures of each new season. I feel blessed to be at a place like Texas A&M and ever so fortunate to have a wife, children, and grandchildren who continue to support me as I continue to answer my life's calling as a women's basketball coach. My journey is not yet complete, but all things considered, I look back and I must admit that I'm quite pleased the baseball thing never worked out for me all those years ago. I think I've made the most of the basketball opportunity first presented to me at South Oak Cliff, and I have very few regrets about everything that has happened on this adventuresome life journey ever since.

INDEX